CW01478521

FOREWORD

This book offers you a summary of more than 30 years' business and business development experience in the UK and Europe – experience which spans businesses of all sizes from small start-ups to large multinationals, from highly technical and specialist to general distribution. As I gained experience I picked up lots of little hints and signals about how well a sales effort was progressing. When I was involved in big deals, there was one sign I always watched for toward the closing stages of the process – when having lunch with a potential customer I always noted whether or not he let me pay. About 90% of the time, if the customer let me pay, I got the business. When the customer insisted on paying, I usually lost. So, the title of this book, 'Who's Paying for Lunch?', illustrates one of the many insights that it will provide to help you understand how to win business and maximise your business potential.

Published in the UK 2014 by

Verve Business Books Ltd
The White House
Mill Lane
Goring-on-Thames
Oxfordshire
RG8 0DD

ISBN 978-0-9929645-0-4

Design and artwork by Artefact Design, Godalming www.artefactdesign.co.uk

Illustrations by Jason Berry.

Printed in China through Printworks Global Ltd

ACKNOWLEDGMENTS

First, I would like to express my thanks all those individuals who told me their stories and gave permission for me to use them in this book.

Andrew Warren & Kieron Brennan for telling me of their experiences at Vertex
Laura Davis of HR Solutions 4U
Mark Llewellyn of Revive
Martin Boddy for his story of Nexsan
Mehran Chandra of Ready Steady Store
Paul Brennan for sharing his experience at Zeus Technologies.

I would also like to thank all those who read my manuscript and offered comment: Kate Youll, Richard Jephcott, Tabitha Moses – with a special 'thanks' to Geoff Flett and Vari McLuskie, who both devoted a great deal of time and effort in proofreading and offering constructive comments and feedback.

Many others, too numerous to list, helped me with referrals and ideas and gave me general encouragement. I also wish to acknowledge their help.

Finally, a very special thanks to Mark Brunton, who walked me through – step by step – the publication process, finding me an editor, designer, indexer and printer and making certain that this book would ultimately become a reality.

Contents

Chapter 3 – Team Selling

Chapter 4 – Sales Targets

Part II – Your Marketplace &
Your Product – Your Strategy

Chapter 5 – Your Market

Chapter 6 – The Offering –
Getting Your Product or Service Right!

Chapter 7 – Pricing

Part III – Your Engine Room – Keeping Your Selling Machine Tuned and Running 146

Chapter 8 – Your Sales Process 151

Chapter 9 – Your Sales Funnel 174

Chapter 10 – Managing the Selling Processes & Sales Operations

Chapter 11 – Putting It All Together

Index

Who's Paying for Lunch?
A Practical Manual for Maximising Sales in Small and Medium Enterprises

Introduction

How is it that some businesses manage to survive and even thrive during hard times? Successful businesses adjust plans, shift focus and adapt quickly. They spot 'opportunity' even in these challenging times and, most importantly, these companies put increased thought, effort and investment into their sales and marketing activities. This book focuses on building a winning organisation to improve revenues and profits.

Let's start by focusing on the objectives of this book – how the book will help you and what it won't do.

In today's market, salvation will NOT come from a 'hero sales' culture in which a salesman alone brings in the sales. Sales people cannot work in a vacuum. Key to their success are an organisation and service offers or products that help your sales people to succeed. Using this approach, the sales person is the final link and a key business interface for a finely honed selling organisation. This book will outline how other members of the organisation can support sales in order to maximise success and turn your business into a 'selling machine'. In fact, it will help to you to create a customer-oriented 'selling culture' for your entire company and encourage all your employees to contribute to the effort.

In addition, this book will describe how focused sales/marketing campaigns and appropriately targeted products can add to measurable success. Additional business benefits can be achieved by:

- Effectively targeting your sales effort
- Tailoring your sales approach
- Directing your marketing effort toward identified targets

... and, all the while, helping all of your staff adapt to these changes.

In good times or bad, all businesses can benefit from examining their culture and customer-oriented processes with an eye to making key changes.

Before we start, let's set the scene.

Is this book for me?

This book is aimed at owners, directors and senior managers in SMEs (small to medium enterprises). You have different challenges staying afloat when you compare yourself to the large multinationals, or even a large national business. But you have some unique opportunities too! Your size gives you flexibility and speed. You can make changes more quickly in response to changing market conditions and there is no question that you can provide better customer service if you want to do so. However, the final measure of this flexibility and responsiveness is sales.

Do you think you could or should achieve higher sales revenues? If 'no', put this book back on the shelf. On the other hand, if you think you should be doing better, then this book was designed for you.

Do you want to create a successful selling attitude throughout your business? If 'yes', then you should encourage your:

- CEO
- Financial director
- Sales & marketing director(s)
- Operations director
- Sales manager
- Customer services director

to read it too!

Of course, you may not have all these roles in your company, but you get the idea. Encourage all the top management to understand and get involved with selling or supporting sales.

This book is not a basic selling skills course. There are already a myriad of companies and books that perform this job satisfactorily. However, having said that basic selling skills are not covered, this book will offer many advanced selling hints, tools and tips around how to use basic selling skills to best advantage.

Why should you involve everyone?

Effective selling involves the whole organisation – and the drive to win can involve changes in behaviour and the way you do things throughout your company. No matter the size of your business, the drive for change must come from the top. If you are not in this position and believe what you read will help, give this book to someone who is and suggest that they read it too. Help take control of the situation and turn your company into a fighting fit, selling machine!

There are four supporting columns that support a successful business:

- o Your people
- o Your offering (product or service)
- o Your target market
- o Your sales processes

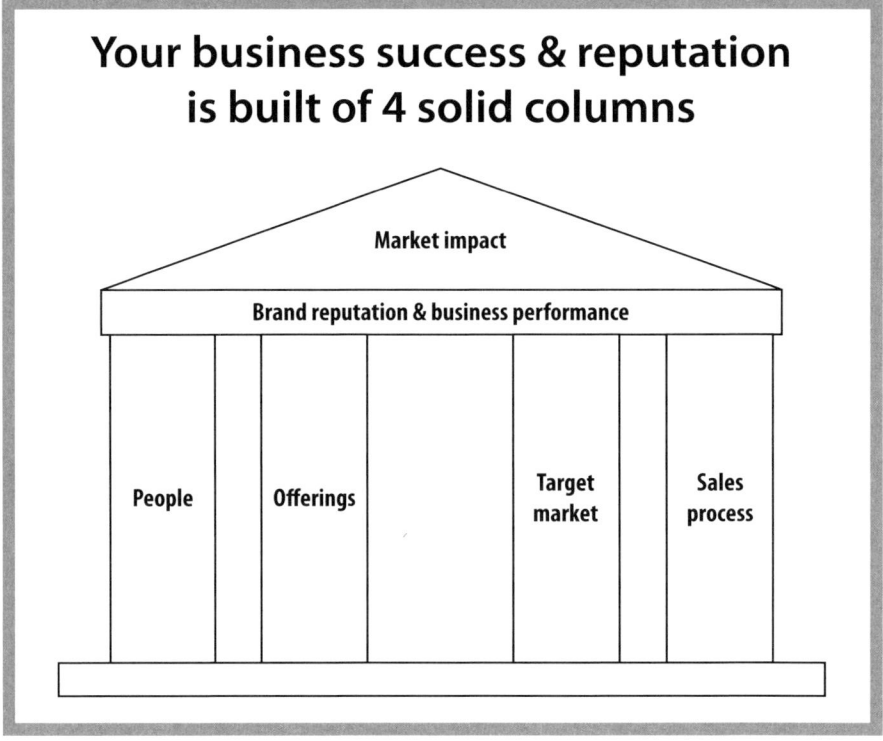

Your business success & reputation is built of 4 solid columns

Market impact

Brand reputation & business performance

| People | Offerings | | Target market | Sales process |

Do you notice that these columns are all the same size? If you place too much emphasis on one or fail to emphasise another, your structure is not stable. This book focuses on all four and provides you with best practice and case studies detailing how best to make improvements in each of these areas.

These four columns work together to maximise your business performance and how your company is perceived (Brand & Reputation). They help you to maximise your impact on your target market. As the diagram illustrates, it's all your staff – not just sales people – who work together to support business performance and your reputation. Strong performance and good reputation combine to help your business make maximum impact.

How to use this book

Throughout this book, we will focus on what you can do to improve your sales efficiency and effectiveness. Of necessity, many different market sectors and selling styles will be examined and not all of them will be right for all organisations. For example, the sales approach will be different if you target the 'man on the street' with a high-volume, retail product rather than if you are a specialist engineering company that sells to other, specialist businesses.

As you read, compare the 'best practice' to your own. To help you do so, at the end of each chapter you will find a section entitled 'End of Chapter Self-Assessment'. If you answer 'yes' to a question, you are doing fine. If you answer 'no' or you are not certain, this response highlights an area you should investigate further. These questions have been devised to help you pinpoint areas of improvement so you can take concrete steps to improve your business performance.

Overall, the book is divided into three sections: your people, your offering & your target market and finally, the procedures you put in place within the business to make the sales process run smoothly. Each chapter also contains some 'top tips' to help you identify key activities for success. These tips kick off each chapter and give an overview of the topics to be covered in the pages that follow. Finally, the body of each chapter provides detailed discussion, definitions and best practice for each topic. Best practice is illustrated by real-life case studies and the 'learnings' of other SMEs.

To begin, let's focus on 'your people'...

Part I

Your People – Creating a Sales Culture

Chapter 1

Creating a Sales Culture

Top tips – Chapter 1

1. Create a shared business and sales language

2. Use introduction of new products and services as an opportunity for Selling Skills briefing

3. Involve all customer-facing staff in some form of sales skills training and updates

4. Create strong, emotional bonds with your customers

5. Hold regular, focused sales meetings with objectives, agenda and actions which are followed up

6. Regularly communicate progress & issues to all staff and use good meeting guidelines

7. Define your values and business language and then use them!

Do you know how your product or service is 'sold'? Do you know who in your organisation is involved and what part each person plays? Could someone be doing more? To be a successful business you must get customers to buy from you and continue to do so on an ongoing basis. You need to know how and why your sales 'happen'. It's 'people' who buy from you, and ultimately people buy or don't buy from other people. This first chapter is about your people and how everyone in your organisation can play a part in sales.

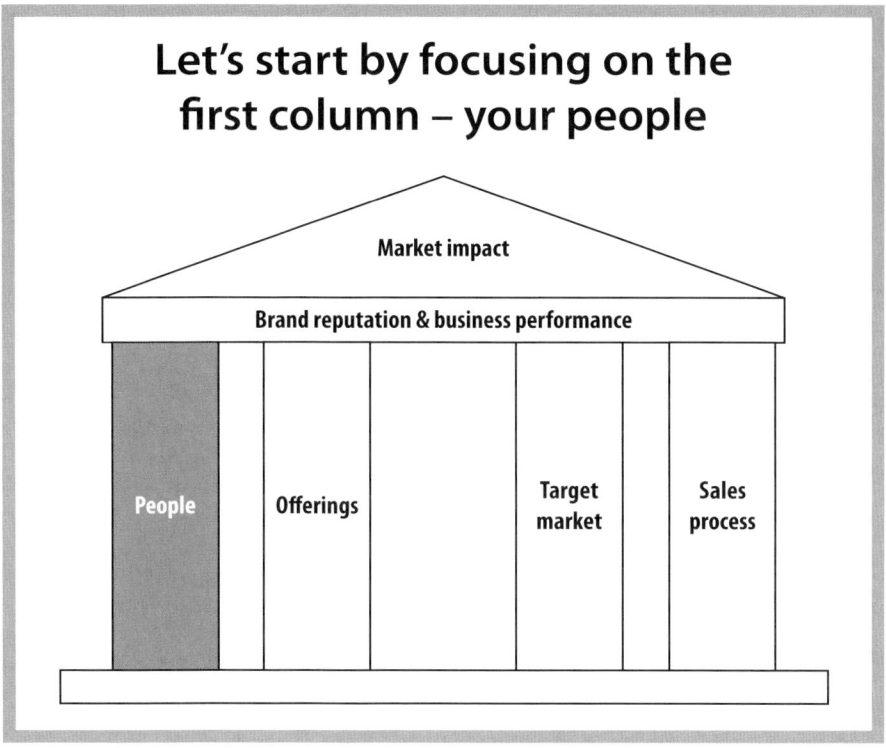

Let's start by focusing on the first column – your people

Market impact

Brand reputation & business performance

People · Offerings · Target market · Sales process

To build the foundation of a successful business, the first support column is your people. In this chapter we will take a brief look at everyone in your company, with a special emphasis on your sales people, and explain how each has a role to play in building your company culture and contributing to your business success.

Let's start at the top with just one person: do you get involved in the selling process? Management can and should take a leadership position by promoting specific values and clearly delineating acceptable business practices. Done well, such leadership can pull together the intellect, energies and enthusiasm of all your employees toward your business goals. Do not underestimate the importance of company culture; it reflects values and practices shared by all your employees.

If you don't get involved personally, do you know how sales happen? Do you understand what makes someone buy from your company rather than a competitor? These aren't silly questions. In many SMEs, the directors and top managers focus on the product or service, concentrating on production and delivery, and figure they will just use the internet or a sales person to do the selling. Sometimes these senior directors are not even very clear about why customers buy from them or how a sales person brings in the revenue. It might as well be magic!

How do you think sales happen?

SALES

MAGIC
PERFORMED
HERE

ORDER

Creating a sales culture

All companies have a company culture. Most 'cultures' share common values and a common language. Many company cultures happen 'by accident'. Few SMEs take the time to carefully define and communicate their culture so it develops haphazardly and, often, can actually get in the way of business rather than help it! Key to any culture are its values and the language it uses. A common language goes a long way to binding people together. Let's look at a non-business example to get an insight into what I mean.

When we speak of 'national' cultures, both the language and values are taught in schools and reinforced by national media and politics. Most people agree, common values and behaviours go a long way to 'defining' a culture. 'The culture' is part of what makes the French 'French' and the English 'English'. It's what everyone sees and experiences at a first glance. So, if a business has a culture too, then your sales people are your company's ambassadors. Does their behaviour reflect the culture and values of your business? If not, so what? Does it really matter as long as they can sell?

Yes, it does matter. Your business culture forms part of your 'brand'. Brand will be discussed in more detail in Section II. For now, just think of your brand as part of the reason why someone buys – or refuses to buy from you. Every one of your employees can have an impact on your brand image and it is important that each employee understands how he or she can affect sales. Here is a story that should make any senior manager cringe.

••

Any one of your employees can make an impact...

A few years ago, as part of its training process for sales, IBM UK made all the new sales people rotate through a variety of jobs, including a few weeks answering phones for the customer services department. Everyone, young and old, junior or senior, British or foreign, took a turn at this job.

One morning while answering the telephone, a senior new recruit from abroad answered a phone call from the secretary of a senior executive who wanted to speak to someone at IBM. Politely capturing the message and reading back the contact name and telephone number, the 'trainee' had to ask her to repeat the name of the company – it was a well-known UK company, but NOT an international name. The woman caller was very impatient and acted as though she couldn't believe anyone did not know the name of her company. She became angry and repeated the name quickly and in a tone which said 'You idiot' to the person taking the message. New to the UK and none the wiser, the trainee asked her if she could please spell it. She tutted in disgust and hung up without answering.

Later, this individual discovered how to spell the company name; it was a major UK supplier of domestic white goods but not well known outside the country. Well, the incident certainly made an impression. Despite living in the UK, this individual refused to buy or recommend a product from that company and repeated the story about the company's 'attitude' throughout the years that followed.

Now, if this individual were the only person that the secretary offended, the impact would hardly have dented their sales figures. However, if her behaviour was symptomatic of the company culture, the effect would have been disastrous to its bottom line – and so unnecessary!

• •

So you can see from this story how creating a selling culture for all employees might have improved the secretary's response and, ultimately, had a positive effect on revenues and customer satisfaction. It also illustrates how, though many of your staff don't need to sell directly, they do need to understand how they can help to sell and how they might make a positive or negative impact on the process. The most important idea for all employees to understand is that the success of the business ultimately affects everyone, so contributing to success is everyone's job.

Before we talk about how other people can help, let's focus on the ambassadors of your business – the sales staff – and how to create and foster an effective sales culture among the sales people themselves. As a minimum, you should have a common sales culture so that all your customers share a common experience with your company.

Sales staff

When I talk about 'sales staff', I mean anything from a director who does all the company's selling through to a full-sized, field sales force managed by a sales manager. This section focuses on those individuals in your business who have direct, face-to-face or phone-to-phone contact with people who might buy from you. Even if you employ 'sales agents' or distributors, read on, this section contains something of value. Let's start with some basics...

Many larger commercial organisations that employ sales people train them, even though these businesses typically hire individuals who claim to have selling skills. Why?

Reasons differ – but usually it's to ensure that all the company's sales people use the same language and terms, understand company processes and learn about the business's products and/or services in a similar way. Smaller businesses often neglect this step, believing that, because their businesses are so small and sales staff few in number, such an education will happen automatically. It doesn't.

When you hire a new sales person, you should consider it a good opportunity to offer training for everyone involved in selling. Select a standard and inexpensive 'selling skills' course which focuses on basic techniques and instruct all sales staff, no matter how senior or experienced, to take the course. At a minimum, this course should include instruction on the following basic techniques:

Technique	Explanation
Qualifying	▶ Making sure the customer intends to buy something
Questioning skills	▶ Leading a sales discussion by directed questioning
Objection handling	▶ Dealing concerns and objections
'Closing'	▶ Asking for the business

If you later hire more new sales staff, do not assume that just because someone has 'sold' elsewhere he or she knows how to sell and uses the same approach as you do in your business. As part of a joining or induction process, all sales staff should have brief sales training, using your products/services as examples. This approach serves a number of purposes – it:

- provides product training which is tailored to selling
- creates a group spirit and enthusiasm about the product/service and your business
- ensures that all those involved have a similar approach to your marketplace

If you have only one or two sales people, this activity can be carried out informally or as part of regular sales meetings. If you have more, say 5-10 or more sales people, you should consider taking a half-day or a day to carry out these activities.

In fact, the best way to ensure that all your sales people have a common skill level and use similar terms is to provide regular sales training updates. Such updates can be short – as little as a couple of hours – but do conduct them regularly – quarterly or half-yearly, depending on the pace of growth and change in your business and your market. A common sales language and approach will go a long way toward developing a common culture – particularly among staff who spend quite a bit of time out of the office interacting with other businesses. It also provides an effective way to communicate, providing a 'business shorthand', and can save everyone time.

Furthermore, sales training updates can be integrated into a variety of standard business events such as new product launches, annual sales meetings or general company announcements. In the case of product launches, this approach gives the added advantage of explaining the new product in 'selling terms' – setting the sales staff in realistic customer situations or role plays, during which they learn to sell the new product rather than just learn 'product features and benefits'.

It pays to create a common sales culture

Many large corporations have institutionalised this approach because it is necessary when you have hundreds or thousands of sales staff. However, even if you have only a few individuals involved in the selling, you can still benefit from some of the techniques. Mehran Charania, CEO of a small self-storage business, quickly learned about the benefits of a customer-oriented company culture.

••

Ready Steady Store praises the impact of a good company culture

Ready Steady Store (RSS) is a young self-storage company set up in 2006 by Mehran Charania, now CEO. After considerable effort, RSS has grown steadily at 15-20%/ year and it now runs at 80% occupancy, while the industry average is about 60-65%. When asked to comment on this success Mehran states: "One of my biggest learnings throughout this journey is that initially, I didn't appreciate the impact of 'company culture' on the success of a business and it wasn't easy to create a company culture. I will be the first to admit that I questioned and blocked the need for so many company meetings but I now understand that they were and are vital to breaking down business silos – even in a small business – and creating a holistic business approach. We have now developed a customer-oriented sales and marketing culture throughout the business.

"I know it sounds trite, but I now appreciate how important 'people' are to the business."

••

Your business language

As important as the selling skills themselves, training provides a common language to communicate how well (or poorly) a sale is progressing. To employ individuals who all work with different selling techniques and jargon is like trying to build an effective team who all speak a different foreign language. This situation will present you with a huge hurdle to overcome. It will waste time, cause frustration and may lose you sales. Far better to ensure that all your sales and sales support staff have had similar skills. You can do so by tailoring your training to ensure that everyone understands your business and its sales procedures and guidelines. Above all, you must be certain that everyone speaks the same language!

Your company culture – four steps to getting it right

There are four steps your business should take in order to empower your sales people – in fact, all your staff – to sell effectively:

1. High-level, basic selling skills course
2. Business-focused sales course
3. Product/service descriptions tailored for customer and sales needs
4. Sales support & customer service staff included in some of these activities

The following section will discuss each in a bit more detail.

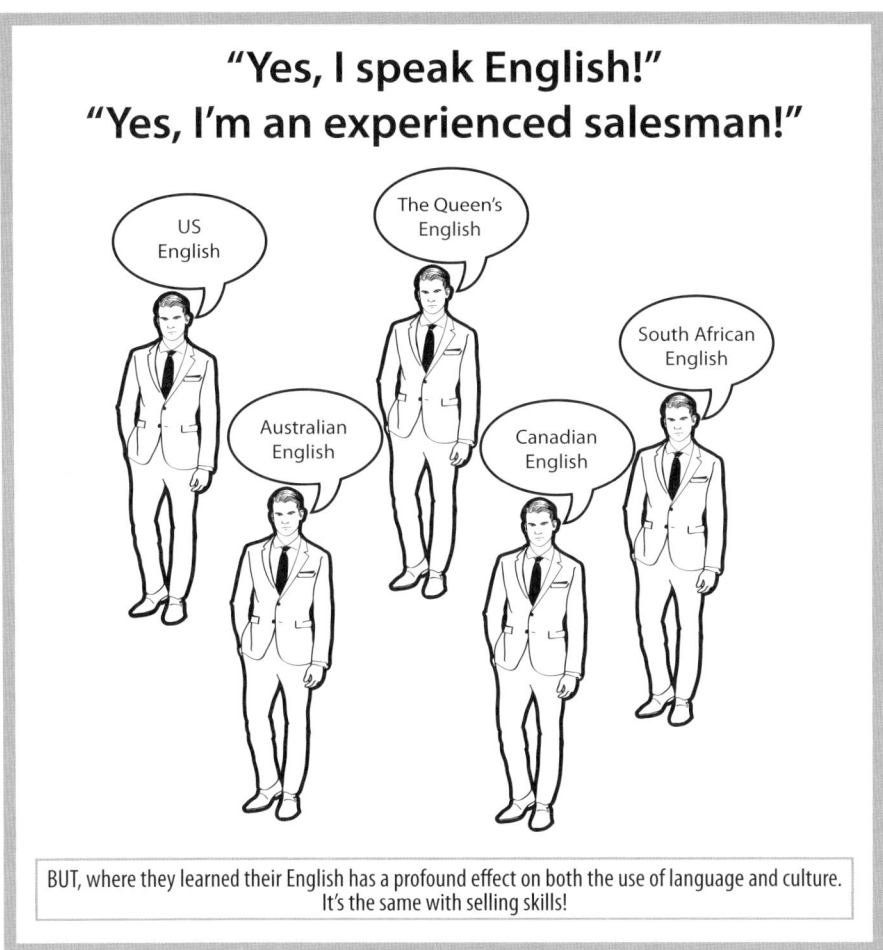

"Yes, I speak English!"
"Yes, I'm an experienced salesman!"

BUT, where they learned their English has a profound effect on both the use of language and culture.
It's the same with selling skills!

High-level, basic selling skills

Selling skills courses are readily available in the marketplace. Probably the best value approach would be to procure one of the market-leading offerings and adopt it as your company standard. You don't need to spend much money or even give up a lot of time to realise benefits. Even skilled sales staff can benefit from a 'training session' which includes your offerings as examples.

Would you let someone 'loose' to represent your company without making sure he or she understood exactly what you sold, company policies or your business values? If you put this necessary information in the form of mock selling situations – like role plays – you get the benefit of offering a sales refresher as well as providing an induction session for your new hire(s). Role-play scenarios also provide a good way to expose/introduce your new employee to the existing staff who take part in the role play, enabling relationship building as well as education.

But what about the rest of your employees? Ask yourself: Does everyone who interacts with a potential customer know how to recognise a business opportunity? Do they understand how to behave when they represent your business to the general public? Let's start with the simplest situation. If a prospect phoned your company and asked about your product or service, would whoever answered the phone know how to deal with the call to ensure a sale? If the staff member is not a sales person, how quickly and easily could the phone call be transferred to an appropriate person? In situations such as this one, it's like having 'a fish on a hook' – you have a potential 'sale' on the end of a phone line. If an inexperienced person holds the fishing pole there is a good chance that the fish will escape. In this instance, what you need is a well understood process for identifying and 'reeling in' this opportunity.

It's not difficult or expensive. If you currently do nothing to address this issue then almost anything you do will show a positive improvement. Some good first steps would be:

1. Make it clear that it's everyone's job to help customers and potential customers.
2. Remind them to be patient and polite no matter
   how angry or annoyed the caller.
3. Make certain that everyone knows about your product and
   service – at least one line that sums up what and why your
   product is good. For example, "At Company X, we offer the
   largest selection of garden furniture in the Newcastle area."
4. Let everyone know 'who' in your company is the designated person that should respond to the call and set up a procedure for referral and/or ring back.
5. Make certain that this designated person receives appropriate selling training.
6. Finally, keep your promise. If you say someone will
   return the call within 30 minutes, then do it!

Anyone who is not a sales person should know your company's process for collecting information from the caller – name and contact details of course – but also what prompted the phone call? Is the situation time-critical? Is it urgent? All this information should be easy to capture during the initial conversation and should then be passed on to sales or the appropriate individual in your business. If someone can't or won't go through these steps, they should not answer your phone.

The employee who answered the phone should conclude by promising to get back or have someone else get back with the answers as quickly as possible. By listening to the caller's needs, an emotional connection has been established. Your employee seems 'interested'. The caller will now be more patient if he is promised a 'call back' or transferred to someone else.

But what if the situation is slightly more complex? Do your sales staff and support staff know how to recognise 'needs' in potential customers? And can they link these needs to something that your product or service can supply? Such a skill is basic selling. All sales staff should know how to do it and most customer support/service staff can be taught to spot these opportunities too.

Business-focused sales briefing

Why not get two for the price of one?

If you need to update your staff about product/service or business changes, why not incorporate it into a session which includes some tailored sales training? In this way, you not only convey factual information, but you do so in a way that makes it easier for the sales person to use when speaking to customers and teaches or reminds him or her of good selling practice and selling skills. In a group, this approach has the added benefit of allowing sales people to pick up skills and tips from each other as well as illustrating to participating office-based staff, some of the challenges faced when selling your offering.

For maximum effect, these briefing sessions should be developed for your own company, using your own products, services and procedures as part of your sales training as well. A very efficient and effective way of 'refreshing' selling skills is role plays. In this manner sales and other staff can integrate product or service knowledge, fictional, 'typical' customer scenarios and practise basic selling skills within a relevant business context. Although there are many ways to offer business-focused refresher courses, role plays are some of the most powerful.

You can produce your own role plays or ask a specialist for help. Typically, someone produces a variety of 'typical scenarios' and background information with a script for the person who plays the customer and another set of background and objectives for the sales person doing the role play. A mock sales meeting then tests the sales person's product/services knowledge, personal skills, selling skills and usually, objection-handling skills. Role plays are also a good way to teach or reinforce 'closing' skills. Asking for 'the business' can be very difficult for some people to do.

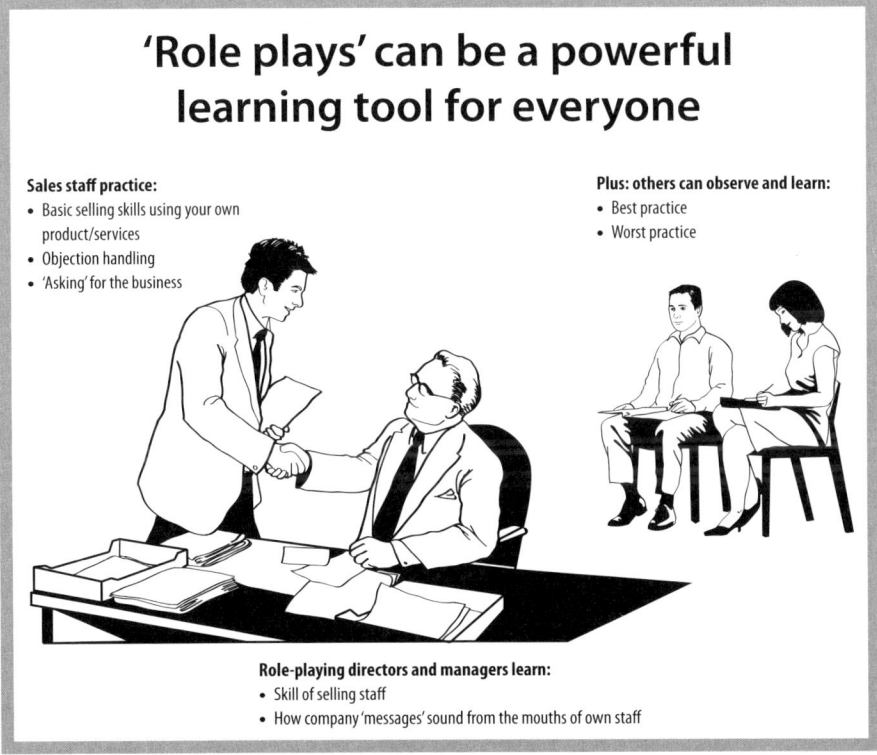

'Role plays' can be a powerful learning tool for everyone

Sales staff practice:
- Basic selling skills using your own product/services
- Objection handling
- 'Asking' for the business

Plus: others can observe and learn:
- Best practice
- Worst practice

Role-playing directors and managers learn:
- Skill of selling staff
- How company 'messages' sound from the mouths of own staff

Often role plays are observed by other sales staff, so it's a learning experience for all and provides an immediate opportunity to give feedback. It can also illustrate to other members of staff the challenges faced by sales in the customer environment.

Product or service descriptions tailored to your customer & sales needs

Do you speak your customer's language? Do you make it easy for your customers to understand the benefits that your products or services will bring them or do your product/service information sheets or brochure merely list 'features'? Features are facts – size, shape price, delivery time are all examples of possible features. Features do NOT change. Of course 'features' tell you something, but not the 'so what'? It is the 'so what?' that makes a product/service interesting to a potential buyer.

Features confer 'advantages'. For example, if you purchase a bright red suitcase, one advantage you have is that you can spot it more easily on the airline baggage carousel. Now, this particular advantage is only a 'benefit' to you if you travel by air and check your suitcase. Otherwise... so what? Somebody must find some other advantage in order to convince you that buying such a visible, red suitcase is a good thing. All features can confer many advantages (and disadvantages!), so there is plenty of opportunity to try to derive appropriate benefits for your target market.

Features are fixed while 'advantages' and 'benefits' will change depending on the individual involved and circumstances. To illustrate the difference I have selected a simple product which you are unlikely to buy yourself so that you have no existing views about the offering. Below is an example of a suitcase – this time in 'shocking pink' (see 'Feature, Advantage, Benefit' in the table below).

You can see from the table that being 'shocking pink' has an advantage in that, like the bright red suitcase, it can be spotted more easily on a luggage carousel. This colour may also be an advantage if you are targeting women, particularly young women, because many young women like pink possessions. However, the colour might be a great disadvantage if you want to focus your selling efforts on middle-aged business executives.

Item	Feature	Advantage	Benefit
Suitcase	No frame	Collapsible	Can fold up and store as 'extra' luggage
	Durable Plastic	Light weight	Can pack more inside without exceeding airline weight restrictions
	Shocking Pink colour	Easily spotted	Can spot more quickly on luggage carousel at airport
	Detachable shoulder strap	Can wear over Shoulder or carry by handles	Can travel 'hands free' if necessary

So what? If you don't manufacture pink suitcases, you may think: "What's the point of this discussion!?!" Well, everything and anything that has features will have advantages and benefits and it takes a skilled process to clearly spell out and elucidate these benefits. You may need to seek help from outside your company to do so, but it is well worth the effort in terms of helping everyone in your business to understand who should buy from you and why they should buy.

We will discuss target customers in more detail in Section II, but for the moment it's important to know that a clear understanding of the concerns and benefits of your target customer plays a key role in successful selling and the creation of effective sales support material such as product description. Almost all the current basic selling techniques rely on a process that creates 'FUDGE' ('Fear, Uncertainty, Doubt & Great Expectations'). A good and well supported salesman can show how your company's product or service will help to alleviate any fear, uncertainty and doubt and support the customer's business aspirations, or 'great expectations'.

Let's return for a final look at this pink suitcase and the target market – a teenage girl. Her fear, uncertainty and doubt might be that she doesn't fit in with her peer group – that her tastes aren't 'in' and that she will be judged as a 'loser' by her peers. If the sales literature and promotion for this pink suitcase show her that a pink suitcase is a 'must buy' item to be one of the 'in crowd', then buying the suitcase will alleviate her fears. Furthermore, if she is the first in her group to own one, she can expect enhanced status ('great expectations'). If selling pink suitcases is not your business, don't laugh – a great many of the items aimed at the teenage market attempt to capitalise on these fears and expectations.

Whatever your business, your whole company should understand and know how to support your sales messages.

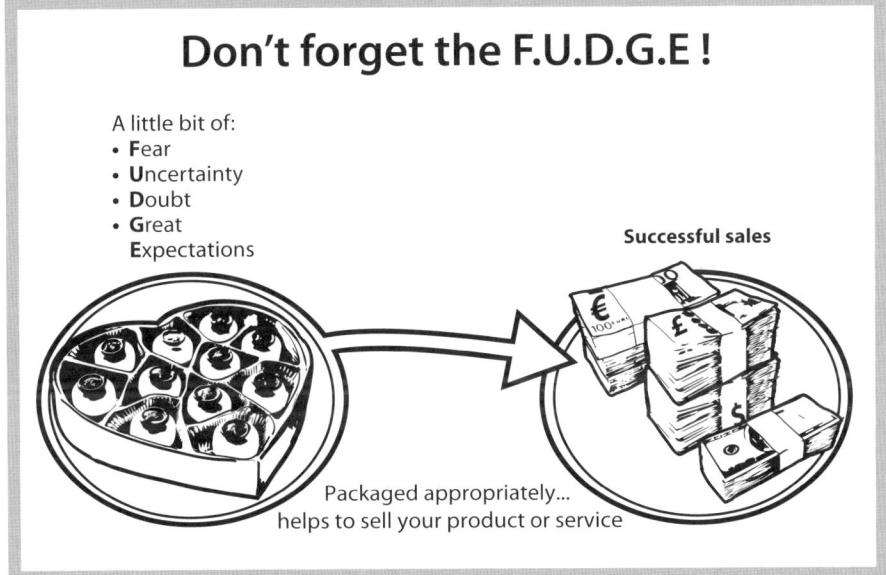

Include sales support & customer service staff in some of the training

It only makes sense! If back office personnel don't understand what a sales person is trying to do, it makes it more difficult for them to provide help when needed. In some companies, there is even the attitude that if a sales person isn't in the office, he or she must be 'skiving', so back office staff feel 'put out' when asked to help. Ideally you want to make certain that everyone understands what the sales person is doing when not in the office and what they can do to help.

Any staff member who speaks to customers or prospective customers should use the same 'language' as your sales people. When customers hear the same terms and language from everyone at a supplier, it sounds familiar – and familiarity gives them comfort. Much of the whole buying processes is about 'feeling' comfortable, not rational thought, so anything you can do to increase this comfort helps to create an emotional bond which is more difficult for a competitor to break.

This emotional bond with the customer can make the difference between keeping or losing business in the future. Overall, customers are heavily influenced by emotions when they make buying decisions, and even good relationships with support departments like finance or accounts can make a difference. Making sure that your business has a 'selling culture' throughout helps to cement strong customer relationships.

How should your tackle this challenge? The answer depends on the size and geographical spread of your organisation. If possible, the easiest way is to include these office-based staff in some of your sales briefings and role plays – even just as observers. With a bit more work, role plays could be adapted to include office-based scenarios so these staff could also take part. As with sales material, make certain that all company 'fact sheets' and product/service information use a sales-oriented, feature and benefits approach and are written in your customer's language.

So, what should you do if you have many office-based staff – particularly if they are distributed over different locations? In these circumstances, it might be worth the added effort of designing and delivering training for them. As with your sales briefings, this training should be tailored to your business, your market, your customers and your products and/or services. The whole objective is to gain a common, customer-oriented mind-set within your company.

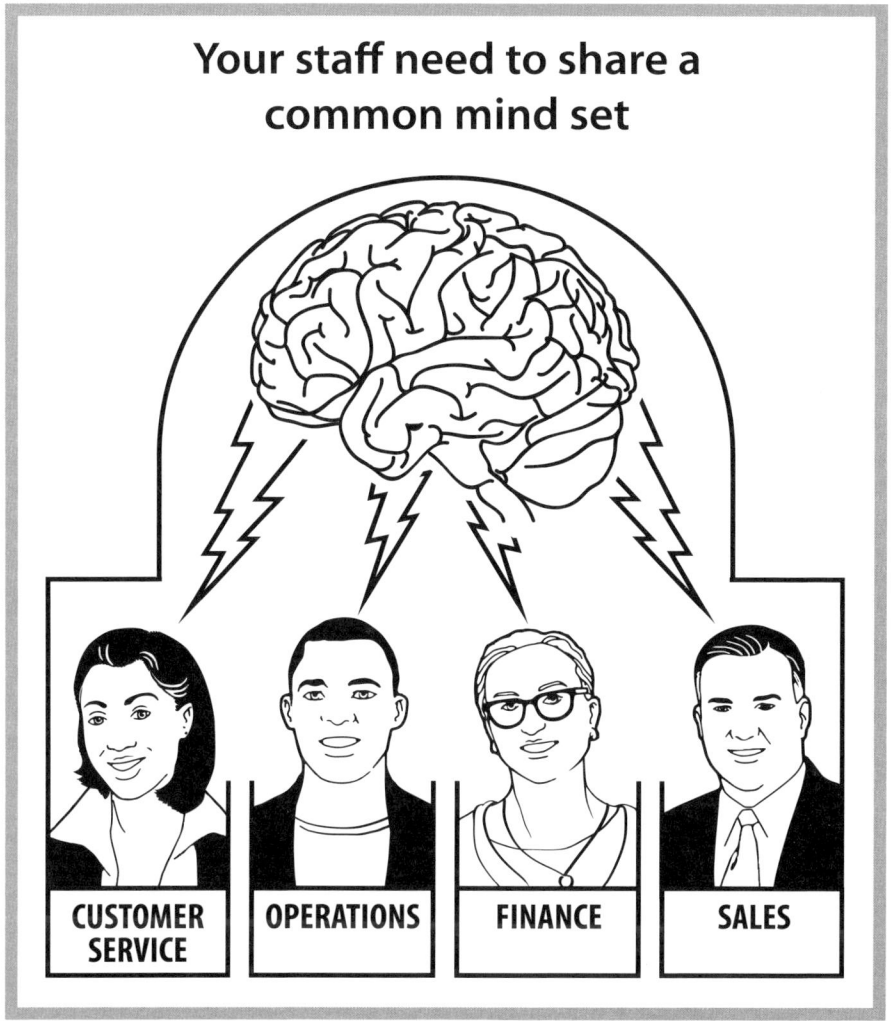

Your staff need to share a common mind set

CUSTOMER SERVICE | **OPERATIONS** | **FINANCE** | **SALES**

How well do you communicate generally within your business?

A good business functions like a team sport. Like the game of rugby, you will only get so far if you don't pass the ball as you move down the field. Could a successful sports team win if not for practice? And do the players practise and win without any backup support — a coach, perhaps, or assistant coach? Specialist trainers? Physiotherapists? There are many other people who stand behind that successful team on the field. Everyone, on the field and off, shares a common goal. No one has to try to win all by himself. Your company should work the same way. Key to being a team player is effective communication.

And... communication is a two-way process. Yes, it's about conveying information, but it's also about listening. Market/customer-facing employees can provide a valuable source of feedback about the market, your offerings successes and failures, and competitor activity. Within your business, listening will also provide you with a better picture of how well individuals are performing their jobs. The challenge for most SMEs is: how to communicate as much as possible efficiently and effectively.

Also, who should be involved in various communications? When should communications be face-to-face and when is phone or email a better vehicle? All this communication can be done efficiently and still be effective.

There are many ways to integrate trainings with updates and we have already discussed some of them in this chapter. Such integration becomes easier still if you include them as part of your regular communications process. For example, for the sales staff, you could schedule a brief (one-hour) update every month at the end of regular sales meetings. For the entire company, you could include some time when you give company 'business updates' to all staff. These face-to-face updates (or video conferences if geographically necessary) are vital to create and maintain a common, business culture focused on your company's best interests.

Ways to build a selling company

Best practice shows that effective communication helps to integrate the company into a single, effective team – like the rugby team mentioned earlier. Let's go back to the rugby example again: despite the fact that rugby is an action sport, there is lots of 'talk'. There are briefings and debriefings before and after practice and, again, before and after games. There are one-to-one talks, group sessions – whatever is necessary to get the optimum performance out of everyone. To be effective on the field, many days' effort goes into producing a few hours' performance. And everyone – players and locker room personnel – feel a part of any success or loss. They are a team, not 'us' and 'them'. Professional teams don't begrudge the investment of time spent talking, and nor should you.

However, holding meetings just to have meetings does not work either. All meetings should have an objective that is clearly stated. If other issues arise that threaten to derail this objective, these issues should be noted and dealt with in a separate meeting. When you call a meeting, you are, in effect, entering into a contract with your attendees to deal with certain objectives within the time period you set aside. If you or your staff can't do so, get help. Time and effort wasted in poorly run meetings damage morale and waste everyone's time. However, just because some companies do not run meetings well does not mean meetings aren't necessary! Learn to do it well and get help if necessary.

In the table that follows, you will see a list of all the different types of meetings what can and should be held in a typical selling organisation. Included are a suggested frequency, delivery method and objectives for each meeting type. This chart is split out into many meetings to illustrate the different components; however, there is no reason why some of these meetings cannot be combined into one – as long as the objectives are met.

Meetings to manage the selling process

Timing	The Event	How	Objectives
Weekly	Weekly sales meetings	1-2-1 face-to-face	Information exchange, 1-to-1 management tasks
Weekly	End of week business review	Group meeting – all sales	Information exchange, planning and resourcing for the following week
Weekly	Monday morning 'kick-off' event	Group meeting – all commercial or whole company	Updates and assigning actions for the coming week
Weekly or monthly as dictated by number of opportunities	Opportunity review	Group meeting with key management and sales person/ team	Determine whether a sales opportunity is worth the time/ costs of pursuing
Monthly	Monthly sales meetings	Group meeting – all sales	Recognition, problem solving, training, issue resolution, resourcing
Monthly	Monthly company-wide	Group meeting, webinar if more appropriate, whole company	Information dissemination
Quarterly	Sales events	Off-site or dedicated day	Training, recognition, group dynamics, morale
Quarterly	Business updates	Group, onsite or as part of another event	State of the Nation, communication motivational
Annual sales	Sales convention	Off-site	Motivational, training, communication, long-term sales planning, new product or service launch
Annual company wide	Business update	Group meeting – whole company	Motivation, information dissemination, performance recognition

The first question you may ask is: do you really need to hold all these meetings? Some of them? Any of them?

Easy answers first. If you don't hold any of these meetings, start doing so as soon as possible. Internal communications are vital to creating a success culture. Start by establishing regular weekly sales meetings. These can be used for both management and review objectives, and with some prior planning a first cut opportunity review can be included.

If you haven't already, schedule a company meeting for everyone and include a 'state of the nation' address – outline how the business is doing, future opportunities and challenges and how everyone can help. This is also a good time to recognise any outstanding contributions – and not just by sales. If you do not already 'walk the corridors' to get feedback from employees, be sure to include ample time for questions and discussion. You might be surprised – sometimes your employees can offer good suggestions that help the business, so you have to give them the chance to voice their ideas.

Ideally, you will do all the things on the previous table – even if you do so by using 15 minutes in part of another meeting. The important thing is that you reinforce messages regularly and that your messages are customer- and market-focused and believable. Don't limit these efforts to your sales people; include as many staff as you can in appropriate sessions. Everyone should part of your company's success.

Vertex, a UK-headquartered international business, provides an excellent example of how appropriately managed, regular meetings can improve revenue and company participation. Over the last few years, Vertex streamlined its outsourcing/call centre business and expanded into new markets. Regular meetings and effective communications became as a vehicle for driving the business and creating a selling culture.

· ·

The Vertex story – better communication for improved sales success

In this division, Vertex created a small, sector-specific sales team composed of account managers (for existing accounts), sales staff (for new business) sales support staff, marketing and technical and delivery managers, and each, as appropriate, drives and manages the selling process. The Public Services Division conducted regular, bi-weekly 'sales' conference calls which included all these people, and all of them contributed to the discussion, offering expertise ranging from 'customer insights' to 'operational impacts'.

In addition, all new opportunities now went through an 'opportunity review' process – a presentation of the opportunity to top management in order to gain their approval and support for the time-consuming and costly sales process to follow. In this way, Vertex could make informed decisions to bid or not to bid for each large opportunity and thereby ensure that business resources were appropriately deployed and that sales staff pursued only approved opportunities.

They also set up a monthly account meeting for this group which enabled them to produce a shared plan and review all activities against this plan. 'Best Practice' was also shared in these regular meetings, which also provided an excellent venue for sharing market intelligence gathered from both the 'delivery' and 'selling' perspective. This approach built 'one team/one common understanding'.

After significant reorganisation that resulted in a much smaller sales force/account team, far more time was spent on preparation for sales meetings and bids than when the numbers were larger. Getting it right was more important that lots of unfocused activity.

In addition to 'Opportunity Reviews', bi-weekly meetings and monthly account meetings, Vertex held quarterly strategy meetings. It is in these meetings that the business is able to share information to better target its services to up-to-date customer needs and changing market conditions.

In addition to all these meetings, there were a number of changes to the whole process.

- All meetings were now 'inclusive' – not just sales staff – so there was now a team of people who felt responsible for the success – or failure – of a bid
- All attendees 'spoke the same language' and shared in the process
- There was a lot of preparation for all these meetings, which all had:
  - a structured agenda
  - objectives
  - actions (which are followed up)
  - circulated minutes
  - Many also had pre-prepared analysis or market hypothesis to act as a focal point for discussions

The new, inclusive culture was company-wide – twice a year the sector head convened a meeting of all staff including central functions such as HR, administrators and finance. These meetings provided a vehicle for greater knowledge-sharing and communication on an organisation-wide basis, enabling everyone at Vertex Public Sector Division to 'walk the walk' and 'talk the talk'. The challenge had been to permeate these changes and the importance of the customer throughout the organisation. 'Success is everyone's job' – 'try to get it right the first time', 'everyone is in it together' and' everyone benefits'. So far, it seems to be working. Both the business results and employee attitudes speak for themselves.

All in all, Vertex reduced its manpower by 50% while increasing its selling effectiveness by 50%. During these difficult economic times, Vertex has held its revenue and increased its profits, with contribution rising by 20% over the past two years. By achieving these numbers in the contracting marketing place mean that Vertex has actually increased its market share by 'selling smart'.

••

Appropriate meetings weren't the only changes made in this division at Vertex and we will hear more of the story later, but you can see that all these increased meetings did NOT get in the way of selling, The bottom line improved significantly; sales increased while costs decreased. Vertex and its sales team focused on the right things and were, therefore, more effective at selling. Together with improved efficiency, increased profits resulted. This success came, in part, from the improved communications and inclusive culture of the remaining staff. Key decisions could be taken more quickly and all behaviours and activities were aligned to a common goal. In fact, the result was so successful that this division was later purchased by a competitor wishing to buy presence in this UK sector... but more on Vertex later on in the book.

The key message here is 'effective communication' is important to sales success – in businesses of any size. If done properly, it's not a waste of time, rather it is key to becoming an effective selling organisation. And you don't have to be BIG to suffer from poor communication. Often individuals in small businesses are so busy, they feel there is no time for meetings, emails or phone calls to their own colleagues. Believe it or not, sometimes there is no communication between individuals whose desks sit side by side! However, appropriate meetings using an agenda and good meeting techniques can work wonders to improve both the efficiency and effectiveness of all and get everyone communicating about business.

A final word about off-site events

A common misconception about such meetings is that the event is 'just a jolly' and, if run incorrectly, that can, indeed, be true. To get the most out of these sessions, you must have clear 'objectives'. In running the meeting, in addition to presentations, allow time to obtain feedback. Try to use smaller 'break out' groups for some of the sessions and try to mix up groups so that people who don't routinely work together are in the same group.

Finally, this day should not be all presentations; nor should the content be all business or only games. In a good event, there is a balance of both 'listen' and 'do', 'serious' and 'fun'. It is OK to have 'fun', and fun should not be confined to drinking and after-hour activities. Business relationships developed at these events can help smooth the daily interactions of individuals when they go back to their day-to-day jobs.

There is no doubt that a working, integrated team works best. In creating and enforcing a common selling culture among all your staff, the 'magic' of sales spreads throughout your company.

END OF CHAPTER 1 – SELF-EVALUATION

EVALUATE YOUR BUSINESS - Tick 1 box for each question
Answer only those questions that apply to your business.

QUESTION	Yes	No	Partly
1. Do all your selling staff have formal sales training?			
2. Does your business provide refresher sales training to all sales staff?			
3. Do sales support and customer service/support staff receive any sales training?			
4. Does your new hire, sales induction process include any sales refresher material?			
5. Does your company have a well, articulated brand and company culture that every employee understands?			
6. Have your product/service descriptions been written with your customers in mind?			
7. Does your sales induction material include information about: your target customer type, your product 'benefits', your competitors?			
8. Does your business use 'new offering' launches as a sales refresh opportunity?			
9. Does your business conduct face-to-face sales meetings at least once/month?			
10. Does your business hold all staff, group events to communicate business performance, issues and recognise outstanding contribution by employees?			

YOUR SCORE: Give yourself 5 points for every 'yes', 2 points for every 'partly' and '0' for every 'no'.

36-50 Points	⇒	Excellent – note areas where you didn't score 5 and plan to rectify if relevant to your business
26-35 Points	⇒	Good – you have some room for improvement. Check those areas in which you ticked 'no' or 'partly' and evaluate how you can improve your score
11-25 Points	⇒	You could do better – there is definitely room for improvement…
0-10 Points	⇒	Get help! You have lots and lots of opportunity to improve your income stream.

Chapter 2

Your Sales Approach & Selling Styles

Top tips – Chapter 2

1. Understand whether you sell 'business-to-business' or 'business-to-consumer'. If both, which is most important to you?

2. Discover whether your target customers consider your offerings to be 'high value' or 'low value'.

3. Select the best sales approach(es) for your market based on customer type & value.

4. Exploit existing customer relationships to sell additional products or services.

5. Be clear about what role your website plays in your business and design it accordingly.

6. Understand the key aspects of selling yourself so that you know how & where it's working (or not!).

7. Back up your sales approach with 'slick' back office and IT support.

8. Don't select a 'sales spproach' because you think it means you won't have to do any selling! To be successful, you will always have to sell your product or service and the benefits of working with your company.

You now understand how your people, your company values, language and culture can impact on your bottom line. You know how to go about helping your sales people improve both their attitude and skills and, vitally, you comprehend the importance of involving as many of your employees as possible – especially your customer service and sales support staff. You know how to start involving everyone in 'sales' so they all feel they play a role in your business's success. But once you have the best-trained, most aware and motivated employees in the world, they need to be used effectively, particularly your sales staff.

Some businesses skip this step.

Some businesses – particularly those run by someone who has invented an innovative product, believe the product is so good that it will sell itself. Have you ever heard the expression "He thought if he built a perfect mousetrap, customers would beat their way to his door"? This common expression exists because it illustrates a common pitfall. The quality of the product does not guarantee business success! A successful business needs to identify and build the best sales approach and selling style to maximise sales of its 'mousetrap'.

Now it's time for you to look at the best way to use your company's sales enthusiasm and skills and select the best sales approach for your business.

Different sales approaches & selling styles

What kind of 'sales' does your business do?

A 'Sales Solution' is not 'one size fits all' and it is different from one type of business to another. Do you sell predominantly to 'the man or woman on the street' or to other businesses? If you sell to businesses, do you sell to large companies or small businesses, or both? The styles of selling are very different – as is the support your sales staff might require. If nothing else, the man in the street and a small business owner are usually spending their own money, while the large business buyer is not! You must tailor your approach accordingly.

Do you sell low-value products and hope to sell lots and lots of them? Or, do you sell high-value or highly configured products or services where you can build a healthy profit margin into your price? Once again, the best approach is different in each of these situations.

There are 3 easy steps to get you started:

1. As a first step, clearly understand whether your approach is:
   → Business-to-business OR business-to-consumer
2. Next, be clear, do you sell:
   → Products OR services OR 'solutions' (a mixture of both)
3. Understand your market approach. Do you sell offerings that are:
   → High value but low volume OR low value, high volume

After clearly outlining what and to whom you sell, you need to think about:

→ Geographical focus and coverage

OK, you've answered these questions. What next?

The best answer may not be straightforward. Some companies use more than one approach, targeting potential or existing customers differently or use a different approach depending on a specific target market (e.g location – is it foreign?) or the potential value of the deal.

Think of what the airlines do as an example of such an approach. They advertise and market to the population as a whole. Most of them also have special sales efforts and 'deals' directed toward high-value customers such as those companies with high volumes of business travel. Airlines also use 'distributors' or 'agents' in the form of travel agencies and partner airlines who will sell seats on their planes. Finally, most large airlines also have 'loyalty programmes' to reward and hopefully retain their high-volume/high-value customers. So, there are four distinct approaches, each carefully targeting a specific group of potential customers.

Airlines – an example of different sales approaches for different markets

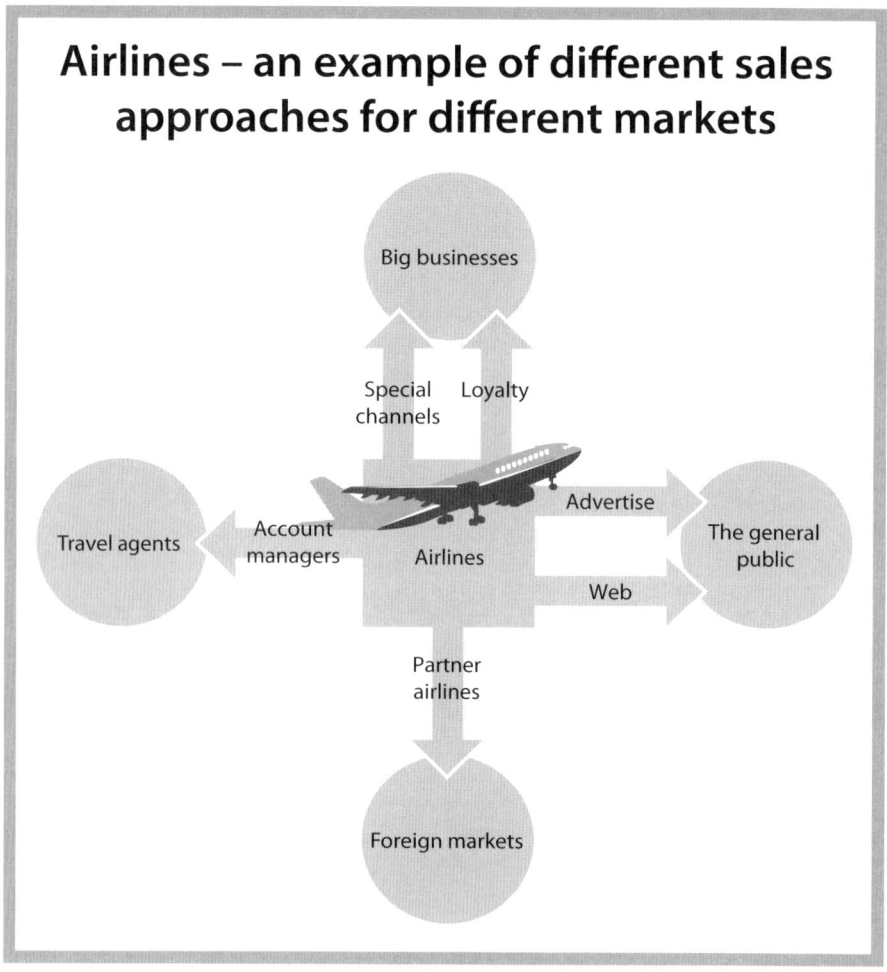

So, how do you decide which approach is best for your business?

First, be realistic. You are probably not as big as the airlines and do not have the staff to tackle all these areas at once. Pick one, maybe two.

A good first step is to decide whether the value of your sale is high or low (NOT cheaper versus expensive). What is meant by value in this instance is: does your target customer consider your offering to be a significant purchase?

An example of such a purchase is buying a car – for most individuals such a purchase is a high-value purchase. This sort of buying is more complex as the purchaser worries over spending the money and considers various options. This same individual would typically take far less time and effort over choosing less expensive items such as new clothes, books or a new mobile phone. The 'value' of the sale depends very much on your target customer. For example, new clothes, books or a new mobile phone might be high-value items to a poor student but nothing out of the ordinary for a successful executive.

Back to determining your sales approach. First, identify your target customer and decide whether purchasing your product represents a high or low-value transaction. Next, decide whether the bulk of your sales will come from existing customers or whether you need to sell predominantly to new customers. The sales approach will be different. Finally, will you be selling to the general public? Or to other businesses?

The diagram below provides an indication of the best sales approach to adopt for these different scenarios.

Once you are clear on the best sales approach for your current business circumstances, you can then identify what type of resource(s) you need. In the pages that follow you will find a section describing each of these approaches. You don't need to read every section if it's obviously NOT relevant to your business. However, whatever your business I suggest you do read the sections on internet and telesales. In today's world use of these approaches needs to be tracked closely and could be relevant to all businesses. So, let's look at each approach in a bit more detail.

New business by direct sales

New business sales are all about finding and converting non-customers to customers. It is the lifeblood for most businesses – even those who make most of their profit from existing clients. All high-value businesses should have some way of generating new customers. For a sales person given this role, the job is challenging.

Consider the situation:

The new business sales person regularly starts the day with a 'blank sheet of paper' and must convince potential customers (prospects) to speak to him or her. Often these prospects are not very happy about giving their time for such a meeting. The sales person must remain polite, persistent (without appearing too pushy) and very knowledgeable about the market into which he or she is selling and the benefits that the product will bring.

Put yourself in his shoes – he must, in one meeting, try to understand the basic business needs in the target prospect so that he can sell to these needs. He must come to any meeting armed with information about the marketplace, competitors, his own company's product/service and, if possible, specific information about the individual and business with whom he will meet. To be successful requires a good deal of preparation. To make that extra appointment each day or week requires a lot of self-motivation. Selecting the right person is critical to good new business selling.

Personality characteristics should include someone who is comfortable meeting lots of new people, someone who is a self-starter, well organised and can think on his/ her feet. To do this job well, the individual must have a good understanding of how to 'qualify out' those prospects where success is unlikely. In addition to standard good selling skills, this person should be adept at 'directed questioning' techniques that gently guide a conversation toward uncovering information and gaining prospect/customer commitment. Above all, you should hire someone who can quickly gain the trust and respect of the buyer. People rarely buy from someone they don't trust.

Managing existing high-value customers

7 Key, personal attributes of a good, new business sales person
1. Self-starter & motivated
2. Independent
3. Personable & polite; builds rapport quickly
4. Good listener & communicator
5. Quick mind, thinks on his/her feet
6. Presentable & neutral demeanour
7. Resilient

Now let's consider the situation in which you already have a number of good customers – won for you by your new business sales person. After the initial sale there is usually a lot of additional revenue to be had from these accounts. As time goes by, your new business salesman keeps selling and you get more 'new business' but you also accumulate more existing or 'development accounts'. Many companies gain significant revenue growth by 'farming' their existing customer base. What should you do?

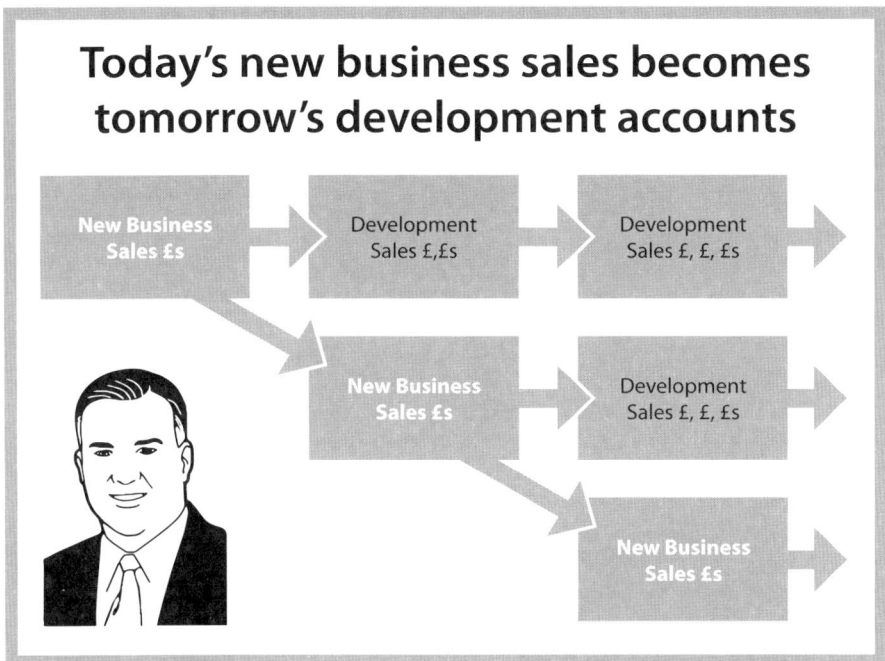

Today's new business sales becomes tomorrow's development accounts

New Business Sales £s → Development Sales £,£s → Development Sales £, £, £s →

New Business Sales £s → Development Sales £, £, £s →

New Business Sales £s →

What do you do now? Do you dedicate a percentage of your new business sales person's time to selling to existing customers? Or do you just ignore these customers and hope that they will ring you when they want something? What are your options?

Options for selling to existing customers
1. Dedicate a proportion of new business sales efforts to supporting existing clients
2. Use back office staff (e.g. customer service) or telesales to continue with sales efforts
3. Hire a different sales person to handle existing customers
4. Do nothing and hope the customer will ring when they want to buy something

So, why not just use your existing sales person to handle existing customers?

In fact, in some circumstances, it might be the best thing to do. If the new business sales person made the original sale, then he/she already has a relationship with the customer and this bond is a good thing. What really matters is: how much business from new customers could this individual bring to you versus how much business the existing customer will bring. If you are a very small business and can afford only one sales person, this may be the way to go. However, be warned, emotionally, it is usually far easier to visit an existing customer with an established, comfortable relationship than to go out 'cold calling'. There is always a danger that the sales person will spend more time than is really necessary in this more comfortable environment and will not maximise new revenues.

If your offering is a simple, straightforward transaction and the value of each deal is relatively low, a good option is to service existing customers with either properly trained customer service staff (lower value, straightforward purchases) or to use a senior manager or director to develop the ongoing relationship with existing customers. However, if your business is big enough and the sales value large enough, it is a good idea to hire a different type of sales person — an 'account manager'.

Why should you bother to have a different sales person handle existing accounts? While selling skills are selling skills, account development represents a vastly different challenge from new business sales. New business sales staff quickly become adept at finding 'opportunities' or moving on, but with an existing customer your sales person doesn't have the choice of 'moving on'. To be successful, these individuals must become good at spotting customer 'needs' and developing these into opportunities. It's often a slower process and requires good people skills of a different kind than for new business. In some cases, a sales person works regularly — often on a daily basis — with your customer, sometimes so closely that there is a risk of identifying more with his customer's business than yours. To be successful, these sales staff must have patience and an understanding of how to build and execute a strategic sales plan.

The 7 key attributes of a good account manager
1. Good planner/strategist
2. Patient & good listener
3. Forms strong, long-lasting business relationships
4. Understands business politics
5. Intelligent
6. Excellent knowledge of all your business offerings and contract options
7. Good at developing customers' needs to show own product/service to advantage

In a perfect world, in addition to new business selling staff, you would have another type of sales person who does 'account management' or 'account development' type of work. Account management is not appropriate for all types of businesses, but when it is appropriate, existing customers become a gold mine in terms of buying additional product or service. Because these companies have already bought something from you, the trust level is high so the barrier to buying more is low. You also possess more information about your customer's business and the issues, and you should have a relationship with some of the customer's staff. All these things make it easier to formulate a winning proposition.

So, when should you invest in a specialist account manager?

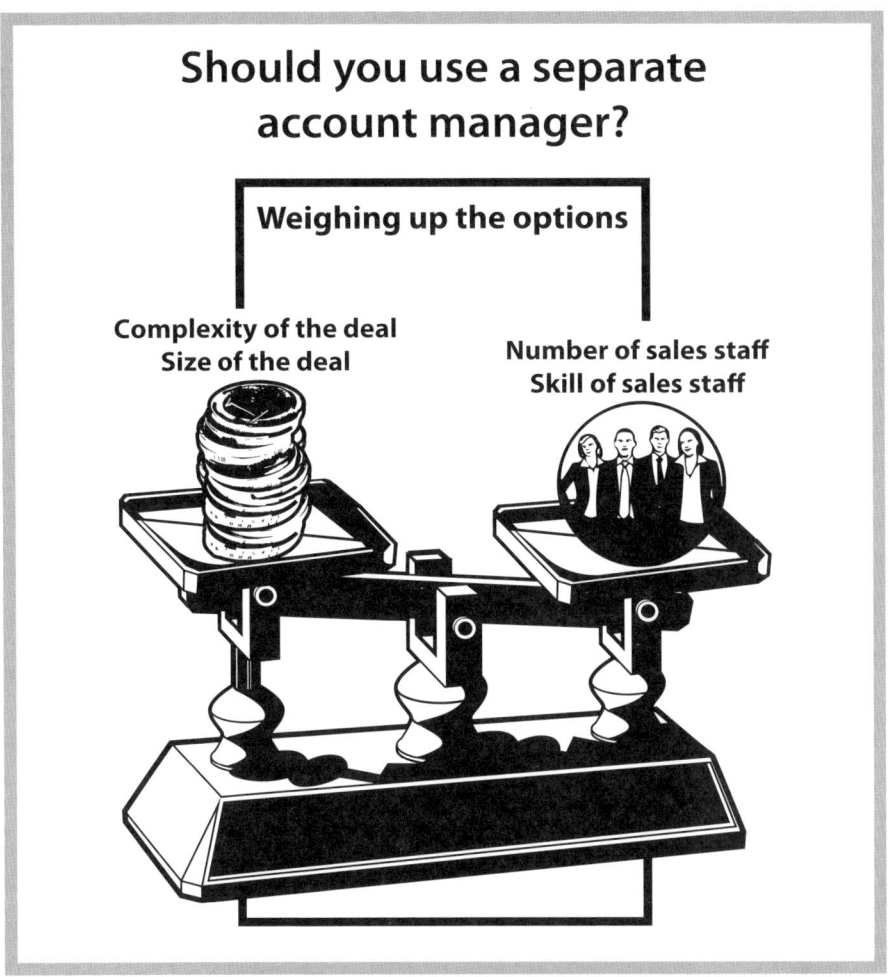

Should you use a separate account manager?

Weighing up the options

Complexity of the deal
Size of the deal

Number of sales staff
Skill of sales staff

Growing revenue by selling more to these customers is much easier and your sales efforts have a far higher probability of success than pursuing new business sales. In addition, on average, existing customers provide a lower-cost way to increase revenue and, because you can learn a great deal about an existing customer's buying patterns, you can more accurately predict the timing of these sales – a real boon for your business planning. Account planning tools (discussed in more detail later) enable businesses to accurately predict the 'what', 'when' and 'how much' of sales in large, established accounts and can allocate business resources and investment accordingly.

So, by focusing on established customers, your cost of sales is usually much lower and it is much easier to forecast sales. All in all, a good position for your business. So, if account management produces a better return on sales 'investment', why waste time with 'new business' sales staff?

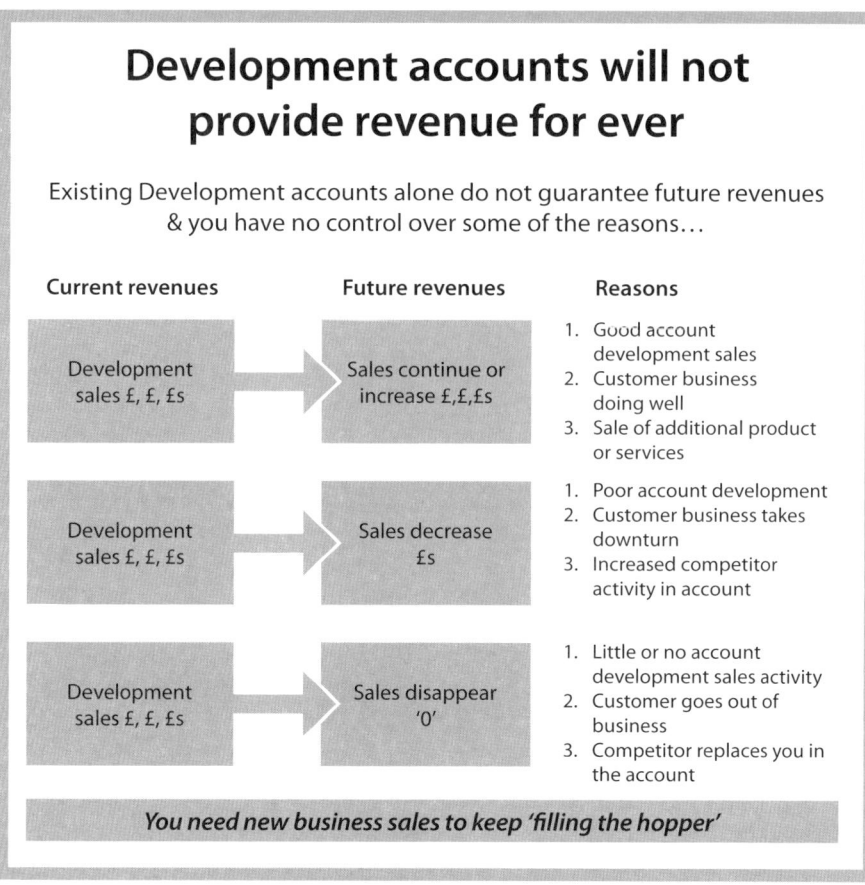

Development accounts will not provide revenue for ever

Existing Development accounts alone do not guarantee future revenues & you have no control over some of the reasons…

Current revenues	Future revenues	Reasons
Development sales £, £, £s	Sales continue or increase £,£,£s	1. Good account development sales 2. Customer business doing well 3. Sale of additional product or services
Development sales £, £, £s	Sales decrease £s	1. Poor account development 2. Customer business takes downturn 3. Increased competitor activity in account
Development sales £, £, £s	Sales disappear '0'	1. Little or no account development sales activity 2. Customer goes out of business 3. Competitor replaces you in the account

You need new business sales to keep 'filling the hopper'

The simple answer is that 'you have to!' If you want to grow or even stay in business in the long run, you must have some way of getting new customers. Existing customers have a way of dropping by the wayside – either through your competitors' efforts or because of their own business issues. In order to have a steady income from 'existing customers' you must invest in some form of new business development. Employing a separate, new business sales person is a common way to tackle this challenge. However, for some business there may be additional sales tool that can be used. Read on to see if you can make use of them in your business.

Agent/value-added reseller/franchise channels

One way of offloading the cost and effort of getting new customers is to use third party agents, value-added resellers, distributors or even franchises to sell your product – and this approach works best when what you sell is 'product', rather than service, although specialist service franchises can succeed too. Each of these third parties offers a slightly different option for extending your sales reach as outlined in the table below.

Agent	Value-Added Reseller (VAR)	Franchise
Independent company	Independent company	Separate company but tied to your business through franchise agreement
NOT exclusive	NOT exclusive	Exclusive
Re-sells your product(s)	Adds service and/or additional features to your product(s)	Product or service – uses your brand features (name, logo, etc) and sells/delivers according to your specification
Sets own price	Sets own price	You set price
No control over agent business	No control over VAR business	Significant control over how franchise runs the franchise
Carries competitive products	Can sell competitive products	Sells only your products/ services
Used to provide sales coverage in distant geographies or when company has NO sales force	Used when additional features or services are required to give your product(s) competitive advantage	Used when want to expand quickly to exploit brand and business opportunity and cannot or do not want to invest in multiple offices/store fronts/ service centres to service the growth

Typically, these agents are remunerated by getting a percentage of the sales revenue they achieve for your product. You may or may not supply special training about your product and then, off they go. The benefits of this approach are that you can offload some of the risk of gaining new business accounts and achieve greater market reach and penetration. These benefits can be significant to a small business with high product costs.

However, the disadvantages must be weighed against the benefits. First, agents are NOT your employees; you cannot fully control their behaviours, actions or activities. You can encourage, but it's very difficult for you to force them to do anything. Also, agents aren't necessarily loyal to your product. To stay in business these companies might have agency agreements with a number of other companies, some of whom may have products that compete with yours. The agent will do what's best for his business and will select what he believes gives his company the best chance of success and the greatest return. You can ask for 'exclusivity', but this type of agreement typically comes at an additional cost for you – usually you have to pay them a higher percentage of your sales total.

Finally, your reputation is linked to how these agents or VARs sell and support your product. You will need to select your third parties with care and monitor customer reaction. One business model that enables you to tightly monitor third–party behaviours is the franchise model.

When should you consider using a 3rd party to do your selling?

1. Expansion into a foreign country

2. Coverage of a large, sparsely 'populated' geography

3. You cannot YET afford the number of sales staff you need to address your market opportunity and you need to act quickly to seize an opportunity

4. 'Franchise' is part of your fundamental business model

A bad reason for selecting this approach is because you don't like selling and want someone else to do it for you!

The 'franchise' is another way of gaining 'exclusivity', but along with greater ties to you can come higher costs. It is not merely a 'closer' partnership with small businesses who will sell your product or service; a franchise model represents a fundamental business decision to go to market in a particular way. It is not as flexible as using an agent where you might decide to 'take over' their territories with your own direct sales force when your business volumes grow. When you choose to use the franchise model you must base your whole marketing strategy around this approach. Your direct customer becomes your franchise partner.

Typically, when you offer a 'franchise' arrangement, there should be a large, geographically diffuse market for your product or service so that these franchises can all make money and not waste efforts competing with each other. Fast food franchises are an excellent example of how typical franchises work. A business, such as McDonald's or KFC, invests a lot of money in 'brand' and marketing so that the public at large will recognise the outlet. Most often, companies who use this model invest a lot of money in training franchise owners, proving equipment or furnishings at a lower cost and specifying signs for outlets so that they all look and feel the same to customers.

Please note this last point: Using a franchise model is NOT a way to avoid selling by offloading it on to franchisees. At best you have merely shifted your sales focus to franchisees who will now be your 'customer'. You still need some kind of new business sales activity when you want to secure new franchisees and you will certainly need 'account management' activities to support and manage your existing franchise network. And, always, always, always you will be responsible for defining and maintaining your 'brand' so your marketing efforts will be very important.

Furthermore, if you become a franchise business you must set a standard for quality and be prepared to 'fire' a franchise for failing to meet these standards. Franchise owners are often obliged to purchase all supplies through the main company. For all this support, franchise owners pay the company a franchise fee for the privilege of running one of the outlets.

All this effort sounds like a heavy investment. Can SMEs really afford to use the franchise model? Yes! One excellent example is Revive, a successful and growing UK SME that introduced 'Smart Repairs' in the UK automotive market. In fact, Revive is a business that started out as a franchise for a foreign company and then moved into becoming a separate business in its own right.

Revive and its franchise model

'Smart Repairs' are small to medium repairs to car bodywork (typically £100–£250) carried out by a mobile team in a specially kitted-out van. Mark Llewellyn, a Rugby-based ex-rugby player, spotted the opportunity while on a trip to Canada in the early 1990s. He started the UK franchise in 1994, and the business really took off after a management buy-out in 2004.

"It's about taking the repair to the customer," declares Mark.

Revive's winning formula focuses on two distinct markets: the end customers for car repairs and attracting and keeping the right, high-quality franchisees. Mark explains that he learned about both 'the business' and what it feels like to be a franchisee during Revive's first decade. So, has the business changed since 2004? "Yes! And it will continue to change."

As Revive has grown, it has shifted into a support business for the franchisees, which:

- Develops and maintains brand value
- Provides marketing strategy and support
- Provides some IT and web services
- Provides financial accounting services (for franchisees)
- Develops, updates and runs telemarketing campaigns
- Runs sales training courses
- Offers 'bulk procurement' services for van/van products
- Trains franchises in how to carry out 'Smart Repairs'
- Provides communications, support and morale events for its franchises
- Supports 'Franchise Steering Group'

New franchisees pay a £23,500 one-time charge. For this they get:

- Licence
- Brand
- Training (both sales and repair)
- Initial 'prospecting' service (one week) and marketing support
- A van

In addition, franchisees each pay £100 per month into a 'marketing fund', which the Franchise Steering Group helps to decide how to deploy. For example, Revive recently sponsored a touring car from this fund. Revive does not provide the financing for this initial 'buy-in'.

This winning formula has fuelled Revive's success and growth. Mark and his team have grown from 13 vans to 105 (75 franchises) and Mark hopes to grow this to 450 vans (140 franchises) over the next 4–7 years.

So, when should you consider this approach?

A franchise is a good method for gaining a low-cost coverage for a sales area, but it works best when business volumes are high and your product or service is straightforward. To be a successful franchise also demands a fundamentally different go-to-market approach when compared to a more direct sales model. However, agents or VARs (value-added resellers) offer a different option.

Agents or VARs are an excellent way of selling over a large or foreign geographical area. In these instances, language, travel costs and cultural issues can be major obstacles to business success. Nexsan Ltd – an example we will discuss in more detail in later chapters – provides an excellent example of how to VARs to enter the US market by a start-up, UK company.

●●●

Nexsan uses VARs to jump-start the new company

The value-added reseller approach was used successfully by Martin Boddy at Nexsan, when he set up a new disk storage rack business. He started from his home in the UK with nothing but a blank piece of paper and his previous experience in the marketplace. Martin's story will be told in more detail later, but the important point in this chapter is that in the beginning, he had no sales resources. He had designed and planned to produce a highly technical product and, although based in the UK, decided to focus on the US market. Martin used VARs in the USA and hired one sales person to recruit and manage these VARs. Over the first 7–8 years of the business, Nexsan grew from no revenue to an annual turnover of more than £50m. By using VARs Martin was able to grow quickly and successfully.

●●●

In this example, Nexsan needed not only sales help in the US but also, because of the complex nature of its product, sales partners who could also add technical services to the sale. It was financially and logistically too challenging for the start-up to consider doing everything itself from a base in the UK, so VARs were the only realistic option.

Telesales

First, when you read 'telesales' did you think 'sales' or did you think 'marketing'? Telesales should not be confused with telemarketing. The two terms are often used interchangeably by businesses trying to hide the fact that they are trying to sell something. Telemarketing is about preparing the market for your product or configuring your product/service better for a particular market. It's an information-only process – both spreading the word and gathering useful market insights – and these processes will be discussed further in the section on target marketing and product description.

This section is about sales and if you wish to sell using the telephone, then you do mean telesales. Typically, this approach targets new business sales. If you sell in a 'business-to-business' environment, tele-selling is rarely used, and never for high-value or complex sales. Even in the consumer marketplace, it is rare that a telephone-based sales person closes a high-value sale on a phone call. It can be done, but selling via the telephone works best in a market where the product or company is well known and the phone call focuses on a 'special offer' or new product/service.

●●●

An example of telesales in the biotechnology marketplace

In the early days of biotechnology, a young, start-up company was well known in the USA among researchers and technicians for providing products and instruments that helped researchers do state-of-the-art genetic engineering and ground-breaking immunology research. Because the business was a start-up, it could not afford to employ sales staff to cover the entire country. Therefore the company used telesales staff to cover geographies that were too expensive and/or too vast to be serviced by regular, face-to-face sales staff.

This qualification is important because most of the prospects and customers, in places like South Dakota and Arkansas, did not expect small businesses to visit them regularly. Because of the market, most of the telesales staff had appropriate PhDs to enable them to speak the customers' language. These 'telesales' staff were not young trainees working to a 'selling script'; they were highly educated professionals who could explain the benefits of new products and instruments to the highly targeted customers. In this instance, telesales worked. Why?

- The products filled a customer need and were often unique – so new business prospects were usually interested in hearing about them and would actually 'buy' during the telephone call.
- The telesales staff were knowledgeable and could speak the language of the customer
- The customers did not expect face-to-face contact because they understood they were 'remote'. However, ANY local provider would probably have had a sales advantage.

For the young biotech company, with the distances involved – thousands of miles – and relatively low 'sales revenue per sale', telesales was the only real, cost-effective way to handle these sales territories. But the young company tackled the situation as best they could by providing the correct calibre of telesales staff.

So, although the biotechnology company 'closed' business on the phone, most often telesales is used as a prospecting tool to identify an individual who might – with the help of further sales efforts, buy a product or service. Double-glazing telesales are a legendary example of this approach in the UK.

Despite its 'hard sell' reputation, if done properly, tele-prospecting can be a low-cost way to make appointments for your new business sales staff. This approach can reduce travelling costs (and thereby your costs) and quickly produce a list of qualified prospects for your more expensive resource – the sales person – to follow up. This approach can be especially useful in a small business when principals or key directors do most of the selling work. HR Solutions 4U is a good example of how, when well done, this approach can help fuel the business.

Telesales and HR Solutions 4U

In 2005, Laura Davis left her career in the retail sector, having spent many years honing her HR skills and experience working in large corporates. She decided that she wanted to work in the SME world – because it was an environment where things happened more quickly and where personal business relationships were important. Determined that she could make a difference, Laura set up HR Solutions 4U.

Laura knew that SMEs needed many of her skills, but the challenges in the SME sector were different. Many couldn't afford a full-time HR person and/or needed specialist skills, but only for a short time. Many of these small businesses didn't even know what they didn't know and the risks that they run because of this 'gap'. Laura set out with a mission to establish her own SME that would provide a full range of high-quality HR services to other SMEs. Her objective? To provide exactly what her customers needed, when they needed it and to do so in a way that enabled them to slowly build a solid HR capability as their businesses expanded.

As her business grew, Laura took on a business partner to assist her. She then began to limit her sales and marketing activities to new business, letting her partner focus on established customers. She discovered from years of experience that it was usually only the managing directors or financial directors who understood the benefits of her solutions for their businesses, and for new business it took a great deal of her time to get a first meeting with these individuals. She solved this problem by using telesales to obtain her first appointments. Over the years, Laura learned through bitter experience how to use this channel effectively.

For example, for telesales, she now uses a company whose business values match her own so that the voice on the end of the phone actually 'speaks' for her business. No scripts are used, but she has invested a lot of time with the individual who makes the calls to make certain that she understands the potential customer issues and how HR Solutions 4U can help. This successful partnership with another SME who does tele-marketing/telesales and arranges well qualified meetings has freed up more of Laura's time to do those jobs that only she can do.

••

Whether or not you should use telesales to sell depends on five critical factors:

1. The price of your product or service
2. The complexity of your product or service and the customer issues it addresses
3. Key competitors' offerings and sales approach
4. The size of your market
5. The number of sales resources you can deploy

Would you buy a Rolls-Royce from a telesales person? In general, the more expensive the item, the less successful telesales will be as an approach. However, there may be exceptions to this rule. For example, if you offer a unique product and have no competition, potential customers may be happy to be contacted by phone. There is no hard and fast rule – you need to look at all the parameters. On the other hand, unique or not, a very complex offering that takes lots of explanation and/or demonstration does NOT lend itself to successful telesales – although use of web-based videos can be a powerful aid. Finally, if you do not have enough sales resources to visit a large percentage of potential buyers personally, then you should consider telesales as one way of 'extending your reach'.

'Telesales' can also be used to extend the efficiency of your direct sales force. If your sales staff do a lot of 'cold calling' in looking for new customers, consider how many phone calls someone can make in a day. Typically a determined telesales person can connect with as many as 15-20 individuals (there will be more actual phone calls, but the target person will be busy, unavailable or for some reason cannot take the phone call). A salesman out in the field would be lucky to see five people without appointments – and a more realistic number is one or two. You must ask yourself if using a sales person is this way is most cost-effective.

Of course, you can use your new business sales person to do the phoning and make these calls, but, typically, a telesales person is paid far less. So, check 'the numbers'. Does it make good business sense to use your sales person or should you be using someone else to set up appointments for 'cold calls'?

If you do decide to use telesales staff, either to obtain appointments for sales people OR to do direct selling, they are often less experienced sales people, and usually know less about your product/service and your marketplace. So, how do you make them successful?

Training is the first step. Make certain that these individuals have training in:

- The product/service and the benefits it provides
- 'Who' they need to speak to within the prospect (job, role etc) and how to identify whether they are speaking to the correct person
- The 'hooks' to get agreement to an initial meeting
- Your company and its processes (e.g. your delivery times, returns policy etc)
- Competitive positioning
- Typical customer 'needs' and issues
- Objection handling

This training provides the 'content' for their discussions.

Next, these people need skills training: not only basic selling skills, but also special skills that help them to 'hold interest' while on a phone call. Many companies use a 'script' to help their telesales staff and this approach – along with other training – can work very well. However, the experience of the individual who wrote the script is critical to success. Finally, to be most effective, you should provide telesales staff with a list of target companies and, ideally, names of individuals within these companies.

• •

Two different examples of how SMEs successfully prepare their telesales

Returning to HR Solutions 4U discussed earlier, Laura, the managing director, solved many of her training issues in her selection of telesales partner. She uses an experienced individual with a mature, business-savvy approach and a style that is conversational, NOT scripted. This individual behaves just like a PA and works to get appointments for Laura to follow up. Laura and this specialist work together to create a target list of companies and identify individuals within these companies. With the help of this business partner she gets appointments with qualified individuals who can buy HR Solutions 4U services if appropriate. In other words, this business partner does the 'cold calling' while Laura follows up the warm leads. Today, approximately 50% of her new business comes through this process.

Revive also uses telesales to its advantage. When Revive achieved sufficient presence in strategic geographical areas in the UK, Mark, the managing director, decided to add the 'Fleet Car' market to his sales efforts. A telesales effort was deployed to contact targeted fleet management companies – the process was scripted and managed by Mark himself, who was already familiar with how to approach these potential customers. As a result of intelligent use of telesales, today the Fleet market accounts for 30% of Revive's business and it's still growing.

In both these successful examples, the managing director was directly involved in the telesales process and carefully prepared and briefed those on the phone.

When to use telesales

▶ Follow-up and qualification of enquiries from marketing/advertising campaign

▶ Obtaining qualified, 'first meetings' for new business sales activity

▶ Selling to awkward geographical area where direct selling by any company is rare

▶ Selling to existing customers if you sell simple, low value items

Retail outlets with sales staff

With retail outlets, most of the 'selling' has already been done via appropriate marketing and branding. Most of the prospective buyers who enter the store believe they know about your product and already have some interest it. It's up to the retail staff to 'close' or complete the sale and to do so they must make 'buying' as easy as possible. These sales people don't need some of the traditional selling skills; they don't have to 'hunt' because the prospective customers have already walked into the shop. What they do need to know is how to convert interest into a sale. In reality, this situation is a cross between 'selling' and 'being bought from'.

Good retail sales

- Captures interest quickly
- Attentive to needs
- Helpful & friendly
- Knowledgeable about products and options
- Does not 'off-load' selling effort on to customer

- Closes the deal smoothly at the pace of the customer
- 'Sells on' related products if relevant
- Is 'helpful' if payment process does not go smoothly

- Continues to be friendly and helpful until the customer leaves the shop & if there are 'returns'

Good retail sales staff should be friendly, attentive and above all, knowledgeable about their products and the benefits of their offerings versus those of the competition. They should be skilled at those customer activities that occur just before they commit – objection handling, negotiation (within specified limits) and making the actual procurement as painless and quick as possible. They should never 'offload' what should be their job on to the customer.

What do I mean by 'offloading'? Say I wanted to find a red dress in my size. For any sales person these words should ring bells – here's a woman who is looking for something specific, so there is a good chance I can sell her something. What should the sales person do? Stick to me like glue! Ask me questions about what kind of red dress I want? "Is it for a party?" "Is it for business?" The more she can find out about me and 'connect', the better chance she has of selling me the dress and other items too. This response only makes sense, right? Then why, in some stores, do sales people respond by pointing – "Try over there!" and then turn to do another job?

We all buy things in shops, so I won't labour the point, I'm sure you could come up with many similar examples. How does it make you feel? Your feelings are important in this situation because 'buying' is typically an emotional process. Someone who is prepared to surrender some money gets annoyed, even angry, when he/she has to wait or isn't accorded the proper attention. So, not only the staff but also the business systems that support the retail staff – the tills, inventory look-up, inventory levels in the shop and credit card systems – should be as slick as possible.

Typically, retail outlets sell tangible products. However, some services can be sold at these sites if the services link to a purchased product. Probably the best-known example of this approach is the selling of 'extended product warranty' – a service based around the repair or replacement of the item being purchased. Mobile phone providers now automatically offer insurance to cover lost or damaged phones whenever a customer buys a new handset. In addition, mobile phone suppliers also sell 'contracts' for phone service – either 'pay as you go' or billed monthly – trying to tie in the procurement of a new phone with a service contract.

One of the best examples of consistently good service in a retail environment is the John Lewis Partnership. In the John Lewis model, all the employees are 'partners' and they share equally (by percentage of salary) in the profits each year. Customer service is part of the culture and employees are trained, empowered and supported in their efforts to provide excellent service. The principle that John Lewis illustrates so well is that, in a large corporation, the whole organisation must support the retail activities – from computer systems to exchange policies to sourcing stock from other locations. Yes, retail shops need appropriately skilled employees, but no matter how well trained and skilled, they can be let down badly by less customer-oriented policies and systems set up by head office.

Tempting as it is, this book is not a vehicle for 'naming and shaming' the worst offenders, but I'm certain that you can come up with many examples of instances where a good and helpful retail sales person was not empowered by the company to help the customer. More and more large businesses today are designed for their own efficiency, treating 'the customer' as a necessary evil in their mission to return larger and larger profits each year to the shareholders. These businesses typically measure customer service as 'politeness' and don't empower customer-facing employees with the ability to solve any issues that might cost the business money. It's frustrating when you are a customer, but it's a BIG opportunity for SMEs who can provide a better, more customer-oriented solution. Remember this advantage if you do set up a retail outlet.

Good service and good products combine to return good sales, but these conditions are only the start. You must also consider location, ambiance and store layout in order to optimise your selling opportunity. Probably your biggest effort will be to get people to come into your shop in the first place and that means extensive marketing and developing a recognisable brand. Customer feedback is an excellent way to test how well you are doing in both these areas and there are some smart ways to obtain this feedback without much cost.

You can think of the 'discounts' or 'offers' you give your customers not only as a buying incentive, but also as a payment for detailed market information. Ask them to provide information as part of receiving the discount or to be included on a list for future 'special offers'. There are also things you can do to keep customers returning; one good example that many companies employ is the 'Loyalty Card'.

The original businesses that offered these cards gained a huge market share as customers switched shops in an attempt to maximise the loyalty benefits. But the market doesn't stand still! Today, in certain retail sectors (supermarkets, retail coffee bars, airlines, to name but a few), the businesses must offer a loyalty card just to get into the game and to retain their business. It's become so popular that there is now a 'Loyalty Card Business', like Nectar – which diverse organisations can join so they can offer loyalty cards without the administrative overhead. Loyalty cards are so common these days that they don't really buy you market share any more, but they are still valuable due to a side benefit – the cards capture individual purchasers' buying information, which can be used for directed sales campaigns.

Internet selling

Strictly speaking, people are 'buying' from an internet site so you are not proactively selling. Rather, you are setting yourself up to be 'bought from'. When items are 'sold' via the internet (or a catalogue), most of the 'selling' has been done by means of 'marketing'. The specific 'marketing' will depend on your business but typically 'marketing' refers to: advertising, brochures and testimonials or any way to get your business known to a potential purchaser. But be warned! Awareness is only half the battle!

You must also design internet systems that are easy to use. Potential customers must be able to:

- Find your website easily
- Look at the appropriate product selection with only a click or two
- Purchase the item in an easy and secure manner
- Have confidence in your supply and delivery systems

After initial customer acquisition (in other words, someone bought something from you), your major challenge will be order fulfilment. That means you must set appropriate inventory levels in the right locations and set up efficient distribution services in order to retain the customer. How do you get the shopper to return to your site rather than someone else's? After all, price and availability checking is not a labour-intensive task on the internet. So, for internet retail business, the critical issue becomes how to you attract shoppers to your site and then keep them coming back.

There is a greater 'urgency' to order fulfilment in internet retail, where potential customers are free to move from online retailer to online retailer until they find the product they want at a competitive price with availability and delivery terms that match their needs. Remember, it's much easier to shop around on the internet than in a 'bricks and mortar' retail environment.

Consider Amazon. If you are an Amazon user, you set up an account with billing and delivery details. You never have to re-enter this information when you place a new order. When you start at the home page, you are given the choice of type of merchandise – for example books, clothes, electronics – and can then search for items more specifically. Shopping is very easy, as is spending money.

When you place an order Amazon provides you with information about price, condition (if it's a 'used' product) and delivery time. It also presents you with a list of other items that are frequently purchased at the same time as the item. In addition, it keeps track of what you have purchased and sends you an email with special offers and product updates based on your purchasing history. Returning items is also a simple process. Most of us will recognise that it is very, very easy to buy from Amazon. But you don't need to be an 'Amazon' to get started!

A big upside to an internet store is that, once the system is set up, it is almost infinitely scalable and has no geographical limitations. It's easy to understand why so many high street retailers are diverting more and more of their business through this channel. However, there may be 'technological limitations'. With the growing proliferation of devices that can 'surf the web', it's vital that any business that wishes to exploit this channel understands what devices its customers will use. The list is long: fixed PC, laptop, tablet, Smartphone – and will no doubt continue to grow. If a user cannot access your site with his/her device, he will go elsewhere, so your business must stay in tune with its customers.

Finally, although, this approach works best for sales of tangible products, service providers can also use the internet – not exactly to sell, but as an advertising vehicle. Need a plumber? Look it up on the net and see who's in the neighbourhood. Again, this isn't so much 'selling' as it is 'advertising' – it works well for small businesses for which the service is well known and understood and doesn't cost tens of thousands of pounds – plumbers, taxis, electricians are all good examples of this sort of service.

However, for high-value or complex products and services, the internet is not a good sales channel. It can be a useful marketing tool, providing interested companies with information about your business, success stories to give them confidence and contact details should they be interested in discussing more, but in a sales process that requires consultation and interactive discussions, face-to-face is a better approach.

Planning your sales

Whatever your approach, you need a plan. Selling is not a random activity, nor is it usually a single-step process. It involves people and money (the 'costs of selling') and, as such, should be managed for maximum efficiency and effectiveness. To manage sales you will need plans.

At the highest level, you need to plan for your annual sales efforts and determine how much money and resources you anticipate needing to support these efforts, but your planning shouldn't stop there.

Focused sales efforts, such as 'campaigns', should also be planned and communicated to your staff, and not just the department that runs the campaign. What happens if you run a 'special price' just as a salesman is about to close some business at a higher price? What happens if you run a sales campaign that is so successful you can't meet demand? Worse still, what happens if your campaign generates sales leads and you create so much interest that you don't have the sales resource to respond to these leads? Planning these campaigns and involving or informing everyone who might be impacted is critical to their ultimate success.

These situations are like breaking a promise and can shatter the trust you have built up with anyone whose order you can't deliver. On the one hand you might think "Great, lots of sales" – however, you might also annoy your customer base when you can't fulfil orders or you raised the interest of someone and then no sales person ever calls. These situations pose a potential image problem in the very marketplace you wish to impress. If your sales approach includes direct sales, you should develop sales plans for each major opportunity. In development accounts, these opportunity-driven plans get aggregated to form an annual account plan that maps out all the activities in a large, important customer account. Such plans spell out, over time, exactly what resources are required to help secure the sale. The plan should also give you an approximate date for closing the business. Items to include in a detailed account plan include:

- Expected 'closing date'
- Key milestone activities with the customer (e.g board meeting, presentation, proposal due date)
- Key decision makers within the customers with an activity plan for ensuring they are 'won over' to your solution
- Activities to manage key 'blockers' who are likely to prevent your winning or who favour a competitor
- Activities to deal with competitive threats
- Proposal production
- Presentation production and rehearsals
- Contract preparation

Finally, plans are not engraved in stone – they can change. When plans change the key thing to remember is to communicate these changes to everyone who has been involved and/or who might be affected by the changes.

Sales approach – a summary

So, which approach is best for your company? The answer depends on a combination of things, including your target market, your product, how big your business is and your growth plans. Product and target market will be discussed in more detail later, but there are some rules of thumb presented in the table below. Usually, the more value and/or the more complex your product, the more benefit you gain from face-to-face selling.

However, if you are a very small business, you may not be able to afford a full-time sales person or enough full-time sales resource to target all your prospects or customers. If this is the case but you have a high-value item, you should NOT sacrifice face-to-face contact with potential customers. Rather, you should prioritise what little sales resource you have to cover these situations and deploy other resources (e.g telesales or customer service) to cover other selling situations. If you need to get to market quickly, perhaps you should consider sacrificing some of your profit and use VARs or sales agents.

If, on the other hand, your business sells to the man on the street or offers a low-value, high-volume product, you have other options: the internet, retail outlets or even franchises. You can also use telesales teams if your product and market lend themselves to this approach.

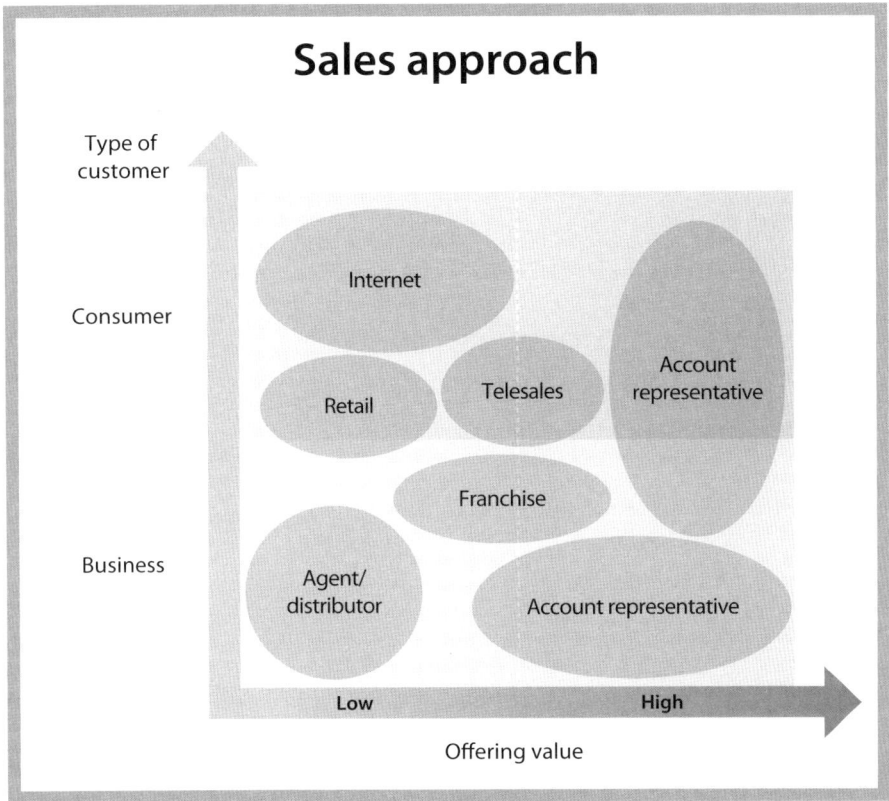

The picture above is meant for guidance only and the actual map of sales approaches will vary from industry to industry. For example, using the airline example cited earlier, you can see how a specific industry maps on to this grid.

Sales approach – the airline example

Type of customer

Consumer

Internet

Package holiday companies

Loyalty programme

Direct phone sales

Business

Travel agents

Account representative

Low   High

Offering value

Although there is some overlap, you can see how airline companies have used different sales approaches to address different target markets

You will note that there is inevitably some overlap between the different approaches – which is a good thing when you want to optimise your chances of capturing business in as cost-effective a way as possible. Your own map may look completely different. After all, not all businesses sell to both consumers and businesses and not all businesses offer both high and low-value options. Lots of options are necessary only when you must address divergent markets and when you offer a large variety of products and/ or services.

A word of warning! Customers provide a wealth of information about your market, competitors' activities and how well your product is being received. When you remove personal contact, it becomes harder and harder to capture this essential data. Loyalty cards can give you buying information, but they don't tell you what a customer **didn't** buy and why.

Whatever approach you use, make certain you have a trusted 'sensor' in your market-place so that you can plan and refine your business accordingly.

In the next chapter we will discuss in detail a special example of a high-value sales approach – team selling. But, before moving on, let's look at some common mistakes made by all types of businesses.

Common sales pitfalls for management at SMEs

1. Hire a 'door kicker' to bring in the business

A common mistake that businesses make is to hire someone who can 'kick down doors'. Have you heard this expression? Does it sound familiar? Does it reflect the thinking of anyone in your company? If so, perhaps you have hired the wrong 'type'. An aggressive 'door kicker' does not inspire trust or encourage the type of relationship your company needs for repeat business

2. Think that selling is 'beneath me'

This sentiment is often expressed by directors or managers who have little understanding or experience of the selling process themselves. It frequently reflects a business culture that has little respect for selling as a profession and therefore, the business hires people to sell who fulfil this image. It's ultimately a self-defeating approach. You may not respect sales people, but think about the message your approach sends to potential customers! Think of the message that it sends to your staff! Your sales people represent your business and need the cooperation of others in the business in order to be successful. Are you hiring people you are proud to put in front of strangers? In front of customers?

3. Believe that the business doesn't need sales people

That may be true. Go back and check the diagram on page 51. If you offer a low-value product and have little repeat business you may be able to get by with good marketing. But be honest with yourself.

You may think you have a great product or service, but your prospective customers will have to be convinced. The history books have many case studies where a better product was outsold by a mediocre one because the company with the best product didn't have a strong focus on sales and marketing or was 'outsold' by a company that had a stronger go-to-market strategy.

4. Expect to offload all your selling activity because you use agents, VARs or a franchise model

When you decide to use third-party companies to do your front-line selling, you should do so because of your inability – either logistically or financially – to fund your own sales force. For example, use of agents, VARs or franchise is often the best choice when you need to sell to remote areas or foreign geography. Franchises are often good to consider when you want or need to provide a service over a large area and just cannot afford to do so yourself.

When you make this decision, you will sacrifice: profit margin, exclusivity and information about your market in exchange for 'coverage'. Do NOT take this decision because you think your own company can avoid undertaking any sales effort itself. You will still need to sell. In fact, if you use a franchise model, you may have a double selling job to do – first to win new franchisees and second to help your franchisees to sell.

In the case of agents and/or VARs, they may offer competitors' products too, so you will have a selling job to convince them to spend as much time as possible trying to sell your product first.

Finally, when you sell using third parties, your marketing costs will be higher than you might spend if you only had to support a direct sales force. Why? Without your own employees facing your customers, you need to create and invest in a strong brand and set up your own systems for market sensing and feedback.

5. *Believe that a website alone will **sell** your offering*

A website can be a wonderful thing. It gives 'substance' to your business and provides information about your company and its offerings. However, a website alone does NOT sell. Selling is about convincing someone that they both need and want your product and that they should buy it. The website can provide a way for people to buy from you, but to be successful you will have to find some other way to:

- Let prospective buyers know your business exists
- Convince them they need your offering(s)
- Demonstrate that your offering is 'best'
- Give them a sense of urgency about buying

You may not have to resort to direct sales to accomplish this task, but you will need to do it somehow. Otherwise, you have just built a good order-taking machine, but few buyers will know you exist. You can achieve a lot with a marketing campaign, email campaigns and telesales to wrap around your website.

In some industries, such as fashion and consumer goods – and items that have been traditionally sold by catalogue – good advertising can help to create awareness around your brand and products. Advertising as well as well-designed web marketing can help convince customers that they need your offerings and show that your products are 'best'. 'Special offers' with time limits can help to create a sense of urgency – but these must be used judiciously or no one believes that your 'special offers' are genuine.

....

END OF CHAPTER 2 – SELF-EVALUATION

EVALUATE YOUR SALES APPROACH - Tick 1 box for each question

QUESTION	Yes	No	Partly
1. Do you have a well-defined sales approach?			
2. Having read this chapter, do you believe it is the best approach for driving sales in your business?			
3. Are you using all the sales channels that could benefit your business?			
4. Does your marketing support your sales approach?			
5. Do you use less costly sales resources (e.g. tele-sales, tele-marketing, customer service) to support your selling efforts?			
6. Does your staff have the appropriate skills/training for your sales approach?			
7. Do your 'back office' systems/IT/policies support your sales staff?			
8. Do you hold regular sales meetings and include staff who support your sales people?			
9. Do you have a website?			
10. Do you have well documented and communicated sales plans?			

YOUR SCORE: Give yourself 5 points for every 'yes', 2 points for every 'partly' and '0' for every 'no'.

36-50 Points ⟹ Excellent – note areas where you didn't score 5 and plan to rectify if relevant to your business

26-35 Points ⟹ Good – you have some room for improvement. Check those areas in which you ticked 'no' or 'partly' and evaluate how you can improve your score

11-25 Points ⟹ You could do better – there is definitely room for improvement…

0-10 Points ⟹ Get help! You have lots and lots of opportunity to improve your income stream.

Chapter 3

Team Selling

Before you read on, examine your own circumstances.

For some businesses, team selling is necessary, but it can be complex and costly. If your sales approach is simple and straightforward and works well with only a sales person or even telesales or the internet, please skip this chapter or read it for interest only.
Why would you need a team of people to sell something?

The truth is if you are involved in certain types of sales situations, you are probably already using 'teams' to sell, whether you do so formally or not. The answer is – you use team selling where it will increase your chances of winning big deals and winning them in a way that minimises your risks and maximises your chances of making a profit.

Chapter 3 will help you to:

1. Identify when and where team selling is your best sales option
2. Select the best opportunities to pursue
3. Organise and manage your selling team
4. Highlight common pitfalls

Sometimes it takes a team to win

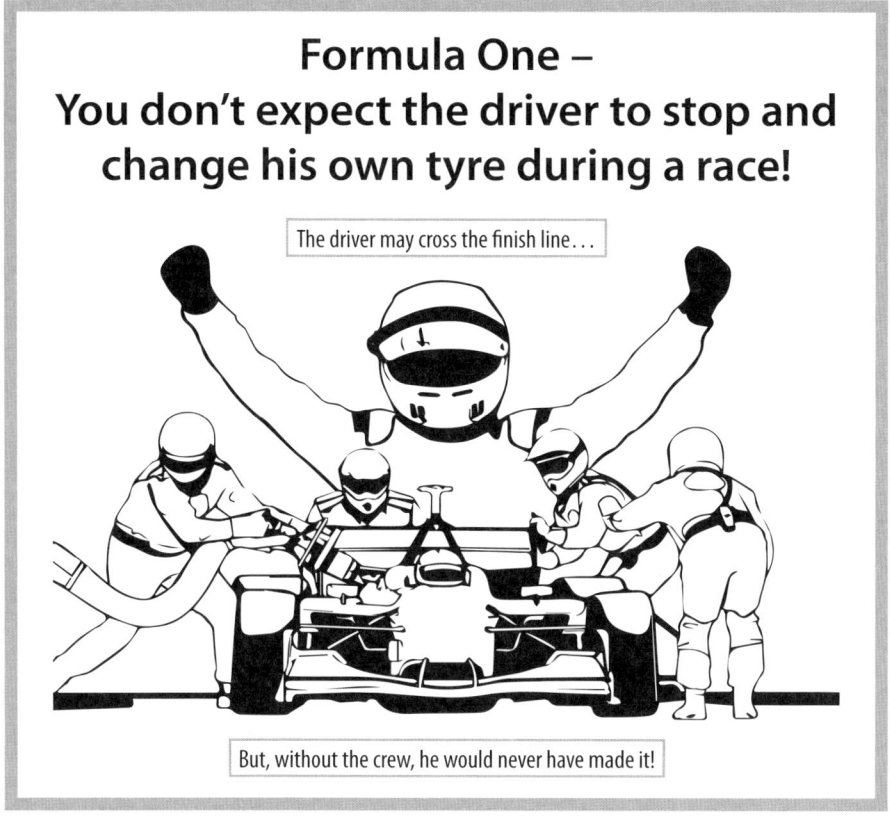

Formula One –
You don't expect the driver to stop and change his own tyre during a race!

The driver may cross the finish line…

But, without the crew, he would never have made it!

Typical team selling scenarios

Team selling occurs when a group of skilled people work together to produce proposals and to sell your organisation's products or services. Like the Formula One team, some selling tasks require a mix of different skills applied at the right time in the sales process, so this team may have full-time participants and/or it may contain many part-time people who carry other business responsibilities. When appropriate, a team selling approach greatly increases the probability of a successful sales outcome. Imagine a Formula One racing driver getting out to change his own tyre or fill his fuel tank. These specialists aren't deployed full-time during a race, but they are prepped and ready to carry out their tasks at just the right moment to maximise the driver's chance of winning the race. So it is with members of a selling team.

Not all sales processes are simple transactions, particularly in a business where the product or service needs special tailoring to suit each client or when the customer's procurement process is so complex that it requires more than one person to produce a quality response. Selling to a customer whose key locations are spread out over a wide geography or multiple countries will also pose challenges to a simple sales approach. In an ideal world, you would put together a team of people to tackle these sales situations, although each of these situations might demand a different combination of specialists.

Don't think: "But my company is too small for all these teams! My staff don't have the time!" Remember, these specialists might work on the team but would also have other responsibilities in your business, and team selling is about organising the sales effort to maximise the probability of sales success while deploying specialists only as and when needed. Team selling requires organisation and planning, but if used effectively it is well worth the effort.

Finally, many SMEs may not have enough sales resource to tackle every opportunity but will want to maximise the chances of winning business. You can leverage these sales skills by using other members of staff to help with some of the selling tasks. And it's not just back-office document production where others can assist. Senior directors and managers can be drafted into the sales process and, if properly briefed, can take part in key sales meetings and advance the sale.

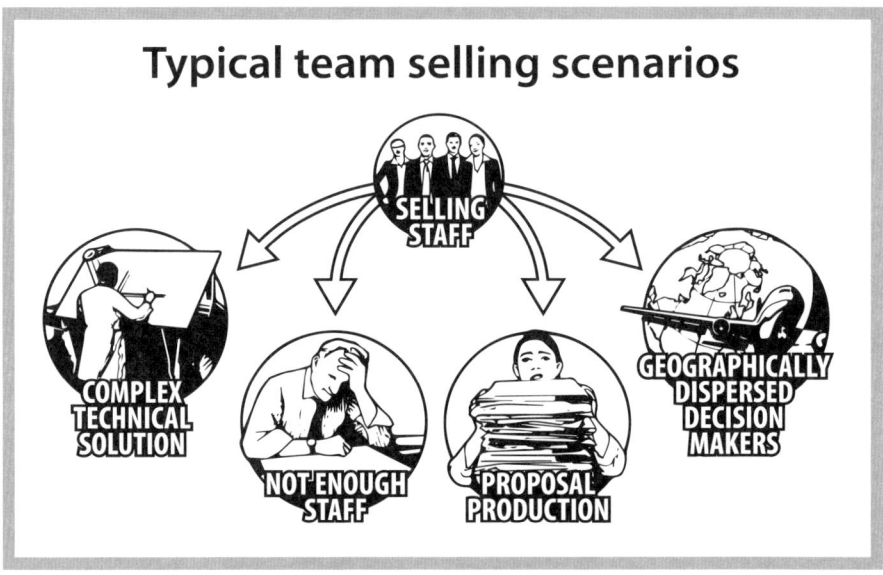

Let's look at each of these scenarios in a little more detail:

1. *Complex solution selling*

Examples of these selling scenarios can be found in heavy construction and specialist engineering companies, as well as application software sales and implementation. In order to 'bid' for the business, technical specialists such as engineers, software designers and consultants must be involved in shaping the solution before it can be proposed. Therefore, although these individuals might not consider themselves sales people, in this situation they are acting with the sales staff as part of the selling team. These specialists are vital to the effort because, without their expertise, no proposal could be written.

2. *Responding to a large, complex bid process*

The worst of these complex bid processes are found in the public sector – however, large complex selling situations may also follow a lengthy and proscriptive proposal process. Typically, there are hundreds and hundreds of questions to answer and all must be answered in a proscribed format or the proposal is disqualified. Therefore, many businesses who respond to these proposals put together a team and divide the work – the bulk of which is document production and not necessarily technical.

3. Selling over dispersed geography or internationally

In some cases, key customer decision makers may be dispersed over a variety of locations, even different countries. If they are involved in the decision, they will want to be involved in the sales process. In this instance, the options are to fly someone who acts in a sales capacity to all the locations, or to find or place someone locally who can act as part of the selling team

4. Limited sales resources

In an ideal world, your sales resource should spend as much time as possible in effective, face-to-face contact with customers and potential customers. This is true whether or not you have sufficient sales staff. However, when skilled sales resource is limited, you must look at ways to enable as much high-quality, customer-facing time as possible.

OK, now you understand why you might need a team to sell effectively and you know that teams may be composed of different skills depending on the scenario, but if you are a small business you might be saying to yourself "I can't afford to employ a whole team like the big companies do!" – and your objection is valid. That's why I used the term 'role'. In most companies, particularly small businesses, regardless of 'job title' people often individual carry out multiple jobs or roles. For example, often someone will be a 'fire monitor' in case of a fire alarm. Fire alarm warden is NOT their full-time job, but the assigned individual carries out this role, stopping his/her usual work, when the fire alarm rings. This is a very simple example. We often have multiple roles at work, particularly in smaller businesses that cannot justify full-time staff for some of the necessary business roles.

So, where do all team members come from?

Usually, they already have a full-time job in the business – a job they must either balance with the team selling work OR neglect for a period of time. It's a frustrating situation, and the smaller the business the more challenging it becomes to balance the sales efforts with the obligations of the 'day job'. Why bother if it's so difficult? Because there are some situations where your chances of winning business you can successfully deliver are extremely low if you rely on a single sales person on his/her own to propose and secure the sale. If you cannot manage to put together a team, you are probably better advised not to waste your business resources pursuing these types of opportunities.

What sales approaches can benefit from team selling?

In general, team selling is only used when you have a direct sales force – either new business or account development sales. While there are some exceptions – for example, in close relationships with VARs and in some franchise situations, typically team selling involves only your own employees.

Which sales approaches can benefit from team selling...

Sales Approach	Team Selling
Direct sales force – new business	✓ Yes, when: 1. Selling complex and/or high value solution 2. Formal, large bid process 3. Geographically dispersed customer decision makers
Direct sales force – account management/ development	✓ Yes, when: The sales opportunity is complex and high value and justifies the resources
Telesales	✗ No – however, telesales can work as team with new business sales staff to help with 'cold calling' and obtain first meetings with potential customer
Agents/VARs/Franchises	✗ No – however, as with telesales, the business can assist Agents/VARs/Franchises with telesales and marketing programs to generate sales leads and appointments.
Retail Outlets	✗ No, not under usual circumstances
Internet	✗ No

What situations benefit from a 'team selling' approach?

There are a number of factors to consider: your own product, the size and resources of your business, the size and geographical spread of your customer's business, the competition, collaboration and any complex, legal or legislative processes that require your compliance. Let's examine each of these factors in more detail to see how you can deal effectively with some of these hurdles.

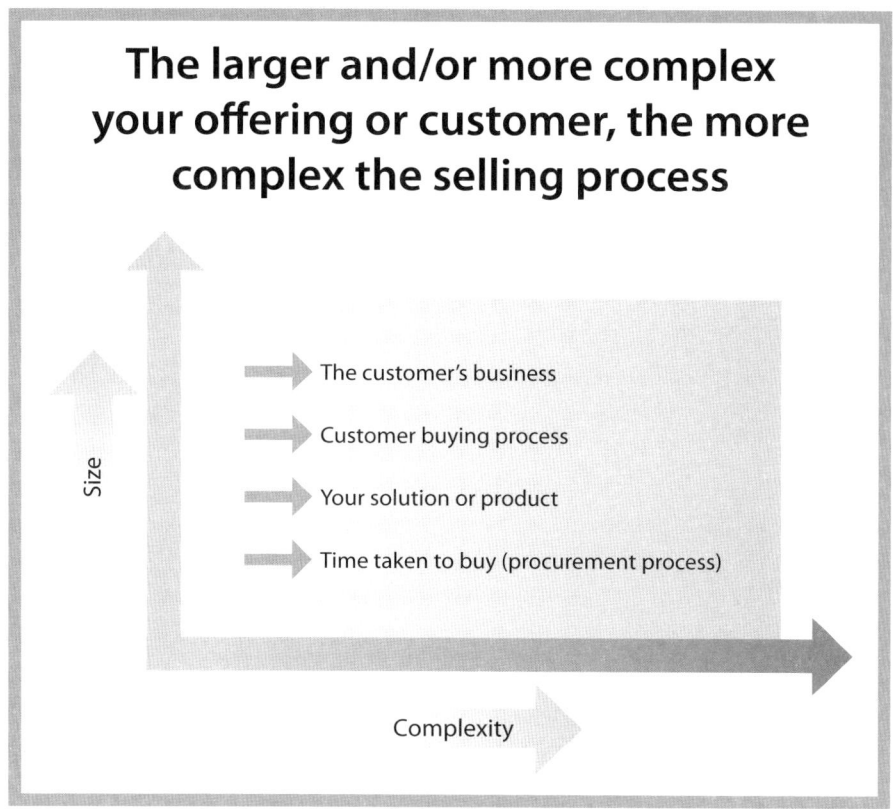

The larger and/or more complex your offering or customer, the more complex the selling process

Size

- The customer's business
- Customer buying process
- Your solution or product
- Time taken to buy (procurement process)

Complexity

Complex product or service

The first thing to consider is something you can control: your product or service. How complex is it? Does it require extensive configuration or tailoring for each client? Do your technical specialists need to be involved in the sale in order to 'cost' and 'validate' what the sales person proposes? Do you collaborate with another company in order to provide a complete solution?

As mentioned earlier, a common example of this style of selling occurs when selling a bespoke customer software solution. Typically such sales also offer implementation assistance. No matter the modern tools available, whoever sells such a solution needs to involve: business process specialists, project/programme managers, software designers, systems architects, implementation specialists and, of course, at least one sales person. All these individuals will interact with the potential customer in order to configure the proposed solution and, therefore, all of them should be considered part of the selling team.

• •

IBM team selling

Over the past decades IBM was cited as a top selling organisation and its sales people were considered a 'gold standard' in business-to-business selling professionals. What many people don't realise is that, at IBM, all sales people worked with a customer-oriented technical specialist – the systems engineer. IBM customers understood that the systems engineer provided them with technical advice while the sales person was there to sell and to 'pay for lunch'. What customers may not have realised was, like the sales person, the systems engineer went through a year of training that included selling skills. Although not sales staff per se, these individuals understood that they played a role in the selling process and worked as part of a team with sales.

••

Today, the job titles within IBM have changed in line with IBM's approach to its market, but in many markets the sales approach remains powerful. As an SME you may not be as big as IBM, but you can still use some of these techniques in your team selling approach. Paul Brennan, an ex-IBMer who went on to work as sales director, CEO and later chairman in a number of different SMEs, applied what he learned at IBM to make smaller businesses successful.

••

The old IBM team selling approach works for small start-ups too!

Paul Brennan started work for IBM in Australia as a systems engineer. At that time, IBM systems engineers were a unique breed – they trained in understanding technical aspects of IT solutions as well commercial and customer-facing skills. This training provided Paul with a sound commercial background in the IT space as well as giving him an opportunity to work in Europe. When he moved to the UK, Paul applied to IBM UK, accepted and then trained to be an IBM salesman. At that time, IBM Sales School was essentially, a pragmatic business school and Paul credits all his time at IBM of the 1980s and 1990s as "giving me all the tools I needed to do the jobs that followed my IBM career. IBM gave me professionalism – a professional approach and discipline that I applied with equal success to large businesses and start-ups."

Paul went on to lead Zeus Technologies (ZT), which we will discuss in more detail later. When he arrived at the business, ZT had no 'sales engine' so he set about transforming the sales and marketing team. Going back to his IBM days, Paul applied his learning by turning ZT into a business in which everyone played some role in the selling process. Previously, the 'rock solid' and very credible engineers had been relegated to a back room to focus on 'engineering'. After Paul took over, in the transformed business, the engineers played a key role in the sales process as part of the selling team.

"It was classic IBM," Paul explains. "The salesman/system engineer approach – commercial acumen linked to technical expertise – a winning combination."

••

Some tools for selling teams

The more complex your product or service, the more people you may involve in the selling. In very complex deals, businesses often collaborate with other companies so that together they can offer a more complete solution with one of the businesses acting as the 'prime contractor'. Having multiple individuals involved can provide many benefits – adding expertise, perspective and support during customer meetings. The tools and techniques described in this section will assist you in successfully managing anything from a team of two through to a large, complex team.

But it's not only your product/service complexity that makes team selling a necessity. If your target customer is large with lots of people involved in the buying process, you face another type of challenge. What is the best way to sell to so many people, all with jobs in different departments, and possibly at different levels within their organisation?

It's important to acknowledge a particular person's status and you can inadvertently undermine it if you send the same person to sell to the security guard as the managing director. This example might be an exaggeration, but you understand what I mean.

Complexity in the customer

A good tool to use when planning a sale in this situation is a 'Buyer Map'. In selling situations one size does not fit all, and it's important to analyse and understand the impact of your sales efforts.

When you deal with a large number of individuals within a customer it's helpful to map them out, listing their positions in the hierarchy and their role in the buying process. It's also helpful to indicate whether you believe they support you, support a competitor or are undecided. Many sales people avoid bad news and try to ignore buyers who don't like them or their company – a bad idea. When you identify a problem, you can begin to do something about it, and that's one of the ideas behind a Buyer Map.

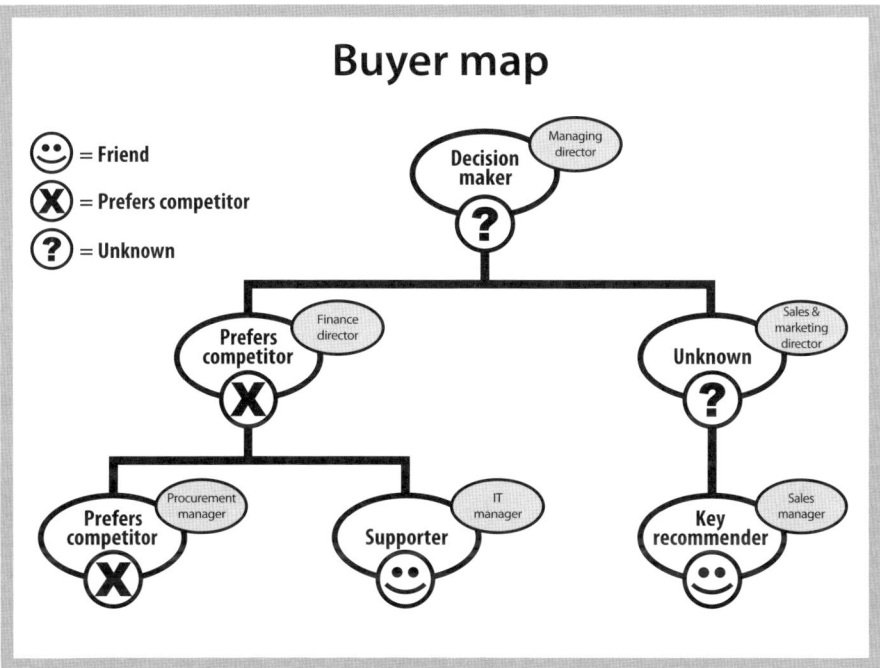

Look at the Buyer Map in the example. You will see that some of the individuals 'like you' but none of these individuals makes the final, buying decision. In fact, your friends are two levels below the decision maker. You will also observe that there are some individuals who prefer your competitor and, sadly for you, one stands between your friend and the final decision maker. Not an easy situation for one sales person to handle alone. If he or she is friendly with people two levels below the decision maker, he/she risks jeopardising this good relationship by attempting to meet with the boss's boss.

The best way to handle this situation – if possible – is to use a more senior person in your company to make the sales call on the decision maker. Your contacts will understand that bosses want to speak to bosses so you can maintain the goodwill of your main contacts while your company sells directly to the decision maker.

What if someone in the customer won't support me?

This individual is also known as a 'blocker'. So, what do you do about the blocker? The undecided individual and those whose views you don't know? Finally, how should your sales efforts manage the people who believe they prefer your competitor's offering? Simply, you – or an appropriate person from your sales team, keep selling to them. I will briefly detail how a sales person would handle such a situation to illustrate how use of the Buyer Map can help clarify which basic selling techniques to use. First, make certain to map your sales team on to the Buyer Map in an appropriate way.

For example, if one of the individuals is highly technical, then try deploying a more technical member of your selling team to form a relationship with this individual. There is a good chance that you can convince the 'undecided' person, once you understand what it will take for him or her to make a decision. If you understand 'why' someone favours the competition, you can also attempt to change his mind. The most difficult character is the blocker and in order to deal with him you need to understand his motives. Are his reasons rational? If so, you can attempt to convince him with rational argument.

Are the reasons emotional? Perhaps this individual doesn't like your sales person. Before you think this doesn't happen, let me assure you, it does. As a female sales person can tell you, sometimes gender works to her advantage and sometimes customers are offended because they can't deal with a man. In these instances the best tactic is to deploy a male member of the team to 'face off' with the individual involved.

Prejudice exists. It can work for you and against you. You have to decide whether you want to take a moral stance or work around it to win the sale. It's your choice. In general, a good sales person may not like it, but he or she does what is necessary to get the sale. If you suspect this sort of prejudice, substituting another team member to meet with this individual might do the trick and a well-constructed Buyer Map will help the selling team determine who should be deployed in each situation.

Finally, someone may 'block' for political reasons – that's company politics. Sadly, this reason is all too frequent. For example, sometimes if director A says 'yes', then director B will always say 'no'. The only way forward in such a situation is to minimise the impact of this individual when carrying out your selling. Some of these techniques will be covered in Part III, but most fall outside the scope of this book. For now, ensure you use a dynamically updated Buyer Map and a well-crafted plan to coordinate important sales efforts in customers where more than one person is involved in taking decisions.

Geographical dispersion

When your customers' facilities are spread out over many regional locations with key decision makers sited around the country, it may be too expensive and time-consuming for a single sales person to travel to all these locations. In this instance you might use additional sales people sited near the remote locations so that you can sell more efficiently and effectively. If you can find someone in or associated with your business, who seems 'local' – particularly to a customer's regional office that is used to being ignored due to a remote location – the apparent local presence creates more 'intimacy' between the sales person and the local customer and this personal bond can help you win the sale.

Foreign locations

Foreign subsidiaries represent a more extreme example of geographical spread, with language and culture differences thrown into the complexity. If you face this situation you must first determine which country actually makes the decision. To win this business it helps if you have some presence in this country. It is not impossible, but it is more difficult to win this sort of deal as a foreigner who is selling remotely – unless, of course, your competitors are in the same situation.

When you are local to the decision maker you must determine how much weight he or she gives to the foreign offices. Believe it or not, sometimes the head office pays very little attention to its international subsidiaries. However, in many cases the foreign opinions are important. Where such is the case, you should be prepared to travel and to get help from someone who speaks the language and understands the culture. You may use a foreign distributor/partner or a consultant; whomever you use, you must include them in the activities of your sales team and make their roles clear.

Complex customer procurement process

Some customers have a rigid, lengthy procurement process. Buying via an RFP (request for proposal) or an ITT (invitation to tender) typifies this approach. Usually, companies that use this approach have a large, powerful procurement or purchasing department 'handling' the purchase on behalf of an internal customer. The process is full of challenges and very costly to pursue for both the company and potential suppliers. Government procurement represents an extreme example of this approach.

What are the dangers of engaging in such an approach?

1. You rarely get to speak directly to the person who wants your product or service. Most of the time you deal only with 'purchasing specialists'.
2. You have little control over what the final solution should be because it's already spelled out in detail in the procurement document – and many times this solution is risky or not the best solution.
3. Often the real decision has been 'taken' but a procurement process is necessary for the buyer, 'just to follow the rules'. If one of these requests 'falls on your desk' out of the blue, be very suspicious.
4. Another situation in which the decision has already been taken is one in which the procurement department want to engage other suppliers so they can 'force down' the price or negotiate special terms with the preferred vendor. Try to identify these situations so you do not waste time and money.

A complex procurement is typically a lengthy process that requires lots of paperwork, proposals, guarantees and a prolonged contracting process should you be lucky enough to get that far. It costs a lot of money, time and effort to respond, so make absolutely certain you have a good chance of winning before you start the process.

However, there are times when you may decide to bid in such a process and when you do, the best approach is a team to help spread the effort. If you have only a small sales force you will not want to tie up all the sales person's time focused exclusively on one deal – it's too risky. Chances are you will require the part-time skills of many individuals to contribute to the sales effort. At a minimum, you should assign someone to coordinate the document production and chase various contributors (sales, technical etc.) for input. If many people are helping 'part-time' you should definitely use the ARCI (RACI) tool, which will be discussed a bit later in this chapter.

Making your sales resource go further

By definition, SMEs are smaller businesses. Many cannot afford to employ enough appropriately skilled staff to support the team selling efforts. But that's OK – there are other ways to tackle this challenge. You have already seen an example of how IBM used its more technical systems engineers to supplement the IBM sales people's efforts. If you have technical specialists they could be trained to provide some support to the selling process.

Depending on your business, you could 'outsource' some elements of the team. In chapter 2 you read how HR Solutions 4U worked closely with a specialist telesales company to obtain new business appointments with the decision makers in target companies. By working as a team with this outside company, the MD of HR Solutions could spend her time most effectively selling face-to-face in a qualified sales meeting. Forming a partnership with another SME whose products/services complement your own may also help you to supplement your sales efforts – but be careful! The company who deals face-to-face with the customer effectively 'owns' the relationship, so you must trust this business partner to represent your business's best interests.

In chapter 2 we talked about how Revive used telesales to obtain good leads for its franchisees in order to help them be successful.

You also have many 'in-house' options for helping this critical resource go further:

- Telesales to get appointments with appropriate individuals in the right companies
- Back office 'sales support' to help with time-consuming sales administration
- Back office 'sales support' to fulfil commitment to customers such as sending out material (brochures, letters etc.) to interested buyers
- Back office support to help with logistics such as reserving meeting rooms, hotels, travel arrangements and photocopying
- Bid support staff to help project manage proposal preparation, gain formal approval for bid commitments and coordinate specialist resources

In all these instances, other people will be involved in the selling process and they will need to understand what role they play in helping to win business.

Summary: Situations that benefit from a 'team selling' approach

▶ Large, complex customer with many people involved in the buying process

▶ Large, complex customer with multiple sales opportunities

▶ Opportunity which covers large geography, especially multiple countries

▶ Specialist(s) must interact with customer in order to configure the solution/write proposal

▶ Customer has a lengthy, onerous buying process (e.g. government)

▶ Your sales resource is stretched to thin to undertake the selling by him/herself

The roles

When a team is deployed to sell, it is vital for everyone to understand his or her role and responsibilities. In addition, everyone should be clear about his/her team members' roles and responsibilities. Although it sounds obvious, it's worth stating that all team members should be clear about how the whole team functions and how each member should interact with team-mates and the customer. The following few pages provide greater detail about the team, roles and tools to help ensure that everyone works together to sell effectively.

The overall objective in establishing different roles and tasks is to maximise the 'face time' of the sales professional with the customer, as well as to ensure that everyone involved in the selling team helps rather than hinders the selling process. How might this work?

In a small team of two or three, typically there will be a sales person and a technical specialist or two. For bigger deals, you could involve many specialists, both technical and sales, who help part-time or full-time, in both the proposal and selling process. All these individuals will often have a 'day job' as well, so as much administrative work associated with the selling should be delegated to a more junior or less costly staff member. Big bids will have lots of logistical tasks – such as reserving meeting rooms, photocopying, managing diaries and making appointments – and these too should be delegated where possible.

If the selling team grows to more than three people, there should also be someone to manage the whole process, from selling to proposal production. This individual, called a 'bid manager', acts as a project manager for the sales process until the business is won or lost. In some cases, this individual provides a 'back office' service and never actually has to come face to face with the prospective customer. In more complex or risky bids, this individual will also make certain that someone has done a 'risk assessment' of whatever is proposed – hopefully before the proposal is shown to the customer!

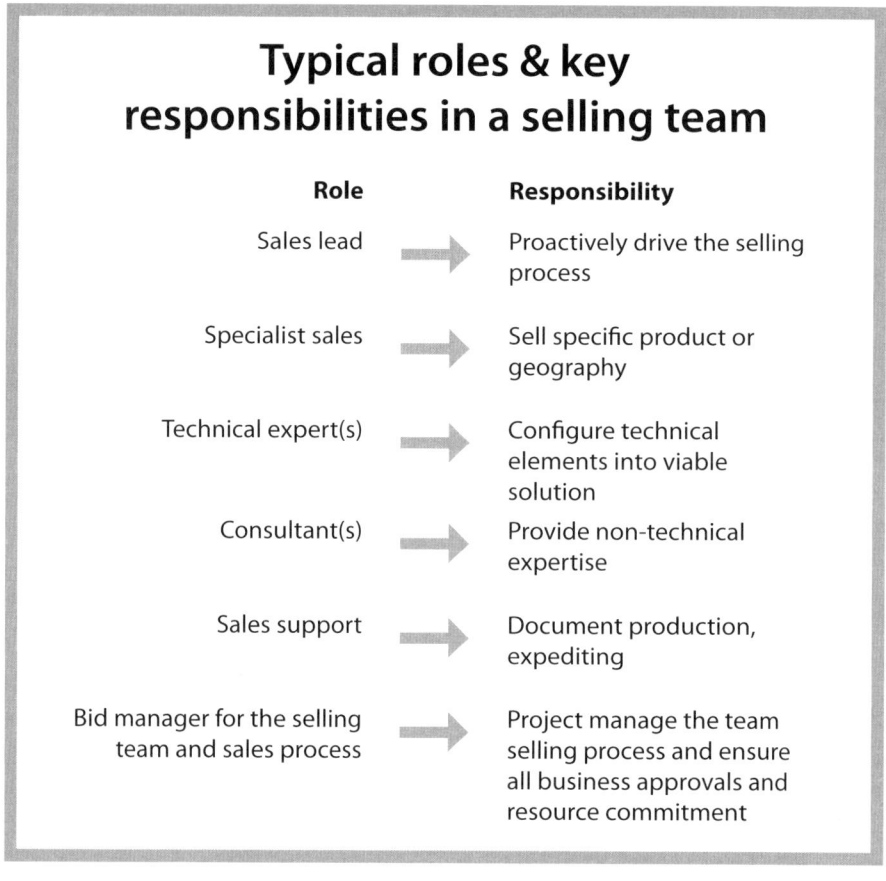

Typical roles & key responsibilities in a selling team

Role	Responsibility
Sales lead	Proactively drive the selling process
Specialist sales	Sell specific product or geography
Technical expert(s)	Configure technical elements into viable solution
Consultant(s)	Provide non-technical expertise
Sales support	Document production, expediting
Bid manager for the selling team and sales process	Project manage the team selling process and ensure all business approvals and resource commitment

ARCI – a tool for setting up successful teams

ARCI (also known as RACI) is a methodology used to set up and manage teams. The acronym stands for: "Accountable" "Responsible" "Consulted" "Informed". To use ARCI, you begin by dividing up the necessary activities into high-level 'tasks'. Then, for every high-level task, the group assigns one person to be Accountable for the successful delivery of that task. Others may do the work – they would be Responsible. Both individual team members (and others outside) may need to be Consulted at various stages of the work – for example, some form of 'approval' or 'risk assessment' may need to happen before a proposal is shown to the customer. These individuals will be assigned a 'C'. Others will just need to know what's going on, but don't necessarily need to be involved in the task; these individuals are Informed (I) as necessary.

The cartoon overleaf illustrates this explanation.

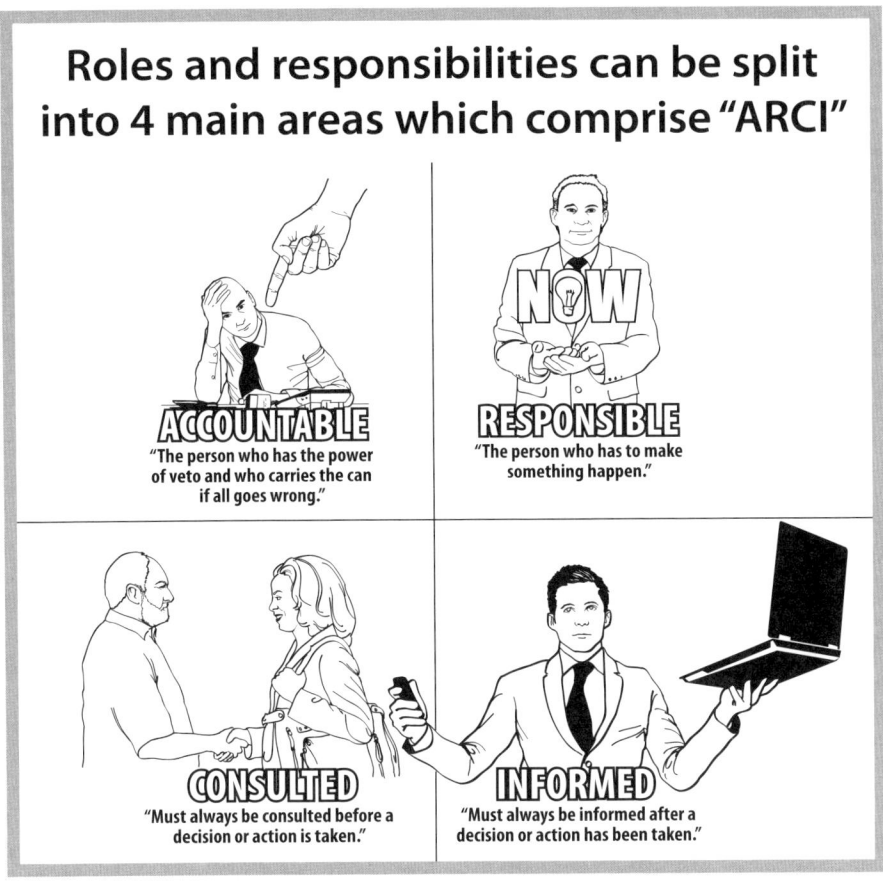

Roles and responsibilities can be split into 4 main areas which comprise "ARCI"

ACCOUNTABLE
"The person who has the power of veto and who carries the can if all goes wrong."

RESPONSIBLE
"The person who has to make something happen."

CONSULTED
"Must always be consulted before a decision or action is taken."

INFORMED
"Must always be informed after a decision or action has been taken."

ARCI provides a simple tool for clarifying roles and responsibilities as well as managing tasks throughout the selling process. It also helps uncover potential issues about who is in charge of the overall process. You may think it's obvious, but remember, this team may contain individuals who are very senior and/or experts in their own right – each may feel that he or she should have the final word in a dispute. The bid manager who is driving the selling process can become 'confused' and begin to believe he/she is in charge of selling. Such conflict and misunderstanding are very common and the ARCI helps to make accountabilities clear. Winning organisations take the time to define the roles and responsibilities of their sales team members; it makes the team more effective and increases the chances of winning the sale.

How often do you hear someone say, "I thought he was supposed to do it!" Again, use an ARCI diagram to map out who does what and you will hear this defence less often.

Who is in charge?

With, potentially, so many people involved – even part-time – it's important for all of them to understand that whoever has the 'A' for selling should call the shots. This individual should be responsible for ensuring that there is a Buyer Map and Sales Plan as well as a ARCI for the sales opportunity. When multiple sales staff are involved or other specialists who might do some selling, there can be differences of style and opinion. Remember, the man who carries the can calls the shots.

Who is in charge of a technical sale?

This story was related by an experienced sales person from a large business and technology consulting and services company. The particular incident refers to a call he made when he was accompanied by a young technical specialist. The salesman made the mistake of not briefing the specialist thoroughly because he brought the young man along just in case the customer asked about a specific problem. In reality, he was just taking precautions and didn't expect the specialist to have to say anything.

The salesman was senior, he was sales, he was in charge... or so he thought. As he settled into the meeting with the customer, he started asking 'directed questions' – a sales technique for leading the conversation while letting the customer do the talking. But every time he asked a question, the specialist piped up and answered it instead of letting the customer speak. The salesman asked the customer a question, the specialist answered it, and on and on it went for about 10 minutes.

At this point the salesman excused himself and asked his young colleague to step outside for a moment. The specialist acted smug, pleased that he had demonstrated how clever he was and self-satisfied that he clearly knew a lot more than the salesman knew. During the brief 'aside' the salesman asked him why he thought the salesman was asking the questions. At that point the technical specialist finally sensed that something wasn't right. The salesman then explained that he rarely asked a question in these situations when he wasn't already certain of the answer. What was important he explained, was that the customer gave the answer – in the customer's own words. He let the young specialist know that he had effectively undermined the selling process and that when they went back into the room he should only speak when asked a direct question.

They returned to the customer meeting and soon things were back on plan. The specialist remained silent and the customer got the chance to speak.

The point of this story is that this meeting was NOT about conveying technical expertise or specifically solving a customer problem, it was about advancing the sales process. Therefore, no matter who else from the selling company accompanied the salesman – whether it was his managing director or a scientific director – the salesman should have the final say in how the meeting is run. In some instances, the salesman may do very little talking and his colleagues may do all the talking, but the important point is that when they speak, they are 'following a script' that progresses the sale – the broad outlines of which have already been agreed before the meeting.

ARCI offers a simple tool for clarifying roles and responsibilities

ARCI provides:

- Clarity about who does what

- Commitment / no hiding

- Resolution of conflicts

- A way to get stuff done!

Activity	Example: ARCI			
	Anne	Brian	Claude	David
	(Technical lead)	(Sales lead)	(Sales support)	(Financial support)
Prepare risk assessment	R	A	I	I
Get technical sign-off	A/R	C	R	C
Complete costings	C	R	R	A
Write executive summary	I	A/R	R	R

Top Tips

- Only one A is possible

- A person with too many A's needs to delegate, otherwise he/she will become a bottleneck

- Multiple R's possible, so work can be delegate

- A person without A's might have a support or expert role; otherwise look carefully at the role and contribution. Ask yourself: Should this person be on the team?

It all sounds straightforward, doesn't it?

Do you use this kind of tool in your company now? If so, you can pat yourself on the back and skip to the questions at the end of chapter 3. However, most companies do not regularly use ARCI and very few use it for the selling process. Whatever your situation, there are other good practices you can employ.

Don't forget to agree common standards and terminology for use within the team; simple things like: common action list formats and agreed, common terms for describing your offers can save time when compiling information from different sources. Common standards and regular team communications go a long way to helping cement the diverse members of the selling team. For example, when responding to a long and complex bid whose preparation takes many weeks, regular bid meetings help to maintain the selling team's focus and ensure that tasks are being completed on time. Furthermore, these meetings enable information sharing of intelligence gathered during various customer meetings that can give valuable insights into how to shape the final bid.

Beware of combining different selling styles…

If you regularly deliver projects as part of your business, think of the selling opportunity as a 'project' and treat the 'bid' or 'selling process' as you would a 'project' by using some of the disciplines regularly employed in project management. You can read more about the process of selling in Part III of this book. If you apply some of these principles, you will discover that everyone works together more efficiently and effectively and it reinforces the feeling of being part of a team and part of the success of the sale.

A common source of conflict stems from different selling styles and approaches. Experts who sell themselves as consultants, or just experts who provide technical assistance, are used to proving their value by demonstrating how much they know. You have already seen an example of this style a few pages ago in 'Who's in charge of a technical sale?' The selling style is very much 'tell' and hope that in telling the potential customer will be so impressed he will ask: "Do you think you can help me?" In other words, experts position themselves to be 'bought from' and manage a conversation so that a customer closes the sales and asks to buy.

Professional sales people who sell 'solutions', products, services – but not themselves – typically use a completely different style. Often they use a technique called 'directed questioning' in which they ask a series of questions during a customer sales meeting. This technique enables the sales person to lead or direct the conversation WITHOUT doing all the talking. Good sales people spend a good deal of their time listening and repeating back what customers say in order to check for understanding. It is important for a number of reasons.

First, you get the customer to say what he wants and needs and then play back his/her own words. This approach is far more effective than just telling him what he/she wants or needs. Second, most people like to talk and think more highly of someone who spends a good deal of time listening to them, asking interested questions. So this approach also establishes good rapport with a potential customer. Finally, as mentioned earlier, if it is done well, the sales person actually controls the direction of the conversation and can discover lots of useful information about the buying process and how to win the sale.

Such techniques are part of basic sales training. In fact, during training sales people are often told: "You have two ears and one mouth – use them in that proportion when meeting with customers!" The earlier story demonstrates what can happen if you merge the two selling styles in one customer meeting and basic sales training alone will not solve this problem. ARCI, preparation and planning will.

Different styles/different points of view

And different personal styles can be a good thing – as long as it's clear who is calling the shots in any given customer encounter. Remember our discussion of the Buyer Map? Sometimes one style works well with a particular customer while another style rubs him up the wrong way. Two different viewpoints in a customer meeting can also be very useful, with one person noticing different, but important, points that another may miss. Different styles and skills when used with appropriate tools and plans can increase sales effectiveness.

What happens after you win the business?

Consider the customer experience of the selling process. If it is done well, many specialists and sales people will have spent lots of time with various customer staff. You will have built trust – trust between his company and yours – but more specifically, trust between the individuals involved in the selling. The customer got used to having you around. So, what happens when he signs a contract? Does everyone disappear? Will he suddenly see fewer people and all strangers? If you don't plan well, even at this stage you can drop the ball and the customer relationship will sour unnecessarily.

If you have successfully sold a major programme or project that involves implementing a highly technical solution – for example, a new air filtration system for hospital surgical theatre or implementation of a new application software product – chances are you will use a programme director/manager to oversee the delivery of your solution. What happens if this individual rolls up just after the contract is signed and the customer doesn't like him? Or, as often happens, the newly introduced programme director complains that he can't deliver the programme the way your sales team has sold it? Yes, both these things can and do happen all the time. However, there are steps you can take to prevent such catastrophes.

First, introduce the programme manager into the selling team at some point midway through the selling process. In this way he has the time and opportunity to build a relationship with your key customer contact and, because he won't leave after the contract is signed, can smooth the transition from selling to delivering. Second, if the programme manager is involved in the selling process he will have participated in the proposal process and should be comfortable with the proposed solution.

Motivating your selling team

Last, but not least, you need to consider motivation. Every member of a selling team is vital to its success. If this description doesn't fit someone, the individual should NOT be on the team. You will often be asking more of these people than usual – for example, working late or weekends to meet deadlines while trying to balance these demands with a different, 'day job'. Keeping everyone motivated is critical to the success of the team.

However, when you use a mixed team of professionals, some or all of them part-time on the sales team, it means that each will be measured and paid in a different way. In some cases the sales person will have financial incentives to win the business while the other individuals will just be paid their salaries – win or lose. Such circumstances can lead to bad feelings and bad team dynamics if the situation is not recognised and managed. 'Managing' and 'motivation' is NOT just about money, it's also about recognition.

Getting your targets and rewards right is critical to success. Chapter 4, which follows, discusses this vital topic in detail.

Team selling: Common pitfalls

- ▶ Roles not clearly defined or understood by all
- ▶ Somebody wants to have all the A's (accountability)
- ▶ Poor communications within team
- ▶ Lack of common standards within the team
- ▶ Lack of smooth transition from selling to delivering the solution
- ▶ Failing to motivate & reward the whole team

END OF CHAPTER 3 – SELF-EVALUATION

EVALUATE YOUR TEAM SELLING - Tick 1 box for each question

QUESTION	Yes	No	Partly
1. Do you use team selling? And if NO, should you? (If NO to both, then skip the rest of these questions			
2. Does everyone in the team have a clear definition of his/her role?			
3. Does everyone on the team recognise that he/she is part of a selling process?			
4. Do you have sales support staff in place to maximise the customer time for selling staff?			
5. Do you use a Buyer Map?			
6. Do you prepare a well-articulated and communicated sales plan for your team selling?			
7. Do you have someone identified who is project managing the sales team and/or bid process?			
8. Does your selling team communicate regularly and effectively with both team members and other invested individuals in your business?			
9. Does your business employ a 'transition strategy' to ensure a smooth shift from selling to delivering your solution?			
10. Do you have a plan to reward or recognise all members of a winning selling team?			

YOUR SCORE: Give yourself 5 points for every 'yes', 2 points for every 'partly' and '0' for every 'no'.

36-50 Points	⟹	Excellent – note areas where you didn't score 5 and plan to rectify if relevant to your business
26-35 Points	⟹	Good – you have some room for improvement. Check those areas in which you ticked 'no' or 'partly' and evaluate how you can improve your score
11-25 Points	⟹	You could do better – there is definitely room for improvement…
0-10 Points	⟹	Get help! You have lots and lots of opportunity to improve your income stream.

Chapter 4

Sales Targets

Top tips – Chapter 4

1. Set a sales target which your company can deliver – too low and too high are both bad policies

2. Set your sales target based on a combination of:

   ▶ sales history

   ▶ the current market

   ▶ customer status

   ▶ competitor activities

   ▶ your business strategy

   ▶ the experience level of your sales staff

3. Use 'recognition' as well as money to reward

4. Remember to recognise/reward others who contribute to the sales success

5. Targets that are too low as well as too high can reduce motivation – good sales people will leave if targets seem 'unfair'

6. Account managers for existing customers can achieve 5-10 times the revenues of new business sales people – target accordingly.

7. Don't keep moving the goal posts!

8. Be sympathetic to unplanned events (e.g. disasters, deaths, etc) and readjust targets

---

How much do you want to sell? Think about it – if you answered: "As much as possible!" Is that really best for your business? Can you deliver 'as much as possible'? What happens to your reputation if you can't? And if you stretch all your business resources, what happens to quality control? And if quality goes down, your reputation and, eventually, your sales will suffer. Like Goldilocks and the Three Bears – what you need to sell must be 'just right'. And figuring out 'just right' is where you need to start before handing out all your business targets, including sales targets.

Getting sales targets 'right' is a serious management challenge – remember, these targets will drive behaviours. Set them too high – unrealistically high – and staff will 'give up'; set them too low and you will undoubtedly lose out or pay too much for new business because no one will be motivated to go out and sell more. In these circumstances, those managers who have done some selling themselves find it easiest to determine what is a fair yet challenging target.

Business targets

Let's go back to basics. Why set targets for sales? In fact, why set targets for anything in your business?

There are many good reasons:

- Targets act as markers and measures in your annual and long-term business planning
- They help you to manage your business and ensure a balance of supply and demand
- Targets in all areas of your company reward balanced growth
- Most people are competitive and well set targets can motivate staff to achieve that little bit more
- Well-set targets, when achieved, help boost company morale

Above all remember, targets should be a means to an end and not an end in themselves. Setting good targets is a skilled and challenging job and many, many people do it very badly. Remember, people like to know they are doing well and, unless the target is impossible, they will work hard to achieve it. This advice goes for all targets and measures that you set to manage and encourage your staff. Sales targets are just one example and the rules for sales apply to your entire business.

Setting business targets

The end result of good target setting is to drive the behaviour you need to perform optimally. In a business, 'optimally' means balancing all the different activities while driving them toward delivery of a common goal. What this means is you have to get all your planning right, starting with your high-level business plan, and carry out 'top down' planning for all your departments, including sales. Then you need to do a reality check.

Do some bottom-up planning and then cross-check by looking at details and making adjustments. Ask yourself: Have there been any major shifts in the marketplace?

- New product announcements?
- New competitors?
- New government regulations or taxes that have impacted your customers?
- Job changes or retirement of your contacts in key customers?
- Impending strikes, shortages?

The list goes on and on, but for your own marketplace you can probably isolate five or six key factors that will have a positive or negative effect on your sales.

What must you consider when setting business targets?

- ▶ Changes in your market
- ▶ Size of your market
- ▶ Position in product/service life cycle
- ▶ New legislation or taxes which affect either your business or your customers
- ▶ Changes in your pricing/discount policies
- ▶ Competitors activities (e.g. new products/offers/pricing/policy changes/ increased capacity)
- ▶ Situation with key customers – business and individuals
- ▶ Your own business's ability to supply orders
- ▶ Changes in your own sales staff

Once you are happy with your annual 'top down' and 'bottom up' business planning, you can begin to set an overall sales target. Remember, any 'growth' in sales targets should be matched by a growth in your business's production/delivery capacity or you will eventually pay the price with disappointed clients and loss of business.

The next step is to break down the high-level sales target and distribute it among your selling staff.

Distributing the sales targets

How you break down and distribute these targets depends on your sales approach. Retail shops pose different opportunities from a business-to-business sales model. What is true is that if you use more than one sales approach you should not assign the same targets for each. For example, it is a well-established fact that new business sales take a greater investment than sales to existing customers. Not only is the probability of winning a sale less for new business, but the sales person's ability to predict and manage the timing of the sale is lower. Therefore, in general, new business sales targets should be lower than those of established accounts.

One thing to remember is that you should only assign a target to someone who has the possibility of reaching it. If a sales target is impossible to achieve, at best you will demotivate your sales staff and, at worst you will lose them.

Distributing your sales targets

Major account manager's target

New business sales target

Agents' target

Minor account manager's target

You should also take into account when an existing customer is 'in trouble' and will not spend much money with you in a given year. It's no good targeting the account manager with a hefty sales target if you know the customer will buy nothing. In these circumstances you must take some difficult decisions: do you remove the account manager from the account? Give the account manager additional accounts to manage or some different work? Or do you 'invest' the account manager's time in this account without the return in hopes that your loyalty will be rewarded in future years? These are business judgments you must make and you must balance the costs and risks.

If you use agents or VARs, apportioning your sales targets can be a balancing act. You will also have to make certain that your targets, though challenging, are achievable or the agent will simply not sell your product. You must also make sure you give the agent or VARs any support needed (brochures, specification documents, technical support) as well as training in your products or services. In any case, always consider both the opportunity and an individual's chance of influencing the outcome – the two do not always coincide.

First, sales targets can be more than just 'revenue achievement'. In fact, you may decide to set targets on profits, rather than revenue, in order to discourage discounting. In product businesses, another approach is to target on 'number of items' sold. Some companies use a combination of all three. Furthermore, you can also set non-financial targets and pay your sales person against these targets too. Non-financial incentives will be discussed in more detail later.

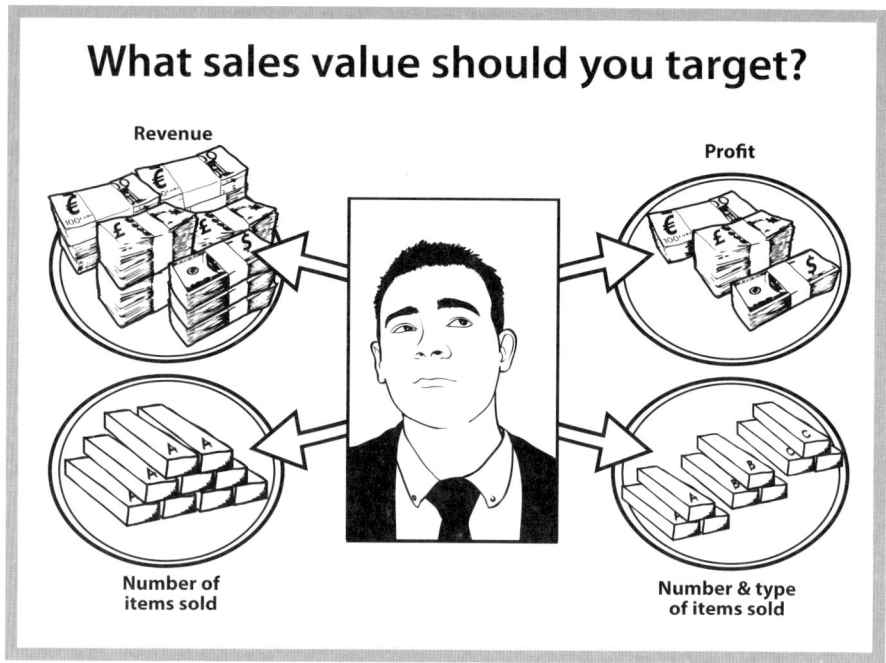

What sales value should you target?

Revenue

Profit

Number of items sold

Number & type of items sold

Next, you must decide how much of a sales person's salary will depend on achieving whatever targets you set. Should you pay a straight salary, and make none of his/her income dependent on how much is sold? Or should you go to the other extreme and pay all the salary based on some quantifiable target – revenue, profit, number of items or a specified combination of these measures?

There are advantages and disadvantages in each of these approaches, and the best for your business depends on:

- The maturity and predictability of your market
- The sophistication of your sales management
- How precisely you need to control/manage your costs
- The skill of your sales staff

…And many, many other variables. All approaches have both advantages and disadvantages that you should consider before setting targets and deciding how to recompense your sales staff. The following table illustrates some of the situations in which you might select one approach over another and lists a few of the potential pluses and minuses.

Sales force compensation methods

METHOD	USEFUL WHEN	ADVANTAGES	DISADVANTAGES
Combination (eg 60/40)	▶ All sales staff have similar earnings potential ▶ Provide incentives but still manage sales force	▶ Provides some security ▶ Provides some incentives ▶ Expense fluctuate with revenue	▶ Sales expense less predictable ▶ May be complex to administer
Straight Salary (no commission or target-based remuneration)	▶ New sales people ▶ Going into new areas ▶ Sales people perform more than just sales	▶ Maximum security ▶ Sales manager has maximum control ▶ Predictable sales expense ▶ Easy to administer	▶ Low incentives so needs supervision ▶ Selling expense remains at same level regardless of sales revenue
Straight Commission (all commission or target-based remuneration)	▶ Aggressive sales required ▶ Company easily cannot control sales force activities	▶ Maximum incentive ▶ Can encourage behaviours to sell certain things	▶ No security ▶ Company has minimal control ▶ May encourage poor service ▶ Selling costs are less predictable ▶ High turnover of sales staff in difficult years

Whatever approach you select, it might change from year to year as your business grows and/or the market changes. That's fine. It's good to review target setting regularly and to make adjustments. But you must consider your timing when you make these changes so as not to discourage or anger your sales force. What do I mean?

How to set the 'right target' for sales

Sales targets should be a two-way contract. You will affect someone's take-home pay and this individual will impact your business revenues – both of you have something to lose if the contractual terms aren't clear, fair and understood by all. More than that, meeting targets can be motivational – helping to give sales staff that added incentive to see just one more client or make one more phone call each day. Give staff unrealistic targets and the will figure "why bother?".

Good practice in setting sales targets

▶ Set the target at a level that the company can fulfil

▶ Set the target at a level that's achievable (although it can be challenging)

▶ Pay for achievement commensurate with effort & risk (e.g. new business versus established account)

▶ Do make reasonable 'adjustments' for unforeseen changes in your ability to deliver or the general market

▶ Make payment dependent on following business guidelines & processes

Remember, don't begrudge paying someone what you may believe is a lot of money. If this person has fulfilled his or her part of your contract this individual should have won your company even more money! If not, then you set the targets incorrectly. If you repeatedly find yourself in this situation, you should probably seek help in setting your targets. Even so, occasionally, a sales person works hard and/or has a lucky break and sells a big deal. Pay the bonus, even if it is more than you earn! Why? If you set targets and then keep making adjustments so that sales staff can't achieve them, it will eventually backfire and your sales people will think... yes, you guessed it... "why bother?".

Does this mean you have to set targets low just to keep sales staff motivated? Absolutely not! Too low a target is as bad as too high. Good sales people are competitive and will work harder if you set a challenge that is within their reach. Your challenge is to get it 'just right' so that you get maximum revenue with good profit, good behaviour, motivated staff and solid market information.

Easy? Absolutely not! Setting targets is probably one of the most difficult tasks to get right. And given that exact 'rules' will vary with business type, market conditions and your staff, there is no simple formula. However, there are some key 'do's' and 'do nots' that will help, which you will find at the end of this chapter.

How much can an individual actually influence a sale?

Marketing and advertising can increase sales, but face-to-face sales contact increases probability of success

If all else is equal...

Many

Web sales

Retail sales

Agents
(When deployed in challenging geographies)

New business sales

How many people targeted

Account manager

One

Low   High

Individual sales person's impact

Bear in mind, there is no point offering great incentives or targets if the sales person cannot influence a sale. Some sales approaches offer little scope for sales staff's talent. When a sales person cannot directly influence the sale, you still need to have a target for this channel – you just need to consider who else in your business should carry this sales responsibility.

Use targets to drive good business practices as well as £s

Other activities you might want to encourage for **new business** sales:

- Reporting customer reaction to your product/price/service details
- Feedback of competitor activities/price/discounting
- Market conditions
- Getting a set number new customers, even if the initial sale is small
- Raising awareness of your offering in a particular market or geography

Account managers who sell to **existing customers** should also be motivated to:

- Produce and maintain an up-to-date 'buyer map' (see chapter 3)
- Produce and follow an annual sales plan (see chapter 2)
- Spot or develop new opportunities within the customer
- Report competitor activity and customer business conditions
- Handle significant customer complaints

All sales staff – both new business and account management – should be 'motivated' to follow your business processes and submit reports, plans, timesheets and expenses in a timely and quality manner. Remember, targets drive behaviours and, as much as you want profitable revenues, it does you no good to achieve them at the expense of good business practices.

In addition, you can get valuable market information from your customers – information that you can use to modify your offering, approach or price and feed into your future business plans. Make certain that your staff are motivated to supply you with helpful and accurate market feedback.

Of course you want sales staff to bring in profitable revenues, but it's also good if they do other things as well. For example, it might secure more business for you later if you also encourage telesales and/or new business sales people to identify new, well-qualified prospects. Well qualified prospects are individuals or companies who know they need a product or service such as yours, have spoken to someone from your business and know you could supply their needs, so all you need to do is convince them to sell to them. Therefore, you cannot merely target 'number of phone calls made' or number of different businesses visited.

But be careful. A real danger in both these sales approaches is to set as a target simply the number of phone calls or sales calls made. This kind of targeting can encourage the wrong sort of behaviour, with sales people and/or telesales making calls to totally inappropriate people just to reach their targets. Think about it. What would you do in their place?

If you do set a simple 'sales call/visit' target, your staff will try to meet these targets any way they can, making phone calls and/or travelling to visit companies or individuals who will never buy anything. This sort of activity is not only a waste of your time and money and demotivating to your staff, but also 'lost opportunity' because these individuals could have used the same time and effort to contact well qualified sales opportunities.

Direct sales

If you sell directly to customers or other businesses, you should use different rules to distribute sales targets to 'new business' sales staff than you use for 'existing accounts'. Depending on your industry and offering, various studies confirm that – sales skills being equal – it takes 6-10 times as much effort to get business from a new customer as from an existing one. Any target setting should acknowledge the difference. A good account manager can make certain that you retain and maximise business from existing customers.

For both new business sales and account management you should consider:

- The experience of the sales person
- How long the sales person has been working for your company and how well he or she knows your products and systems
- How many opportunities have already been identified and their value (the 'Sales Pipeline') and which ones they are working on
- What's happening in your marketplace
- What's happening with a particular individual or business
- Competitors' activities
- New government legislation
- Your own business's ability to supply orders

Your business is not operating in a bubble and you must remain vigilant to any factors that can impact your sales and make adjustments. Sensing activities in your market is not solely so you can re-adjust your targets downwards – although in some cases you may need to do so – it's about listening and keeping an eye on everything. In some circumstances, market feedback can give you an opportunity to revise upwards.

Agent/VAR/franchise sales

You must be very careful when you sell using agents. These businesses are actually your customers as well as your sales staff. They can choose whether they want to sell your product or someone else's, so you need to ensure that they prefer to sell yours. Price is important, of course, but personal relationships and ease of doing business with you also play a major role. You should appoint an 'agent manager' who is really a specialist type of 'account manager' and should be measured as such. This agent manager should carry a sales target for your business on behalf of the agents that he or she manages.

Although they sell for you, agents are not your employees. Therefore, you must remember that when you agree a sales target with an agent, the process should feel like a negotiation, not 'orders'. Remember, they **do work** for you, but they don't **work for** you.

Handled properly, working with 'sales agents' can be a true business partnership.

• •

Nexsan case study

In 1998, Martin Boddy left Trimm Technologies to start Nexsan. While working at Trimm he spotted many business opportunities in the information technology market so he decided to strike out on his own and build a business around one of these opportunities.

From nothing, he hoped to establish a 'next generation' in storage racks/cabinets for computer systems. These new 'racks' would enable 'hot and cold plug-in boards' and thus, no downtime when adding or subtracting storage and other components from IT systems. In 1999, such an offering was revolutionary. Having come from this industry, Martin mortgaged his house, asked friends for help and began to design the new system. Based in his own home, he had nothing substantial in terms of a business. No employees, no support and no sales.

At Nexsan, Martin started by selling 'from the drawing board' literally, using a video derived from the CAD drawings to illustrate the new product. In this way he could 'pre-sell' his new offering, a product that actually took one year to produce. On the plus side, because it was not held back by the constraints of a slower, manufacturing business, Nexsan (Martin) could listen to customer feedback and could 'trim' and 'adjust' the product quickly to better suit the market. The focus was on technology, not manufacturing, and the business flourished and after only a few years.

Martin took his proposition to the USA, where he found more interest and raised an additional £4.5m. As part of the funding, he opened an office in Delaware and set out to hire a US salesman.

So what approach did Martin use to find a salesman in the USA, having spent more of his time in UK and Europe? Once again, he made use of his connections. Initially, his Scandinavian salesman made the early forays into the US market. Then, he used his old connections from the Trimm business days to find a salesman from a complementary US company. This salesman understood the product and had a business relationship with many of the prospective Nexsan customers.

This US salesman had also developed a comprehensive sales lead system to support VARs for his product. Using this system to 'register VARs' so they could sell the Nexsan product, he was able to get VARs to cooperate, rather than compete for various opportunities. With this cooperation, all parties were able to maintain a healthy profit market rather than engage in a price-cutting war with each other.

After a short while, VARs became such an important selling tool that Nexsan set up systems and events (e.g training, communication, new product launch) to better support this VAR network!

By this stage, Nexsan finally added 'storage disks' to the configured 'racks' they provided. There were now two key target customers – VARs and systems integrators – and by 2007, the business had grown from £0 in 1999 to £50m turnover.

● ●

The Nexsan story also provides a good example of a company that used customer feedback during the selling process so it could design and offer a better product. It is also an excellent example of how to work with and support VARs.

Retail sales

If you have a retail business, you may assign targets by shop location and/or product line and leave it to the shop to motivate individual sales staff locally. In retail, opportunity will vary from location to location and even a location's attractiveness can vary from year to year. Consider the complaint of Oxford Street retailers during the London 2012 Olympics. Many people stayed away from London to avoid the crowds attending the Olympics, and those who made the journey were often across town at one of the Olympic event locations. Therefore, typical footfall on Oxford Street was down and so were sales.

Within a location, staff can be targeted on such things as:

- Friendliness and helpfulness
- Maintaining appropriate displays
- Keeping the shop and public areas tidy and well presented
- Managing 'returns'
- Vigilance with regard to shoplifting and credit card fraud
- Providing customer and market feedback to management

Internet sales

When you sell via the web, an individual cannot affect the actual purchase. Marketing plays the major role in enticing prospective customers to your website and buying your offering. Marketing is very different from selling – although the two go hand-in-hand and will be discussed a little bit more in Part II of this book. In a web-based sales approach, marketing in the form of visible advertisements, endorsements and Twitter create an awareness of your business in your target marketplace so that potential customers seek out your site and buy from you. You can still hand out targets, but they would more likely go to marketing specialists and/or product managers in your business.

Target setting 'Do's' and 'Do Nots'

When you set your targets, DO:

1. **Make certain that the rest of your business can deliver the goods.**
   Back orders and failure to fulfil customer orders cause dissatisfaction and more work for your sales person in responding to dissatisfied and impatient customers. It also eats away at your reputation in the marketplace and, if 'back orders' become the norm, it will have a negative impact on sales.

2. **Agree bonuses and/or commission based on sales and activities/measurements to ensure that your sales staff adhere to business policies and processes.**
   Sales people should have obligations that include timely reporting, market sensing, customer feedback – in additional to generating sales revenues. However, you have an obligation to make certain that you have spelled out your company processes and guidelines when you agree the bonus payment criteria.

3. **Think carefully about the bonus payment you have promised to make if a sales person achieves the targets.**
   The amount should be commensurate with the effort and risk PLUS whatever you need to pay in your industry to attract these skills. And whatever you pay, your business must be able to afford it. Remember, if the sales person brings in good business that nets you more than you pay in bonuses, then don't begrudge the money. You both win.

4. **Treat the 'target' and accompanying details as you would a contract.**
   Write everything down. Sign it and ask the sales person to sign it too, and then comply with it.

5. **Consider exceptional circumstances.**
   Sometimes, the sales person has obeyed all the rules, worked exceptionally hard, and then something happens over which he or she has no control or warning – death of a key person (personal or at the customer), illness or disaster. Be compassionate and be reasonable. Most contracts have 'Acts of God' clauses and so should your agreed sales targets. Behave as you would with a good customer – renegotiate the terms.

So, we've talked about some good practice. But what shouldn't you do?

How NOT to set sales targets

▶ Same as last year

▶ Same as last year plus x%

▶ Built only from 'top down' plan without 'bottom up' refinement

▶ Because we NEED to sell this number to:

   ▶ please the Board

   ▶ clear stock

   ▶ stay in business

▶ Based on 'how much' you believe a sales person should earn

▶ Make it unachievable!

DO NOT:

1. **Set a target based on the previous one.**
   It's always dangerous just to do what you did last time, last month or last year. Customers, competitors and markets all change and you must adapt your business and incentives to meet this change. Never merely 'add a percentage' to last year's numbers just because you want your business to grow by that amount. If this approach has worked for you in the past that's probably because, initially, you set your targets too low.

   It is OK to raise targets by a percentage if you have a good, balanced reason to do so. For example, if the market spend is increasing or your key competitor has gone out of business, then by all means take advantage of the new circumstances and plan to raise your business output accordingly – but always understand how you arrived at a number and be able to justify it. That's why it's critical that you do both 'top down' and 'bottom up' calculations to build both your business and sales plans.

2. **Set a target based on how much you need to sell.**
   Your business 'need' does not legitimise a target number. A very desperate, yet very common mistake is to pick a number because that's what you need to achieve in order to pay the bills or keep your investors happy. Using this approach you are just as likely to underestimate your number as overestimate. I can't say it often enough: build your targets using 'facts and judgment', not 'hopes and needs'.

3. **Base your target on 'top down' market assessment**
   without doing a 'bottom up' validation.

4. **Pay your sales staff what you BELIEVE they should earn.**
   I make this statement because many executives believe that a sales
   person earns too much money. Always pay your sales staff what
   you need to pay to get a good one – no more and no less.

   Then, incentivise them so that they bring in good business and revenue
   for you. If a successful sales person wins a big deal and earns a big bonus,
   don't resent it or play games so you don't have to pay it all. Never move the
   goalposts mid-game. Such behaviour sets a standard for everyone in your
   business – a standard that says: "I don't have to keep promises or honour my
   contracts." Is this the company culture you want? So what if this person earns
   even more than you do that year – you set the target and will benefit from
   increased revenues and profits, you have planned for success and achieved it.
   So what's the problem? As long as you built sensible targets, your business
   gains even more money than the sales person, you shouldn't worry about it.

In setting targets, always remember you want to keep and encourage good sales staff –
sales is one profession where a good performer can always find a job. The main reason
good sales people leave is because they believe that their company did not 'make good'
on its bonus or commission promise. If a good sales person leaves, not only will you
have to replace him or her, but you will also have the added cost of recruitment, hiring
and training a replacement, and even a good replacement will take some time to get up
to speed. So, if you have high-performing staff, deliver on your promises so they will
stay with you and deliver the sales.

Don't make promises you don't plan to keep!

Moving the 'goal posts' or setting up
obstacles to achievement is not
good practice in the long run.

Reward versus recognition – it's not just about money

Why have targets? Targets are a measure, but they also motivate. Up until now, most of this chapter has focused on money as reward for achieving a target, but money is only half the story. People want to be recognised and appreciated for their efforts and this is true for both sales people and those people behind the scenes who help realise the sale. Many companies have 'sales person of the month' and 'sales person of the year'. Other companies take recognition a step further by recognising technical specialists or customer service staff who made a significant contribution. Many companies have special trips – with or without partners – to recognise high-achieving sales efforts. Remember, you want to encourage all your employees to cooperate in the effort to get good business, and recognising 'right behaviour' encourages this cooperation.

Do you have a regular way of publicly thanking such people?

Other staff who may 'sell' & team selling

When setting targets, you should consider how best to motivate and build cooperation among other staff who 'sell' or help with the selling process. These roles include:

- Specialists involved in team selling efforts
- Customer services staff
- Bid managers and people who do back-office proposal production
- PAs and administrative assistants
- Specialists already on a customer's site who are delivering something already sold

Imagine how any of these individuals would feel when/if a sales person gets lots of public accolades and a big bonus when they too have worked very hard to help win the sale. It can be demotivating and cause bad feeling among the rest of the team – but with a bit of thought and effort, this downside can be avoided.

First rule: you don't always need to give them money! In fact, it's often better if you don't, because these staff do not usually work on an incentive basis. Instead, you can do the easiest thing by publicly praising appropriate behaviour and effort. If you want to take it a step further, you can give awards like 'dinner for two' or 'spa days'. Some companies set aside a prime parking spot and award its use (for a week or a month) as recognition. We have already discussed Vertex and its success in creating a selling culture, and Kieron Brennan of Vertex was emphatic about the importance of recognising the team effort in selling. He told me: "Today, people work harder, but they find it more fulfilling. Some of the fulfilment comes from working together as a team and some from **team-based rewards**. Everyone works in the team, all partake and share responsibility and all share in the reward."

There are many, many things you can do that don't involve paying cash but act to motivate non-sales staff. Use them! They can bring you great rewards.

END OF CHAPTER 4 – SELF-ASSESSMENT

EVALUATE YOUR SALES SUPPORT - Tick 1 box for each question

QUESTION	Yes	No	Partly
1. Do you set sales targets?			
2. Do you establish an overall sales target using both top down and bottom up calculations?			
3. Do you distribute your overall sales target commensurate with an individual's ability to deliver it?			
4. Have you ever revised a sales target downward due to market conditions or individual circumstances?			
5. Do you always set sales targets that your business can satisfy? (i.e. do you have enough product/service capability?)			
6. Do you target and reward behaviours as well as revenue results?			
7. Do you regularly recognise or reward non-sales staff who have assisted with the selling effort?			
8. Is good sales performance given public recognition in your company?			
9. Do your sales staff provide you with high-quality market/customer information?			
10. Do you use sales/customer support feedback to adjust your business planning?			

YOUR SCORE: Give yourself 5 points for every 'yes', 2 points for every 'partly' and '0' for every 'no'.

36-50 Points	⇒	Excellent – note areas where you didn't score 5 and plan to rectify if relevant to your business
26-35 Points	⇒	Good – you have some room for improvement. Check those areas in which you ticked 'no' or 'partly' and evaluate how you can improve your score
11-25 Points	⇒	You could do better – there is definitely room for improvement…
0-10 Points	⇒	Get help! You have lots and lots of opportunity to improve your income stream.

Part II

Your Marketplace & Your Product –
Your Strategy

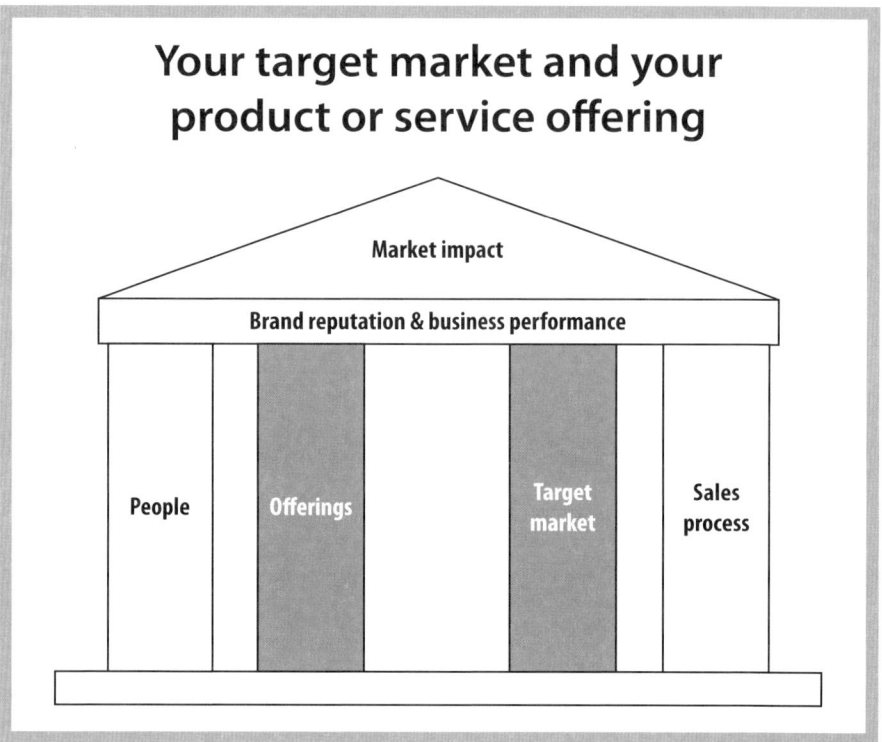

Introduction

I have intentionally grouped these two supporting columns of business together because your target market defines how you position your product. If you make laptop computers, your basic product is a laptop computer, or if you provide car cleaning services, your basic product is car cleaning services – however, the positioning of the product in terms of description, benefits, pricing and supporting services should vary significantly in line with satisfying your target market.

Let's elaborate using the example of the car cleaning business. There are a myriad of ways in which you could focus your efforts, many of which require vastly different sales and marketing approaches, and I have listed just a few of the options below. You could:

- Set up a car cleaning service in one location and try to attract passing motorists
- Provide 'at home' valet services to domestic households and travel to your customers' locations
- Focus on a high-end car type – say, BMW or Jaguar – and offer valet services to the dealers for cars brought in for service or used cars to be resold
- Target a particular customer type, such as rail commuters, and locate your services at car parks near major rail stations.

The unique selling points in each of these situations would, in fact, be different. For example, the speed of the service and price would be a top consideration if you wanted to attract passing trade. For home valet services the convenience, quality and time saving could be a major selling point, while cost is likely to be less of an issue.

Now let's look at a product sale to understand the market impact. For a company that manufactures or distributes laptops, there is similar variation in target markets. You could focus on:

- University students
- Domestic users
- Local users
- Specialist applications and these users
- Everyone!

This last suggestion – 'everyone' – is a very, very common mistake for new, small businesses. While it's true that everyone might be a potential customer for your product or service – 'everyone' won't recognise it! That is because none of us see ourselves as 'everyone'. We all see ourselves as unique, with our own wants and needs. So your need for a laptop will be different from your brother's or your 24-year-old daughter's or your friend's teenage son. You get the point – each of these individuals has different 'wants' and 'needs'. So, while your product or service may have many different features and these probably won't change, the features you emphasise will change with the target market. The benefits you emphasise will differ and so will your unique selling points. The best thing you can do is stand in the shoes of your customer for a moment and try to see your offering as your customer sees it.

Now, consider the Microsoft PC and the Apple Mac – as personal computers, both will do the job, both have email software, spreadsheets, word processing – basically everything that a typical individual computer user might want. However, until recently most business users bought the Microsoft-based systems while 'trendy younger businesses', artists and designers selected the Mac. Apple knew it could not take on the conservative, established users on 'day 1'. So Apple set itself up to appeal to 'youth' and 'creatives' instead of trying to take the more staid and established business market head-on. Now, after years of successful growth, the Apple Mac has moved into Microsoft's traditional territory.

Remember the 'Apple' story if you think your product is for everyone. Your product alone is not enough – you also need a strategy to break into the marketplace. The example of Apple versus Microsoft illustrates a successful market strategy – focus on your main competitors' weak spots and tailor your offering to satisfy this market segment. As you gain market share, expand your focus if you wish, but don't try to take on the entire market all at once.

Yes, Apple and Microsoft are two big, international companies, but the principles are valid for businesses of all sizes. Remember Revive, the car bodywork repair business that was discussed in the earlier chapter. Who do you think wants scratches on a car repaired at a reasonable price? Just about everyone, of course. But did Revive start out by targeting everyone? No. Instead it focused on used car dealerships – a market segment where focused sales effort would yield multiple car repairs rather than just one. By understanding the entire market, you can decide which segment plays best to your strengths and then develop a strategy for market penetration and growth. Once you have defined your target market and its issues and needs, you can describe your offering in the best way to address these needs, structuring the benefits of buying from you to appeal to your target customer.

You have to fashion your approach for potential customers – perhaps there is competition present in some areas but not others – and as I have already said, different market segments have different buying criteria. As a small business (and even in big businesses) you can't afford to have too many versions of your marketing material, advertisements etc – it's expensive and confusing. Nor does a business benefit from spending money on service offer descriptions that don't 'hook' the prospective buyer. Can you answer the following questions about your product or service?

- Why should someone buy from you?
- What benefits are you offering them?
- What needs are you fulfilling?
- What are your unique selling points for these potential customers
- Do your brochures, website and/or promotional material make these reasons in a clear and concise way?

How do prospects recognise themselves and their needs in your messages? TV adverts do this well with simple messages: "Do you want white teeth? If so, use our product." "Did you 'celebrate' too much last night? Feel the effects this morning? Then take our remedy." It's easy for a potential buyer to identify whether or not the product is appropriate. However, for business-to-business offerings and more complex solution-based sales, it can be more difficult.

How do you make your product stand out from the rest? How do you make someone want to buy from you who has never heard of you before? The first step is to focus. Select one or two market segments in which you are likely to succeed and aim your message at these markets. Let's start this process with chapter 5, which focuses on how to help you select the best market segments for your business.

Chapter 5

Your Market

Top tips – Chapter 5

1. Don't try to be all things to all people

2. Select your target market and understand it

3. Identify the top 3-5 trends in your customer's marketplace

4. Analyse how these trends create issues/opportunities for your target customer (customer needs)

5. Understand and clearly spell out where and how your offering can help satisfy these needs

6. Do a SWOT (Strengths, Weaknesses, Opportunities, Threats) analysis in your target market

7. Emphasise your unique selling points (USPs)

8. Understand your key competitors' strengths and weaknesses

9. Select the best sales approach to exploit your target market(s)

Have you heard the expression "Selling ice to the Eskimos"? This is one of many common expressions that suggest it's difficult or futile to try to sell something to a market that already has the product locally and in abundance. It can be done – and the expression "He could sell ice to Eskimos!" is often used to describe someone who can sell anything to anyone. However, if you made ice, would you really start by setting up a distribution system to sell it to the Eskimos? Why not select an easier market segment and increase your chances of success.

Targeting different market segments is not just about 'who' would buy your offering: it's as much about where you have the greatest opportunity for success. Of course you should look at:

- Where could your offering be used? (Business type, geography etc.)
- Who has the money to spend?
- Are you well placed to service this marketplace?

But you also need to consider:

- Is there a competitor already in this sector?
- Is the competitor well entrenched?
- Does your offering have anything that distinguishes it from the competition?

It is well worth answering these questions before you create any sales material, develop a website or select a selling approach. You may find that the very best market is the one with lots and lots of competition, while a slightly less attractive market has none. If this is the case it might be worth taking the strategic decision NOT to follow the crowd but to focus on the secondary market. In other words, you need to develop a market strategy.

Developing a market strategy

Developing a market strategy

To identify your optimum target market segment(s) you must consider:

▶ Customer need & urgency

▶ Amount of money available to buy your product/service

▶ Competitors

▶ Sales effort/cost

▶ The value of your offering to the customer

▶ Location

▶ Your current market activities

Few businesses have the luxury of starting with a blank slate – regardless, each should regularly review market strategy against these basic market influences. If you have an ongoing concern, you should also include ways to capitalise on your current market position. Zeus Technologies Ltd – who we already heard a bit about in chapter 1 – provides an excellent example of how a business can develop a new strategy that capitalises on the best bits from the previous business focus.

• •

Zeus Technology Ltd focused on new market segment

Zeus Technologies Ltd, founded in Cambridge in the early 1990s, was one of the early pioneers in the dot.com world. Established by a couple of creative engineers, the business carved a niche for itself in the early, web server marketplace. In fact, Zeus Technologies provided the first commercial server to the market – one of the first in the world. The company successfully weathered the dot.com downturn around the change of the millennium, but, after a number of funding rounds, had stagnated. In 2004, one of the funding VCs brought in Paul Brennan to act as chairman and temporary CEO.

Zeus Technologies (ZT) already had a brilliant team of engineers – 'rock solid'. Its previous management team had targeted the business against the global hardware giants like Cisco and tried to take on the world with only a few million pounds in the bank and a small office in the UK. Paul, an expert at repackaging technical solutions, decided that a different strategy was in order and looked at the market from the different angle.

2004 was the beginning of 'Cloud Technology' and not many vendors owned the 'cloud space'. Zeus Technology's key product was software that acted as a web server and load balancer. So ZT began to focus on Cloud applications and repositioned itself as providing a 'traffic manager' – introducing the concept of PVC (physical virtual cloud) and shifting the goalposts in the marketplace. In this way, ZT began to sell 'futures' based on scalable entry into the Cloud world, where customers paid only for what they used. Thus, rather than taking on the global network hardware manufacturers in a head-to-head competition, ZT jumped ahead and began to sell the 'next generation' solution. This approach proved extremely successful.

• •

And, you don't need an existing business to be successful. Ready Steady Store is a self-storage business that opened its doors in 2006. Before the business purchased or built any storage facilities, Mehran Charania, the CEO, did a thorough market analysis and created a market strategy that would ultimately give him market growth many times those of his well-established competitors. He based his initial strategy around location.

• •

Ready Steady Store – successful market targeting

With self-storage in mind, Mehran Charania studied the UK marketplace and discovered a number of large population centres that were not being serviced by any of the significant existing self-storage companies. In addition to focusing on population density, Mehran's strategy was to 'cluster' his locations in twos and threes and to target middle and higher-income neighbourhoods. All locations had to be in a clearly visible spot with good 'footfall' – ideally near a major retail park or busy road with signage on display to passing traffic. After he completed his analysis, eight sites were purchased between 2006 and 2007, with an eye toward establishing self-storage centres.

So, did this strategy work? The answer is an emphatic 'yes'. Since opening its doors the self-storage income has risen steadily. Ready Steady Store has grown at 15-20% per year and it now runs at more than 80% occupancy, while the industry average is about 60-65%.

• •

You can see from the case study that Mehran carried out a thorough market analysis in order to establish a marketing strategy so that Ready Steady Store could successfully exploit a gap in the UK self-storage marketplace. He targeted areas not serviced by his leading competitors and situated his storage facilities in areas frequented by his target customers, thereby increasing his probability of success.

You can do the same thing. A careful analysis of your selected market segments can help you tailor your approach to best service this marketplace. Then modifications of your product/service descriptions, your sales approach, your pricing and even your contracts can lead to increased business and even lower costs. The key skill is understanding how to turn market conditions into business opportunities.

Understand your customers' needs and tailor your approach

Turning market conditions into a business opportunity

Within your marketplace, who is spending money and what are they spending it on? Shifts in spend can often be identified by known changes in your prospect/customer's marketplace. For example, has there recently been new legislation that impacts your target market? Purveyors of 'energy audits' and products for cleaning up air and water have recently seen an increase in business due to recent 'Green' legislation. Other change drivers include: cutbacks in spending by key customers of your customers (e.g public sector), new markets, changes in your competitor status... there are many.

To maximise your success in your target market, you must clearly identify your prospect/customer's key issues and how these businesses will be making their buying decisions. So, where do you start? You can start with a PESTLE analysis – look at the Political, Economic, Social, Technical, Legal and Environmental factors prevalent in your customers' environment that could have an impact on how and what they buy. It's easier than it sounds and well worth the effort.

Example: PESTLE analysis

POLITICAL	ECONOMIC
▶ Changes in political regime (with speculative tax and legislative changes) ▶ Changes in foreign/EU political regimes ⇨ impact customers' customers	▶ Condition of local economy and upward/downward trend ▶ Employment rate ▶ Interest rates
SOCIAL	**TECHNOLOGICAL**
▶ Demographic changes (e.g. rural ⇨ urban) ▶ Immigration	▶ New, emergent technologies (e.g. social media, mobile internet, online communities)
LEGAL	**ENVIRONMENTAL**
▶ New legislation (e.g. building specifications impact on builders and construction, air quality impacts car dealerships, etc.) ▶ Areas of pending legislation	▶ Pressure to be 'green' and environmentally aware ▶ Focus on 'carbon-neutral' business growth

As you can see, these are all factors that can't be controlled by your customers (or you!) but can cause them to worry and experience 'pain'. As a result of this 'pain' the customer will have issues as well as opportunities. These customer issues/opportunities can, in turn, be transformed into 'customer needs', and once you understand your customer needs you can describe your product or service features to show how it addresses these needs. (This final point will be discussed in more detail in chapter 6.)

For example, the fact that some consumers are environmentally aware and want to buy appliances with the lowest possible impact on the environment is a 'customer opportunity' for an appliance vendor. The fact that these consumers have this belief becomes one of their 'needs' when they want to purchase a new washing machine, for example.

In another example, if a property developer planned to convert old properties into flats, the new 'energy efficiency' legislation would be an issue. It would force me to make extra effort (and spend more money) to create a more energy-efficient living environment from an old, energy-inefficient house. This 'customer issue' translates into a 'customer need' for products and service, which help the builder to achieve compliance with the legislation in as cost-effective a way as possible.

So, from the list of items on your PESTLE, a next step is to:

- Identify the top 3-5 business drivers, or activities happening in your customers' environment that will have an impact on them
- Then develop a list of the key issues and/or opportunities
- Rewrite these issues as 'customer needs'

Once you have a list of your customer needs, you can make sure that you describe your product features to address these needs.

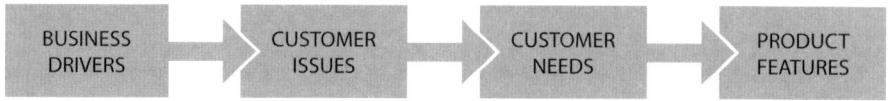

BUSINESS DRIVERS → CUSTOMER ISSUES → CUSTOMER NEEDS → PRODUCT FEATURES

All the examples listed in the PESTLE have created real issues for UK-based businesses/customers over the past decade. Let's look at a real example of an external event that created issues and opportunities in more detail.

Example of business driver

The massive flooding suffered by much of England over the past few years has caused devastation in certain locations and some of those directly affected include:

- Local residents
- Local businesses
- Insurance companies
- Emergency services

So, for the householders and businesses who were flooded, the water caused some immediate 'issues' – for example, no business premises (if a business) or no house (if a residence), and no transportation if their car/delivery vehicle was destroyed or damaged. For a business, there was loss of business income during the time the premises were unsuitable. For a home, there was no place for the family to eat or prepare food, bathe, store personal possessions – in other words, nothing to support daily living. These are all issues and the issues created 'needs'.

So, what needs did these issues create? The need for: a temporary, dry, safe place to live, perhaps a new car or a rental car until the damaged vehicle could be repaired, new carpets, soft furnishings, new flooring, furniture – all new items to replace what was destroyed. And somebody had to go into the damaged properties to collect and throw out the flood-damaged materials. Once emptied and cleaned, the premises then needed to be repaired. In addition, of course, there were the administrative and financial processes of obtaining the money to live and effect repairs and negotiate settlements with the insurance companies, if the victims were insured.

For others – those not directly impacted by the flood waters – the situation provided an opportunity to satisfy some of these needs. Those who actually benefited from the disaster include:

- Local building services (carpenters/electricians/plumbers)
- Building supply companies
- Car dealerships and rental companies
- Furniture stores and household supply companies
- Local, functioning B&Bs, hotels and other places of temporary residence
- Waste haulage businesses and skip suppliers
- Professional cleaners

This example illustrates how some people's issues can become others' opportunities. While not always as extreme as flooding, 'external forces' affect your marketplace all the time and – whatever your market – chances are there are three or four common key 'opportunities' and 'issues' affecting all your customers at any time. Identify the external drivers or 'events' and you can clearly define both the issues facing your customers and the 'needs' these issues cause. With these needs you can then examine your offering to understand how best it can satisfy these needs. If it doesn't, then you should probably look to a different market segment for your business.

The SWOT analysis – an excellent tool

SWOT analysis

Strengths	Opportunities
▶ _____ ____ __ ____	▶ _____ ____ __ ____
▶ ____ _____ _____	▶ ____ _____ _____
▶ _ ____ _____ ____	▶ _ ____ _____ ____
▶ __ _____ __ ____	▶ __ _____ ___ ____

Weaknesses	Threats
▶ _____ ____ __ ____	▶ _____ ____ __ ____
▶ ____ _____ _____	▶ ____ _____ _____
▶ _ ____ _____ ____	▶ _ ____ _____ ____
▶ __ _____ __ ____	▶ __ _____ ___ ____

A SWOT analysis provides a good starting point for analysing your position in your current market and for your opportunities to address new market segments. SWOT stands for 'Strengths', 'Weaknesses' 'Opportunities' and 'Threats' and offers a framework for examining both your business in relation to the market and your offering (We will use it in chapter 6, too, to examine product/service offerings). Let's go through the process and quadrants in more detail, and in this chapter we will use the SWOT for your business in relation to a specific market segment.

First, some definitions:

- A 'Strength' is an internal capability about which you are confident and which is relevant to the specific market segment (e.g you have the newest machinery in the market or, as in the example of Ready Steady Store, you are the only self-storage company in a given geography)
- A 'Weakness' is something that you recognise as an area of vulnerability for your organisation (e.g you don't have the skills to do social media marketing but you target the teenage market segment)
- An 'Opportunity' is an external situation that gives your company an advantage in a market segment (e.g your product contains a new feature that gives great cost savings to your customers – like doubling the fuel efficiency of a car engine)
- A 'Threat' is the possibility that some external action/company/event will put your business at a disadvantage. (e.g a new market entrant makes aggressive introductory offers in order to gain market share)

The key to successful use of a SWOT is:

- Sufficient data
- Different perspectives
- Focus
- Honesty

A practical exercise

So, now it's time to try a SWOT for your business. How do you start?

First, call together a team of knowledgeable people from all parts of your business (e.g operations, sales & marketing, finance, customer service – as relevant to your organisation). The attendees do NOT need to be in management, nor do you necessarily have to invite all management. Two to three people in the session are OK if you are a small business, more is better – but don't try to manage more than seven or eight individuals for this process. Tell the attendees about the SWOT process and what you hope to achieve by doing it.

Then go through each quadrant in the SWOT diagram and ask: what strengths (weaknesses etc.) does the business have in this market? Ask for everyone to contribute. One answer might be: "We are local" – so write "local" in the strengths quadrant. Under weaknesses, one might be: "We are perceived as small" – so write "size" in the weaknesses quadrant. Work through each quadrant and collect and discuss input from all your team. What do you know about 'Opportunities' in your target market? Is there a growing opportunity for your product or service, even if you haven't captured this business? Where is the growing opportunity? Do you know? It needn't always come from your prospects or customers, but might be enabled by a weakness in a key competitor that you might exploit.

Remember, this SWOT is about your business and how it is positioned in a specific market sector. It is not about your offering – it's sometimes difficult to keep the discussion focused. By doing this SWOT analysis you will gain a picture of what you need to do to be successful in a given market segment. The SWOT might even raise the question of whether you should even be in this market segment. Once you have positioned yourself in a market, you can then refine your approach by carrying out a similar analysis of your offering.

Carrying on with the earlier example, let's look at an example of a market SWOT for a small building firm near the areas of flood devastation. You will need a bit more information about this hypothetical business in order to do the SWOT. So, what does this fictitious 'full services building company' do? Up until this point, the small business built new houses and filled in slack times by doing renovations and extensions – both domestic and small commercial. This experience makes them very familiar with most of the building types damaged by the flood waters. In addition to carpenters and bricklayers, the firm has access to electricians and plumbers and skips, scaffolding and an architect. In other words, if necessary, the firm could do everything necessary to (re)construct a building or extension, from nothing to a completed structure. The business is located near the flooded area, but its own premises were NOT flooded and all the equipment is intact and functional. Let's begin to fill in the SWOT quadrants.

STOP HERE and do the SWOT before turning the page.

SWOT analysis example: Local, full service building firm in a flood damaged market

Strengths	Opportunities
▶ Local ▶ Flexible ▶ Good reputation ▶ Full service solution ▶ Quick response	▶ Joint venture with professional cleaning service ▶ Link with insurance company as supplier of choice ▶ Possible 'recovery grants' or funds to help stricken area
Weaknesses	**Threats**
▶ Limited resources ▶ Limited access to some locations	▶ Competition may link with insurance companies as supplier of choice ▶ Slow payment/no payment by individuals & businesses affected ▶ Larger, national firms may 'move in' to capitalise on the opportunity

The lists on this SWOT are not exhaustive and are meant only to give an indication of the type of information that's meaningful in each quadrant. In reality, such a firm probably has little choice about 'where' it's doing business, but it does have a lot of choice about how it does business as you can see from the 'Opportunities' quadrant. In the past the business worked directly with customers who wanted houses or new business premises or renovations.

This change in market circumstances, the flood, gives this company the opportunity to form new business alliances – with other local firms, government agencies or insurance companies. Such alliances might change the culture of the business – but, before the management can discount pursuing these options, they also need to consider that their competition – perhaps big, national competitors – might form such alliances and thereby cut them out of a great deal of business. There isn't a 'right' answer – the right way forward really depends on the appetite of the business and its future strategy. However, the SWOT analysis of company position versus the market gives the power of choice to the business managers.

··

Ready Steady Store and the power of marketing

Mehran Charania at Ready Steady Store emphasises the power of this market analysis when he confesses: "I became convinced of the power of marketing – despite the temptation to 'cut back' when the recession set in, I actually increased the marketing spend. For me, with a strong financial background, it was very difficult to trade off 'expense management' (e.g cost controls) and short-term gain for marketing expense and bigger numbers in the medium to longer term, but it was the right thing to do."

"You can't stay still!" advises Mehran. "A business like ours has to review, review, review and test whether plans and strategies are still appropriate. Business tactics and people management must constantly be adjusted to reflect market changes."

....

After the market SWOT – what next?

By doing the SWOT you should now have more clearly defined your target market segment(s). Furthermore, you may also have more clearly elucidated your market strategy; for example, are you really the lowest cost provider? Perhaps a better strategy might be to position yourself in a specialist niche (like Apple when it targeted designers and 'creative' users). Maybe your SWOT shows that your company adds lots of extra value to its customers, so you could justify charging more.

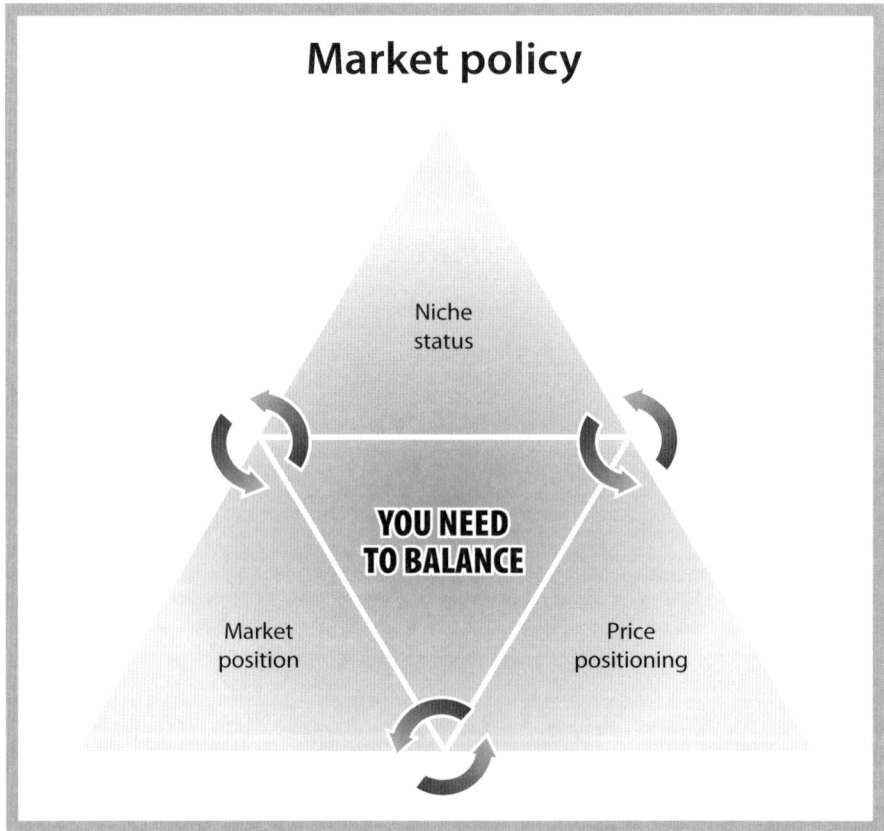

It is always useful to do and regularly review a SWOT of your market. Even if your business is doing well the work won't be wasted; you need to make adjustments keep it in line with the shifting marketplace. Review your market strategy as well!

Now, be honest:

- o Does your business have a formal 'market strategy'?
- o Or has it just happened?

If it's 'just happened', you are part of a very, large group of businesses. Many, many businesses start off focused on their product and service and then just start selling. Be careful – in these circumstances just being like one of the crowd is not good thing. If you do not understand your market – the opportunities and threats – then you will be at the mercy of those who do. Many businesses go bankrupt each year and you don't want to be a part of that crowd.

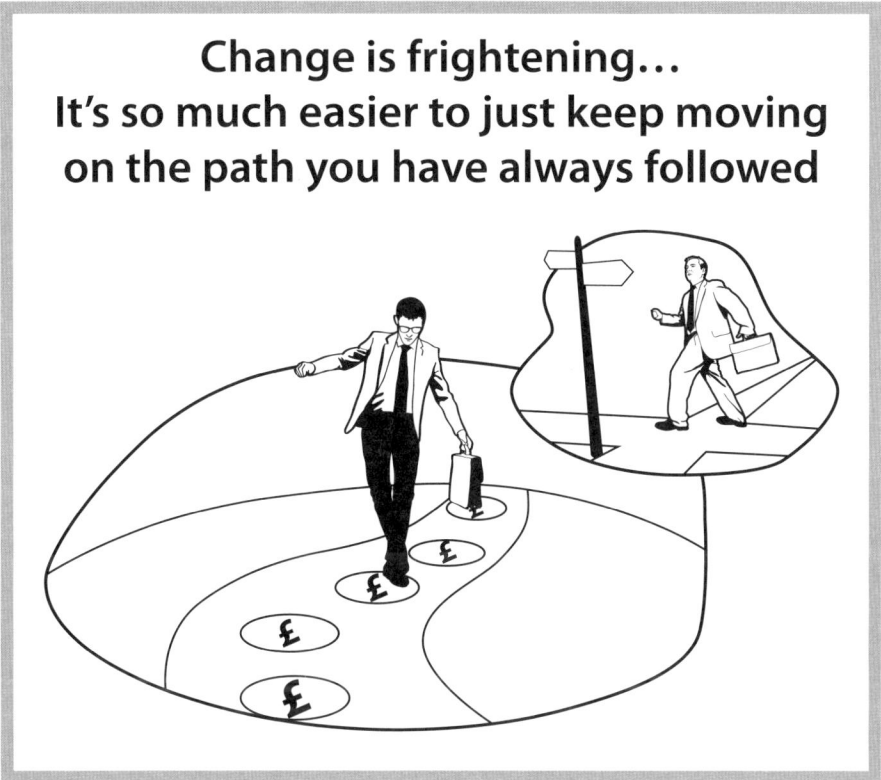

Change is frightening…
It's so much easier to just keep moving on the path you have always followed

If you do have a market strategy, is it actually followed? You would be surprised at how many businesses commission such a study, only to put it on the shelf and then carry on as they always have done because change seems too difficult. If this situation sounds familiar, why didn't you act? Why bother with the strategy? As I have already stated, in good times you may get away without one, but you won't extract as much from your market as you could. You will definitely leave 'money on the table'. And in bad times you run the risk of being outmanoeuvred by competitors who do have a good market strategy.

Vertex's re-evaluation of its market provides a good example of the benefits that can be achieved, but also the changes that might be necessary in order to implement a new market strategy.

Vertex adapts its market focus for better results

Remember Vertex, the outsourcing/call centre company from chapter 1? Market focus played a considerable role in its business success.

When it first entered the public sector marketplace, Vertex's activities were all opportunity-driven. The business heard about opportunities – or 'bids' – via standard government procurement announcements and replied to almost everything. This approach resulted in lots and lots of activity, but very little success. Why? Vertex realised that waiting for the formal announcements meant that it heard about opportunities too late – by the time a bid was announced, the competition had already done a thorough job of selling to the prospect, so the formal bid was merely a matter of form. Kieron Brennan of Vertex sums up the situation by saying: "We didn't qualify anything out – the organisation mistook sales activity for efficacy and we busily responded to anything and everything. When it became clear that this activity was not bringing in the business we needed, we stopped this response-driven approach and took stock."

The challenge was: how to discover opportunities at an earlier stage? With only around 50 appropriate 'deals' per year in this sector, Vertex decided to do some research and take a more targeted approach.

First, Vertex more clearly defined and delineated its customer proposition. It soon became clear that Vertex possessed neither the strength nor the capacity to be good at everything, so the business decided to focus on delivering on offering "Citizen Services through Government". With this in mind, if opportunities arose that did not encompass Citizen Services, Vertex would not bid. An added benefit was that by tightening up the definition of its service, it could better describe it to its potential customers, making it 'easier to buy'.

Next Vertex decided to proactively investigate its market for potential opportunities. To do so, it focused on two areas:

1. Organisations
2. Specific individuals within organisations

For example, in the UK there are around 500 local councils, but with a little bit of research it became clear that only those councils with a £200m budget or greater were in a position to buy Vertex services. A further cull was made because some of these councils did not offer 'Citizen Services' as defined by the Vertex service offering.

Finally, in the remaining list of potential customers or 'prospects' Vertex checked each council's 'propensity to be a buyer' against two different criteria: first, if larger competitors already held a strong position within the council it was unlikely that they would change supplier, and second, there were some councils that held a philosophical objection to procuring services from the private sector. This prospecting approach winnowed out still more of the potential 500 prospects, leaving a final list of around 80 councils who might buy Vertex's 'Citizen Services through Government'.

With the refined list of 80, Vertex then built a marketing campaign in order to create awareness within this target list where it was virtually unknown. Again Kieron Brennan reminds me: "Getting noticed is different from what you want to sell," and at this stage what Vertex wanted was to get noticed and to begin a relationship and discussions with the appropriate individuals within these 80 councils. After three months, Vertex had engagement with 25% of this target list. A typical success rate for a good campaign is less than 5%. Clearly, Vertex was doing something right.

....

In the Vertex example, you have not only a refocusing of its target market, but also an adjustment to the Vertex offering to address this new focus. A new market strategy is just the first step – to be effective you must make other changes too. The next step is to examine your sales approach to determine whether it is still effective.

Aiming your sales approach

You need to aim to hit a target

And it's vital to aim very carefully!

You have to 'aim' to hit a bullseye, and the same principle applies to selling. Many sales forces and/or advertising campaigns relentlessly go after the same prospects year after year. And sometimes the rationale for the original lists has been lost in the mists of time. Is this really an effective way to deploy expensive and expert resources?
So first ask yourself:

- Do you do the same thing year after year with minimal improvement, or even declining success?

When you do the same thing year after year and expect something different to happen it's time to re-examine those things you can change. For example:

- Where and how does your sales resource focus now?
- Is there, in fact, a current justification for how you focus your sales and marketing efforts?

You have already heard how Vertex refocused on its market. As part of this process it redesigned its sales approach to improve its success.

•••

Vertex restructured its sales approach in line with new market focus

...Vertex was able to handle this more focused activity with only one specialist salesman, whereas before three sales staff had been employed to handle all the reactive bids. This new situation offered many benefits because Vertex now had well qualified leads with good prospect relationships and early insight to future procurement activities, all, with reduced sales costs. So today, instead of chasing every formal opportunity published during the year, Vertex has about half a dozen well qualified opportunities at any time and is well positioned with all of them.

As Kieron emphasises, "By focusing our service offer and delivery on 'Citizen Services', it became easier to focus on the appropriate individuals – at all levels – within the prospective customer. And by speaking to the right people we were able to gain better insights and intelligence faster, and began to understand when opportunities would happen before they were announced via the formal channels."

•••

Vertex is not the only business to readjust its sales approach. Even in its short business life, Ready Steady Store has adapted its selling approach.

•••

Ready Steady Store studies its market and adjusts its sales approach

How did Ready Steady Store (RSS) market to its target customers? First, CEO Mehran Charania developed a profile of the 'ideal customer' – which he decided was relatively affluent, reliable and steady. This profile provided potential customers who were less likely to default on payments, who would take larger units and who could afford to pay slightly more for good service and an attractive, secure building in a convenient location.

RSS then focused on local marketing and, because of the culture shift in staff at local sites, employed them to represent RSS (and sell!) to the local community. Local staff even had sales incentives, whereas before and traditionally these staff had only answered phones, handed out keys and kept the facilities clean.

•••

Finally, you may have more than one target market – many businesses do. If so, remember that you may want to consider a different sales approach for different target markets. A good example in the UK today is retail banking. Retail banks have started offering different services and financial products to different market segments.

Target market	Interface with the bank	Charge the customer?	Extras included	'Deals' on other financial products	Value of the individual customer to the bank
Any person who needs a bank account	Internet & branches	No	None	Small discount on mortgages and insurance	Low
Individuals with income > £50K/year	As above plus allocated account manager to review financial needs annually	Yes	Insurance products, mobile phone, concierge products	Larger discounts on mortgages and insurance, currency exchange	Medium
Individuals with income > £250K/year	As above with special areas in the branch or special branches and account manager who calls more frequently	Yes	As above plus investment advice	Special deals on a number of products (see above) and investment deals	High

Please note, these markets and values are indicative and do NOT represent actual segments and numbers from a specific UK bank.

As the table above illustrates:

- For the 'average person' there is a 'standard', highly automated, low cost of delivery, basic, banking service.
- For customers who have more money and/or who use profitable services like business loans and banking, banks now offer a higher standard of service – separate, dedicated areas in the bank, special services or perks and sometimes dedicated personnel.
- Finally, truly high-net-worth individuals receive a different level of service altogether. Banks also reconfigure their product offerings to appeal to these different market segments.

All these business examples illustrate the practice of:

- Defining a target (or multiple) market(s)
- Understanding the market
- Creating a market strategy
- Modifying product/service so that it appeals to that market segment
- Selecting or adjusting the sales approach for maximum effectiveness.

If you miss out any of these steps you are leaving money on the table.

We have discussed the market and sales approach. In the next chapter we will delve more deeply into how you can better configure your product or service to satisfy your target customer.

Common pitfalls

DO NOT:

1. **Accept sales feedback about the market/customer situation without questioning and qualification.**
   For example, if your sales staff typically deal only with the purchasing department, purchasing will always tell you that a final decision is a question of money, but that is rarely the whole story.

2. **Select a market on the basis of 'market value alone'.**
   Everyone else with a similar offer to yours will also consider this market. What else do you have that will make you successful in this market? And can you handle the volumes necessary to truly exploit this market?

3. **Select a market that is difficult for you to service.**
   At the very least, wait until you have established a successful, going concern – a common example of this risky choice is those businesses who decide to focus on the US or Far Eastern markets because they are much bigger than the UK but neglect to consider the logistical difficulties, increased cost of sale, increased regulatory issues and cultural differences – any of which can be a barrier to success.

4. **Fail to review your market strategy on a regular basis.**
   Market drivers change, and therefore so do customers' needs and priorities. Put in place a regular marketing review process and re-evaluate your sales approach in light of any changes you made.

END OF CHAPTER 5 – SELF-ASSESSMENT

EVALUATE YOUR MARKET FOCUS - Tick 1 box for each question

QUESTION	Yes	No	Partly
1. Do you have a market strategy and use it?			
2. Do you review your target market regularly?			
3. Do you know your businesses' strengths in your target market?			
4. Do you know your businesses' weaknesses in your target market?			
5. Can you list the top five opportunities in your target market?			
6. Can you list the top five threats in your target market?			
7. Do you have a well-defined and appropriate sales approach(es) for your target market(s)?			
8. Do you have a good system for market sensing so you can monitor changes and threats?			
9. Do you believe that marketing is important to your business?			
10. Have you maintained or increased your marketing budget as your business has grown?			

YOUR SCORE: Give yourself 5 points for every 'yes', 2 points for every 'partly' and '0' for every 'no'.

36-50 Points ⇒ Excellent – note areas where you didn't score 5 and plan to rectify if relevant to your business

26-35 Points ⇒ Good – you have some room for improvement. Check those areas in which you ticked 'no' or 'partly' and evaluate how you can improve your score

11-25 Points ⇒ You could do better – there is definitely room for improvement…

0-10 Points ⇒ Get help! You have lots and lots of opportunity to improve your income stream.

Chapter 6

The Offering – Getting Your Product or Service Right!

Top tips – Chapter 6

1. Describe your offering in your customer's language, not your own (better still, use your 'customer's voice')

2. Link your product features to your customer's needs

3. Always turn features into advantages and benefits for customer materials

4. Understand and quantify the benefits to your customers

5. Highlight your unique capabilities and/or features

6. Listen to the customer and adapt your offering to incorporate input where possible. Best still, get 'customer testimonials' and use these in your sales activities

7. Understand your competitors' offerings

8. Do a SWOT analysis on your own offerings

9. Use the optimum sales approach for your offering

10. Develop sales 'role plays' and other selling aids which incorporate your offerings

---

How do you describe your product/service? Does this description map easily on to the 'needs' of your target buyers? Do you know how they will make a buying decision (the key decision criteria)? Many businesses create marketing material and selling messages and never adjust these documents for the changing marketplace or different market segments. Do you? For the very same product or service your sales and marketing messages are not fixed; they may differ depending on what's happening in your target market and where the buyer's 'pain' is experienced.

When was the last time you modified your sales/marketing material? In bad times and in good, the needs of your market will shift and you should modify your marketing materials to ensure that the benefits you emphasise reflect what the market wants. For example, in the run-up to Christmas supermarkets will promote food and drink for special occasions and then, as soon as January arrives, they will shift their focus to diet foods and healthy alternatives. What's interesting about this example is that the products stocked by these stores during December and January are, for the most part, the same.

Some businesses thrive during challenging times by taking the trouble to emphasise the value on offer and making certain that their customers feel they get their money's worth. Have you re-examined your sales approach and support material in light of the changing market? Even if you have an up to date approach, have you clearly translated your product/services features into benefits that address the current market needs? If yes, has your sales team been re-trained or updated around the new selling approach?

If you can answer 'yes' to all these questions, well done – most businesses cannot. Typically, sales teams are trained or updated once a year – if at all – or at the time of a new product launch. And usually the support material merely focuses on the new product only. Your sales force is the 'mouthpiece' of your company – it doesn't matter how good your offering and how professional and up to date your materials, if your sales force has not been updated they will continue to parrot outdated facts and sales messages. In fact, once you have clearly identified your offerings' strengths you may find you should consider using different or additional sales approaches to extract maximum revenues from your market.

Many of the businesses illustrated by the case studies discussed in this book altered or augmented their sales approaches after a more thorough market and offering analysis. Ready Steady Store (chapters 1 & 5) added internet marketing to its more traditional phone-based sales. HR Solutions 4U (chapter 2) switched to using a third party to help with getting 'first calls' in order to increase its sales effectiveness. Vertex (chapter 5) narrowed down its target market and then used teams to focus its selling efforts on those opportunities where it had the highest probability of winning. Finally, Zeus Technologies (chapter 5) reshaped its offering and sales approach completely in order to avoid selling head to head with the traditional, multinational hardware services suppliers.

Link your product features to your customers' needs

'Customer first' applies when you design your sales/marketing materials and website. So many firms, especially technical firms, make the mistake of describing their product from a 'features' point of view and this approach lacks impact and prospect appeal. What does this mean? Remember the 'pink suitcase' in chapter 1 and the discussion about turning features into benefits? And how a good sales person and/or or marketing material can use 'FUDGE' – fear, uncertainty, doubt & great expectations – to relate your product features to customer needs? If you don't remember, go back and read it again, as it is a fundamental tool for selling success!

Your product or service has 'features' – features are facts – tangible or measurable, like size, colour, opening hours. These are all features and any material should provide the 'advantages' of these features. For example, if a corner shop that declares "we are open all night" (a feature), that means that you can pop in and buy a replacement light bulb any hour of the night or day (an advantage). Features and advantages are really a minimum for marketing material.

Let's look at a product example, a chef's knife; it has a very sharp blade – fact. The knife's sharp blade is an advantage if someone wants to chop onions or prepare a gourmet meal. However, a chef's knife is of little use to someone whose cooking repertoire consists of takeaway and microwave meals. Lesson? Not all people who prepare meals will be potential customers for this chef's knife.

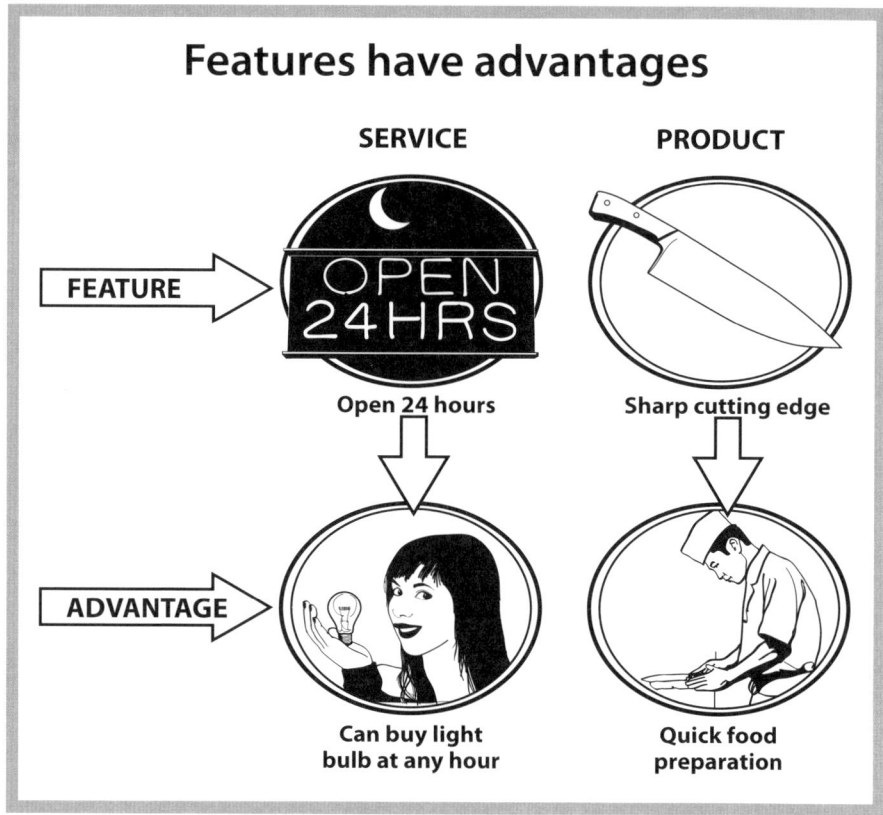

Features have advantages

SERVICE

PRODUCT

FEATURE

Open 24 hours

Sharp cutting edge

ADVANTAGE

Can buy light
bulb at any hour

Quick food
preparation

When you have clearly focused on a market segment, you can further refine your approach and create a more powerful message by transforming these 'advantages' into 'benefits'. So, what's the difference? Well, features will always be features and advantages will always be advantages, but benefits depend on who is using the product or service. In other words, benefits are unique to a specific customer or customer segment. For example, if my house or business does not have electricity, the fact that I can buy a light bulb any hour of the night or day really doesn't matter to me; this specific opportunity does not offer me any benefits. If, however, I run a 24-hour establishment, it could be a genuine benefit to have access to replacement light bulbs at a moment's notice and I would probably pay a premium for this convenience. If we go back to the knife as an example, the chef's knife is sharp – this is great for anyone who wants to do traditional or gourmet cooking and is capable of using the knife.

This point has been emphasised because many businesses confuse 'advantages' with 'benefits'. Don't! A benefit always answers a 'so what?' question. A brief example follows that illustrates this point.

Features & benefits

Example: Soft drink in a 100ml/3oz can		
Features	**Advantages**	**Benefits to a shop owner**
100ml/3oz can	Small	▸ Takes less shelf space ▸ Uses less storage space
Integral pull-off tab	Don't need to have tin opener	▸ None – unless shop owner is frequently asked to open tins for customers
Packaged as a 'single item' not in multiple pack	Can buy just one	▸ Can charge a premium price for convenience
All natural ingredients	There may be none – in fact, might have disadvantages in terms of shelf life	▸ Appeals to health-conscious customers
UK-manufactured	▸ Faster distribution to shops ▸ Few miles between production and customer	▸ Can hold less stock at any given time because replacement can be fast ▸ Can appeal to the 'green' customer ▸ Can appeal to the patriotic customer

Features and benefits are not always obvious. Let's look at an example of a fictional carbonated beverage that is sold in an individual 100ml/3oz can. In the table above, the first column lists some 'facts' or 'features' about the product – things like size, construction of the packaging, contents and origins. Your product/service will have lots and lots of features, but not all of them will be relevant to your target market. For the soft drink example I have focused on five features.

The second column lists some of the 'advantages' of the features. Features may have more than one advantage, as you will see from the two advantages: faster distribution and fewer miles between shop and supplier associated with being a UK supplier. Again, looking at the soft drink example, you can see that some features may even be a disadvantage to the shopkeeper (all natural products) yet still offer a benefit to his/her customer and therefore provide a benefit to the shopkeeper. If you were the manufacturer and wanted to gain a full picture of the value of this product to your end customer, you would try to quantify each of these benefits, including the disadvantages, and come up with a total value to your customer of purchasing from you.

When you examine Table Y, which lists benefits to the shopkeeper's customers, you will see that all the features are the same as those on the shopkeeper's table and some of the advantages highlighted are similar. However, the list of benefits to the 'end customer' is completely different. What this highlights is the fact that any advertising and sales material must be carefully targeted. Who are you trying to influence? Your customer? Or your customer's customer? As you can see when you compare the two different lists of benefits, whatever advertising or promotional material you produce will stress completely different benefits.

Features & benefits – a different view

Example: Soft drink in a 100ml/3oz can		
Features	Advantages	Benefits to shop owner's customer
100ml/3oz can	Small	▸ Fits in a bag or large pocket ▸ Good size to give to young children (no waste)
Integral pull-off tab	Don't need to have tin opener	▸ Only one item to dispose of when finished ▸ More environmentally friendly
Packaged as a 'single item' not in multiple pack	Can buy just one	▸ Don't need to buy more than needed
All natural ingredients	There may be none – in fact, might have disadvantages in terms of shelf life	▸ Healthier than comparable products
UK-manufactured	▸ Faster distribution to shops ▸ Few miles between production and customer	▸ Feel good by supporting a more 'green' product ▸ Feel good about supporting local industry and jobs

You might go a step further in selling to your customer by helping him understand how to sell to his customer or provide sales/advertising posters to improve your customer's sales. If you did so, another feature of your offering would be: "Comes with advertising posters and supporting ad campaign". This feature would give an 'advantage' of 'marketing/selling material included with product'. The benefit to the shopkeeper would then be "it's easier to sell". (Well, as long as the ad campaigns and support materials are any good!) To produce this support material for the shopkeeper, you need to create a second 'Features/Advantages/Benefits' chart focused on the end customer (the shopkeeper's customers).

Highlight any unique feature of your offerings

Finally, is there anything your product or service offers that is unique for your target market? How many times have you noticed a petrol station with the sign "Last Petrol

Station before the Motorway" or "Next Petrol Station in 50 miles"? These signs are an attempt to highlight a unique feature of this business for its target market – the motorist. If you sell 3oz cans of soft drinks but so do all your competitors, the size of your product is not a strong selling feature – it doesn't distinguish you from competition even though it might be beneficial to your customer.

It is very, very useful to identify any truly unique feature(s) that you offer and then, try to match these to your customer's needs. What are unique features? In the soft drink example, if all the other suppliers of canned soft drinks only offer sizes much larger than 3oz, then the 3oz can is a unique feature. So, what market might find this unique feature of significant benefit? Some examples include: airline caterers who need to fit many small, single serving cans into airline storage compartments, small shops or catering businesses who sell takeaway lunches and might want to offer a single serving size as part of their offering, or small corner shops that typically sell only one or two cans at a time.

Be warned: a unique feature is only relevant if it confers a 'benefit' on your target customer. Your offering may be unique, but if the customer doesn't need it, he/she won't care. However, if your unique feature does confer a benefit, you can use it to boost your sales success.

Historical examples of companies who have shot to prominence by leveraging a unique feature include: First Direct with the introduction of online banking in the 1990s, Virgin Records and mail-order records in the 1970s, and more recently Amazon with online book retailers. All these businesses grew rapidly from 'nothing' by offering a unique service. Of course, since then others have copied the approach and the market has shifted, but without the unique feature these pioneering businesses would not have enjoyed a meteoric rise. Since these examples, new technology has driven many, many more examples. Google and Facebook are multi-billion-dollar corporations that didn't even exist 20 years ago. Both shot to prominence by leveraging the growth in the internet – another relative newcomer to the consumer marketplace.

Another lesson illustrated by these businesses is that 'market needs' change and if you are successful, your competition will work hard to catch up. Today, most major banks offer online banking and many providers offer 'downloads' of music from the internet. Even Amazon, a more recent example, has not stood still. Once exclusively 'books', the business has morphed into an online retail business, selling items that range from T-shirts to toasters, natural remedies to music.

The lesson? Unique features can be a powerful selling tool. Identify them and use them in your sales approach and support material. However, markets change. You must review your market and your benefits along with the rest of your marketing strategy on a regular basis in order to remain competitive.

Quantify the benefits of your offering

Having identified the benefits to your target market, it is also very useful to quantify them in terms of how much money/value your offering provides for your customers. Adding up savings or increased business for your customers' business helps you to structure your sales approach and set a reasonable price. (Pricing will be discussed in chapter 7.)

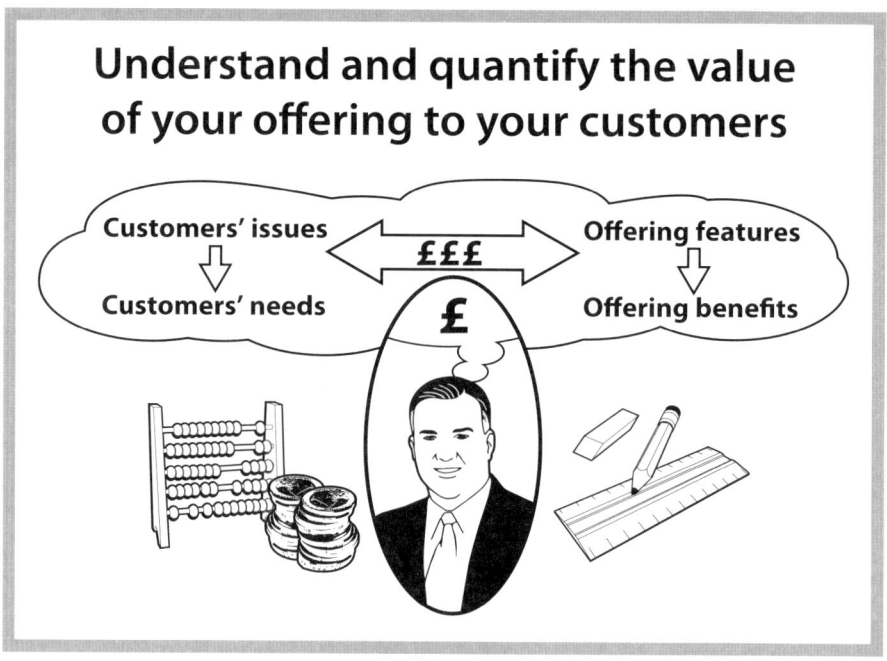

Understand and quantify the value of your offering to your customers

Customers' issues

Customers' needs

£££

£

Offering features

Offering benefits

If you have taken the trouble to understand your customers' issues and needs and analysed your offering's advantages and benefits, you are now in a position to be able to quantify the benefits. These benefits will be unique to specific customer groups or, in the case of large, custom-built solutions, unique to a given customer. In the retail bank example used in chapter 5, for the customer who earned more than £50k per year, the bank was able to provide them with added value (insurance, cheaper financial products etc.) as part of their 'customer package'. So, the bank can tell these customers that – although they may be paying £24/month for their account, the insurances and other services included are worth at least £40/month.

Now it's time for you to go through this exercise for your business, if you haven't already done so.

In addition to quantifiable or tangible benefits, you should also note 'intangible' benefits. Tangible benefits are those to which, with experience, you can attribute a monetary value. Intangible benefits are usually associated with 'feelings' – but don't discount feelings! Feelings can be a valuable sales tool or barrier and must be considered when designing your overall sales approach.

Let me start with the first of the two of simple examples illustrated in the following diagram. This first example is one that many of us have faced – a new car purchase. How do you buy your car?

A few years ago, a UK businessman was discussing commercial strategies with the UK financial director of a German car manufacturer. In discussing his product – the car – the FD explained to the businessman that (at that time) the UK marketing strategy was to focus on a particularly status-conscious sector of the UK marketplace. "Our cars and engines have the same reliability and good design as our main German competitors – that's not why our customers buy our product. They buy for the status," he said. The FD went on to elaborate: "We also 'manage' the used car market so that prices do

not fall too low and impact new car prices. We then increase our new car price so that only a limited number of people can afford, it so that our car retains its exclusive image."
"So," the UK businessman summarised, "if all I wanted was a reliable, well-engineered German car, it would make no difference if I purchased one from you or one from your competitor who is slightly less expensive."

"That's right," he confirmed. "The price differential represents 'prestige' – our customers are paying for prestige."

So, when this car manufacturer set a price in the UK, it looked at costs plus it added a certain percentage for the 'prestige' that the cars provided. Prestige isn't found on the car – it's all in the customer's mind.

Example two, lipstick, illustrates a similar pricing strategy. Most lipsticks cost almost nothing to manufacture and in many cases the packaging is the most expensive component. However, if you look at cosmetic counters you will see that typical lipsticks range in price from £5 to £30-plus. So, what's the difference?

I'm sure many manufacturers would respond by listing an ingredient or two in order to justify the price, but do your own market survey and ask women why they select the £30 lipstick.

For the more expensive brands, the whole shopping experience makes buyers feel sophisticated and fashionable – and that's what beauty products are all about. In terms of the basic features, the lower-cost item available at a major chemist chain and the expensive item purchased at a top-end retail outlet tick all the same boxes: size, colour, texture and longevity – but the shopping experience and the cachet are different. Women pay more for the expensive lipsticks in order to buy glamour, sophistication and chic. Like the German car, you won't find any of these qualities listed among the ingredients.
In both these examples you will note that the status product won the business for 'emotional' reasons. The intangible benefits played a key role in securing the business. But no one likes to admit that he or she uses emotions to make a financial decision. If you lead your sales campaign with intangible benefits, you still need to provide 'tangible benefits' so that individuals can rationally justify the purchase.

Capture all benefits – tangible and intangible

Examples	Tangible	Intangible
Upmarket, status car	▶ Reliable so it gets me where I need to go ▶ Good resale value so good investment ▶ Well made so my children will be safer in case of accident	▶ Shows people I've 'made it' ▶ Makes me feel 'proud' ▶ Feel like a good provider and happier when my children are in car
High-fashion brand lipstick	▶ Colour matches my clothes ▶ Can buy colours to match all current fashion trends ▶ Get free 'samples' when I buy product at shop	▶ Buying this brand makes me feel beautiful ▶ Buying this brand makes me feel sophisticated

Brand

These two examples also illustrate another component of your offering – brand. When a buyer selects the expensive lipstick, she selects a particular brand whose image she aspires to. Similarly, buyers of the German car were buying 'apparent status' because of the brand image created by the manufacturer. At its simplest, 'brand' is a promise you make to your customer about your offering, its impact, reliability, consistency.

As the two examples illustrated, brand can be more than just product or service features – it can convey an image, status or a feeling of safety to the purchaser. All around the world, tourists will go into a McDonald's because they 'know' what they will be purchasing. They know that McDonald's will provide a familiar meal even when they are in an unfamiliar environment.

For years, IBM used to sell many large systems with the phrase "Nobody ever got fired for buying IBM!" and, in the past, that was true. In this instance, IBM's brand meant 'safe' to some of its customers. IBM spent time, effort and money cultivating its brand and this 'safe' component was as much about how its employees behaved and how it conducted its business as it was about the actual IBM product.

Creating your own brand takes time, effort and expertise and you will probably not be able to invest the same as a McDonald's or IBM in brand development. However, you can take steps appropriate to your size to ensure that you present a consistent 'image' to your customers and in your marketplace, and you can decide what you want that image to be. Do you want to be known as a 'reliable supplier'? Low cost? High quality? Your marketing material, your employees' behaviour – all interactions with your market – can be constructed to support whatever 'image' you select. It would take an entire book to explain the process and its applicability to any particular market.

However, as you have seen from the lipstick and car examples, careful investment and work on your brand can prove its worth. A first step toward strengthening your brand is to make certain that you speak your customer's language.

Communicate – speaking and listening

Communication is a two-way exercise. You must use language that your customer understands or you might as well not bother. An easy way to begin your communication is to focus on your target buyer and his/her needs and use your customer's terms, not your own.

To support this approach, both your sales material and sales approach should make a direct and clear connection between your offering's features and your customers' needs. Make it easy and obvious to buy from you – don't make your customers work hard in order to understand and buy your product. And your conversations should not be all one-way. Let your customer speak/communicate and listen to what's said. If you use the internet to sell, understand how your buyers will use the system to make certain that the whole 'buying process' is as swift and simple as possible.

Listen to your customer and adapt your offering where possible

Your product

Customer feedback

Apply modifications where it makes good business sense

Your 'modified' product

'Listening' to your customer doesn't mean that you have to make immediate changes to your business or offering, nor does it mean you should believe absolutely everything you hear.

If you listen often and well, you will be able to judge the accuracy of what you hear. Therefore, it is important to listen constantly to as many different sources as possible. A process for gaining customer feedback and market intelligence will provide you with vital information that can play a significant role in shaping your market strategy. Listen, but don't overreact. Take your time and assemble data so that you gain a big picture of your market and your company's image in that marketplace. If changes make sense, make them.

It's much easier for you to change what you do than to change your customer or an entire market segment. You have already heard how Ready Steady Store made changes by listening to its market. Mehran Charania went on to describe in detail one of his company's responses.

··

Ready Steady Store listens and adapts to its market

"One of these changes has been the shift by customers from phone to internet. Keeping in step with this shift, RSS redesigned its website to take advantage of many internet features including online enquiries and follow-up. RSS had always received good customer feedback, but when reputation was 'word of mouth' the impact of this good service was slow to spread. Today internet-based ratings spread the word more quickly and RSS is beginning to see the impact in terms of speed of attracting new customers."

··

Understand your competitors' offerings

It is not good business practice to ignore your competition. On the other hand, in general, it is NOT a good idea to design your sales, pricing or business model on those of your competition. So what is the right balance?

Ideally, you should base your own business and marketing strategies on your own strengths and capabilities. Understand your market segment and focus on your unique features and how they meet your customers' needs. Then, examine your competition – not just their offering, but also how they sell, their business practices and how they are perceived in the marketplace. With these insights you can then modify your basic approach – tactically – to counter competitive threats.

If you are entering a new market, you might modify this approach a bit, by specifically targeting your key competitor's weaknesses so as to gain a foothold in their customer base. As always, focus on your customers' needs first.

A good example of this approach is M&S and Waitrose with their "Dinner for Two" offers each week. Since the recession hit the UK economy, more and more young business professionals who used to eat out a lot are now forced to economise. Having identified this market segment, food retailers have put together offers of three-course meals or two courses plus wine for two people at a total cost of £10. That £10 is well below what a takeaway or a meal out for two would cost, and most of the selections involve very little cooking, mostly heating up in a microwave. There you have it, a quick, tasty, often 'posh' meal for two at an affordable price – and, more revenues for M&S and Waitrose, because they did not previously compete with restaurants and takeaways in this manner.

And note, neither retailer is offering 'new' products or services – both have merely 'repackaged' and priced existing items to give them appeal to certain customers. These items are usually prominently displayed near the check-out queues so a busy professional doesn't have to travel far to do his or her shopping. So, the products now appeal to the needs of a particular set of customers and are very easy to buy – a good example of how to market and a commercial success.

How can you make the same impact in your chosen market?

Analyse and understand your key competitors' offerings, business and market tactics

A SWOT analysis of your offering is a good first step

In chapter 5, you used the SWOT analysis tool to look at your target market. You can now use the same tool to analyse your offering. What are your product/service strengths? Remember, even if you are justly proud of your offering, if everyone else's product can do what yours can do, it's not a strength, it just gets you into the game.

Let's return to the example in chapter 5 of the soft drink sold in a 100ml/3oz can. Study the following table and have a look at how a product SWOT for this item might look. You will notice that one of the opportunities in this example consists of targeting additional market segments, while a second involves adding a new product 'feature' to the range. To make the first changes would involve analysis of each of these segments, selection of an appropriate sales approach and then reworking the product descriptions and advertising information so as to appeal to each new market segment. The second opportunity – offering an additional, larger sized product option – would probably involve a number of activities within the manufacturing and distribution process as well as creating slightly modified marketing material. The manufacturer would have to:

- Adjust or build a new production line to produce the larger size
- Source materials and design for larger packaging
- Create new product numbers, storage locations and pallet configurations to accommodate a second, larger product.

There would doubtless be other changes within the organisation as well, but you get the idea. Changing a product costs money, so any business must do its homework to ensure it understands the return on such an investment. Furthermore, in a small business these changes would also take up the time of staff who would otherwise be manufacturing, testing, storing, distributing, etc. the smaller version of the product and could, therefore, have an impact on the ability to produce and deliver the original product. It is vital to understand both the upside and the downside of pursuing new opportunities.

Product SWOT analysis – 100ml/3oz can soft drink

Strengths	Opportunities

▸ Smaller size than any competitor
 	
▸ Can supply to shops within 24 hours (sometimes less)
 	
▸ Convenience
 	
▸ Doesn't need opener
 	
▸ Only one item for disposal (tab folds into can)
 	
▸ Healthier than carbonated drinks
	▸ New market segments
	   ▸ Hospitals
	   ▸ Nursing homes
	   ▸ Schools
	   ▸ Food Vans
	   ▸ Train and airline caterers
	
	▸ Add a larger size to the product range

Weaknesses	**Threats**
▸ No straw sold with product (for young children and invalids) ▸ Price/volume ▸ Only 2 flavours offered ▸ No 'low calorie' option ▸ Only available in 100ml/3oz size	▸ Traditional soft drink manufacturer will produce similar sized product ▸ Bottled water suppliers will produce smaller bottle (focusing on 'healthy' option). ▸ Cost of ingredients – fruit juices – will increase due to recent global droughts

When you look at product or service weaknesses, analyse them in comparison to other options your customer might select. Usually, such options come from your competition, but sometimes your customer can elect to try to do something himself or decide to do nothing. You should consider this option to be a competitive threat as well. Customers often believe that doing something themselves costs 'nothing'. Occasionally, when a customer's time is worth 'nothing' – this belief may be true. However, most of the time this belief is a delusion.

Similarly, if a customer truly needs to do something for his business – replace a vital manufacturing component, reorganise staff, buy a new van – this expense is usually justified by a business benefit. Every minute that a decision to purchase is delayed, the customer also delays receiving this benefit. It is important to understand 'how much' it costs your customer when he delays the purchase of your offering.

There are some very simple examples of the cost of 'delay'. If, for example, a customer has calculated that installation of a new, internet-based sales order system will reduce costs by £10,000/month and increase his sales by £100,000/month, then for every month that the decision is delayed, this customer could, by his own calculations, be paying £10,000 more than is necessary and losing £100,000 in business. Understanding the costs of doing nothing or delay is vital and there will be more on this topic in chapter 7.

When you have completed a list of strengths and weakness for your product, and analysed competitive threats in all their forms, take a look at your marketing and sales support materials. Do they emphasise your offering's strengths? Target your opportunities? How about your competitors?

In general, it's not a good idea to mention your competitor's name in your selling efforts. Why give them free advertising? Your sales approach, advertising and support literature should, instead, promote things you do well that you know your key competitor does poorly or less well. A good example is when a supplier helps the customer to 'buy' by including a list of what they should look for in a product/service. This list, of course, includes all the supplier's strengths and some of the competitor's weaknesses.

For example, large multinational suppliers often stress that customers should look for:

- Financial stability
- Breadth of geographical cover
- Investment in R&D
- Large numbers of back-office staff who can help with customer service.

This positioning is emphasised when these suppliers are up against smaller, local suppliers. You can see the use of FUDGE (fear, uncertainty, doubt & great expectations) in this list. Everything is aimed at making a potential buyer worry about doing business with a 'small company' that doesn't have the 'necessary' size and resources. But are these resources really necessary? Of course, that depends, but often they are not.

A small business whose offering competes with the larger business would emphasise:

- Personal service
- Flexibility
- Products and services that focus on the potential customer's needs (as opposed to a large range of products/services that are irrelevant to the business need)
- The importance of this deal to the local business will ensure priority service at all levels of the supplier's organisation. Feel like a 'big fish' in a moderately sized pond rather than swimming with sharks in the ocean.

In the two approaches above, the actual product might be identical, but the emphasis is NOT!

When you understand your market, your offering and your customer you can effectively tailor your sales messages and approach to your own advantage. As in judo, sometimes you can even use your competitor's own strengths to defeat him.

Arm your sales staff with all the right messages. Include the output of your SWOT in revamped sales training, new product launches and all sales support material. Provide your 'selling machine' with the right fuel and they will deliver success.

Common pitfalls

DO NOT:

1. **Use your own internal terms and language for customer materials and sales literature.**
   This mistake is frequent in technical, scientific and engineering companies. It doesn't matter how educated you are – if you can't explain why your offering is good and how it works in simple terms, you will not sell as effectively. You are in business to sell and satisfy customers' needs and make money, not demonstrate your intelligence.

2. **Fail to listen to your customers.**
   The issue is often not that nobody listens to the customer – it's that there is no formal process to systematically record and evaluate feedback and decide whether/how to take action. Remember, you are in business to satisfy your customers – no one else!

3. **Forget to 'check' and 'confirm' customer needs.**
   Don't assume. The UK executive who found out about the German car manufacturer's marketing strategy – to keep its brand exclusive – found out because he prepared a sales presentation in which he assumed that the business wanted to grow market share. How wrong he was! Simple confirmation of the customer's needs would have saved him time and effort and made him look better prepared.

4. **Compare yourself to your key competitor(s) in customer literature or sales material, unless this comparison forms a key part of your sales strategy.**

5. **Fail to train your sales staff using your own product or service.**

END OF CHAPTER 6 – SELF-ASSESSMENT

EVALUATE YOUR PRODUCT/SERVICE OFFERING - Tick 1 box for each question

QUESTION	Yes	No	Partly
1. Have you mapped your offering (product and/or service) features on to your customers' current needs?			
2. Have you carried out a SWOT analysis for your most important offerings?			
3. Do you update your SWOT and marketing/offering analysis at least once a year?			
4. Have you analysed your key competitors' offerings, businesses and market approaches?			
5. Do you have a process for capturing customer feedback – both positive and negative?			
6. Do you have a process for capturing competitive activities?			
7. Do you have a process for modifying your offering/approach/activities as a result of important feedback?			
8. Is your offering description and customer literature written in the customer's language?			
9. Is your sales support literature written in terms that address the customer's needs and in the customer's language?			
10. Do you incorporate new offering launches into sales and customer service training material?			

YOUR SCORE: Give yourself 5 points for every 'yes', 2 points for every 'partly' and '0' for every 'no'.

36-50 Points ➡ Excellent – note areas where you didn't score 5 and plan to rectify if relevant to your business

26-35 Points ➡ Good – you have some room for improvement. Check those areas in which you ticked 'no' or 'partly' and evaluate how you can improve your score

11-25 Points ➡ You could do better – there is definitely room for improvement…

0-10 Points ➡ Get help! You have lots and lots of opportunity to improve your income stream.

Chapter 7

Pricing

Top tips – Chapter 7

1. Remember, cost and price are different – the two need not have a straight line relationship

2. Try to 'quantify the benefits' of your offering to your customer and consider these benefits when establishing your baseline price

3. 'Intangible' benefits should be spelled out too

4. Calculate the costs of selling and delivering as well as producing your offering, so you know when you are 'buying the customer's business'

5. Select a pricing policy and be consistent

6. Whatever your pricing policy, make certain that all your employees believe that your product and/or services provide value for money

7. Establish a discount policy which is consistent with your pricing strategy

8. Never discount without 'trading' something for your loss of revenue

9. Protect your investment in your brand

Even in these economically challenging times, achieving business success is not as simple as just lowering your prices. There is also a danger of focusing on cutting costs within your business, assuming that any investment is unwise. It's not. To prosper and ensure that your business has a future, now is the time when you must invest in sales and invest in increasing your revenues and profits. You have already read how Ready Steady Store increased its marketing spend in response to the recession and, in doing so, maintained its high occupancy of storage units while many of its competitors experienced drops in revenue and occupancy. Maintaining and even increasing your revenues is possible, but you must look hard at your pricing and discounting policies as well as your sales and marketing efforts.

Traditional wisdom dictates that pricing should take into account three variables:

- Your costs
- Customers
- Competition

While this is true in principle, there are many misunderstandings about what constitutes each of these variables.

Your baseline – calculating your costs

Before we start discussing pricing policy, let's return to some fundamentals. Do you know what it costs you to make, sell and deliver your offering? Many, many small businesses start by costing only the 'production cost'; in other words, the price of manufacturing and raw components. Sometimes these businesses also include storage costs and raw goods inventory. The more sophisticated add in the sales costs but still neglect to factor in all the management and administrative costs. In addition, if you have to borrow money from the bank to fund your cash flow, the cost of borrowing should be included. Frequently, owner/directors fail to pay themselves a regular salary so fail to include a notional cost for themselves in their pricing. Finally, spoilage, 'risk' and contingency – if relevant – should always be factored into your cost.

The cost of delivering a product or service should include an accurate apportionment of EVERYTHING to each offering you sell. This value is your baseline cost. If you sell the item/service for less you will be losing money and will eventually go out of business.

Calculate all the costs in making and selling your offering

Once you understand what it really costs to deliver your product or service to a customer, you may establish a baseline price. This baseline price should be higher than your total costs. The difference – whatever it is – represents your profit, and some profits should be retained for re-investment so it should NOT all go directly into investors' or owners' pockets. You cannot afford to set your price lower than this baseline price value. To do otherwise, you are, in effect, paying customers to buy from you and this is not a sustainable long-term business strategy.

In fact, until you understand this minimum price and its components, you will not be in a strong position to price, negotiate or discount. Understanding the true cost of your product/service may help you to identify issues elsewhere in the organisation. For example, if you cannot offer a price that is approximately the same as your competitor, it could tell you something about your efficiency in producing the product. Or... it could tell you that your competitor is selling below cost and perhaps you should let him win a few large deals at these prices. No business can sustain selling at a loss forever, and this approach could put your competitor out of business.

How should you determine your profit margin? The answer will depend on:

- Your pricing policy
- Market conditions
- Competition

However, now that you have calculated an accurate minimum price, you can have a look at your customers, the competition and the market and determine a pricing policy.

Your pricing policy

What's yours? You may have a number of options, depending on your marketing strategy. Do you want your company to be known as the lowest price provider of good-quality goods? This strategy has proved very effective for The John Lewis Partnership with its "Never Knowingly Undersold" philosophy. Or do you want to be perceived as a 'prestige brand' like the German car manufacturer I mentioned in the last chapter, or a 'pile them high and sell them cheap', low-cost supplier, like retailers such as Pound-land? There are many pricing options, all of which must support the image you wish to portray in the marketplace and should be aligned with your brand and marketing strategy. Whatever your policy, you must consider – but not necessarily copy – your leading competitor's pricing.

Your baseline price is composed of many layers of 'cost' plus some profit

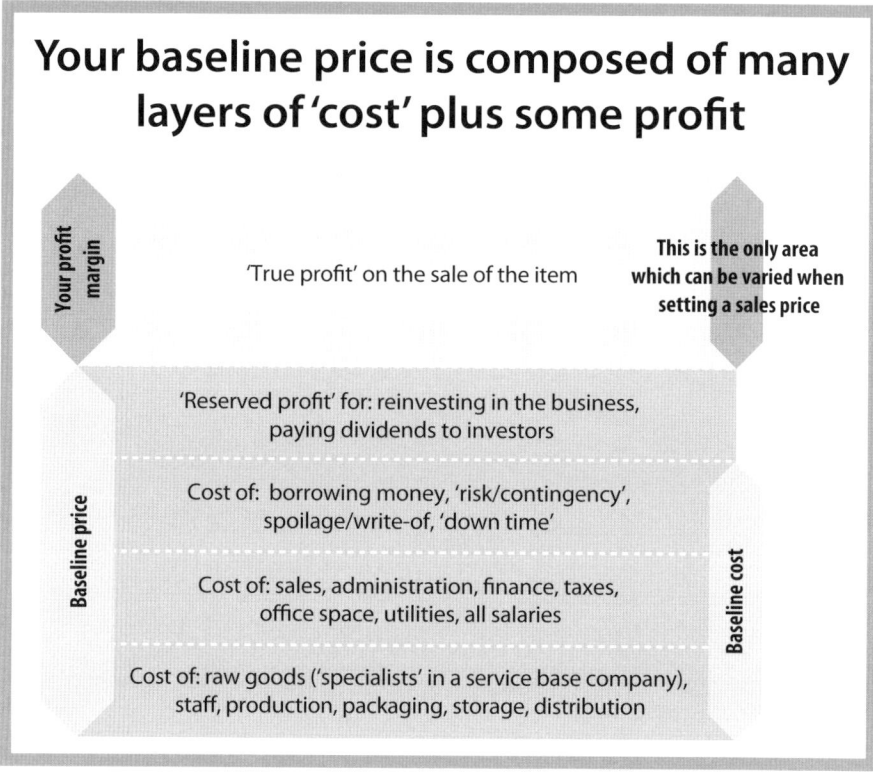

Your profit margin

'True profit' on the sale of the item

This is the only area which can be varied when setting a sales price

Baseline price

'Reserved profit' for: reinvesting in the business, paying dividends to investors

Cost of: borrowing money, 'risk/contingency', spoilage/write-of, 'down time'

Cost of: sales, administration, finance, taxes, office space, utilities, all salaries

Cost of: raw goods ('specialists' in a service base company), staff, production, packaging, storage, distribution

Baseline cost

In fact, there are some instances when mentioning a competitor allows you to capitalise on your competitor's marketing and pricing policy. A good example in today's marketplace is the one of premium brand supermarkets who put up notices on the price tags that say: "This price is equal to Tesco's price – the current, leading 'value brand' supplier." Such an announcement is tantamount to writing: "It's OK to buy your product here – not only are your getting a good shopping experience with high-quality goods, but you aren't paying any more for it!"

Whatever you chose, your pricing policy should be clearly spelled out and followed or you will not achieve your anticipated benefits.

For example, in the 1980s and 1990s, the policy of the UK subsidiary of the German car manufacturer I discussed in chapter 6 was to keep raising its prices until only a select, fixed proportion of the UK market could afford to purchase its cars. The approach meant that while profits were high, market share remained static. The directors of this business realised that maintaining a fixed market share was part of their business strategy.

Should the policy have been less clear, or if the sales staff were motivated purely by sales numbers, it's possible that the sales director would have tried harder to increase market share by selling more cars at a slightly lower price. If successful, this behaviour would have increased the number of people driving their brand and, ultimately, made their cars more common and less exclusive. If exclusivity decreased, the company would find it more and more difficult to charge a premium price.

Just as marketing strategy can change, so should pricing policy. When you are new to a market, you might price slightly lower as part of your attempt to gain market share.

Alternatively, if you want to gain more customers but do NOT want to give the image of being a low-cost provider, you can offer 'special' deals that bundle products together. For example, the "Dinners for Two" at M&S and Waitrose 'bundle' products together to offer two courses plus wine or three courses for £10. This price is significantly less than the sum of the individual prices for each item. Thus, these retailers do NOT need to reduce their baseline price for individual items, but discount only to those customers buying the whole meal.

'Introductory offers' are another way of luring customers to make purchases, discounting without lowering the item's price. Then, after taking up the special introductory offer, if the customer decides to continue buying the product(s), he or she is not surprised by the higher, 'original' price of the item(s).

Finally, 'pricing' is not always only about the initial selling price. Returns policy, support, added services, etc. – all these should be valued and factored into the 'deal' and you should make certain that your customers value these 'extras'. Airlines' loyalty programmes represent a good example of how something other than price can drive behaviours. Some people will pay even pay more to fly a particular carrier in order to obtain 'points' for 'free' flights and other rewards. Credit cards that offer 'cash back' are another good example. Many people use one card in preference to another because they get a 'rebate' – a small percentage of the total spend – returned to them periodically. Some car dealerships now offer three-year warranty and servicing as part of the car purchase deal – a setup that not only adds value to the purchase but also conditions the buyer to return to the dealer for annual servicing.

Discounts should be 'give and take'

Standard discounts

If you plan to offer discounts, make sure you have a reason to do so and be certain to make this reason clear to your customers. For example, you may offer a discount based on volume – "Buy more than a dozen and get a 10% discount on everything!" – or on timeliness – "We must clear our warehouse. Buy before month end and get a 20% discount!" Why go to this trouble? If you don't, you run the risk that the buyers will feel 'uncomfortable' with your usual price. They will become suspicious and ask themselves: "Did I pay too much before? What is the 'right' price to pay? What is the real price?"

All pricing activities should be conducted with the knowledge that other customers will eventually find out what price others are paying, and the last thing you want is to make someone feel a fool for buying from you. Like all good selling processes, discounting is a form of negotiation with 'give and take' on both sides. The discounts can form part of your policy or be negotiated on a one-to-one basis – but there should always be rules.

The most common reasons for 'discounting' include:

- Volume commitment
- Timing (i.e. buy before year-end or end of season stock)
- Payment terms (e.g. payment within 10 days or up front gets % discount)

These sorts of discounts are easy for you to justify to your customer and easy for you to calculate the additional benefits to your business. For example, a volume commitment over time can enable you to better plan production or procurement and save you money. Customer purchase of end of season stock – even discounted – can help you free up space for new season's items. When a customer pays you quickly you have these funds to use in the business – either paying off or minimising the necessity for costly loans. In each of these examples, by adhering to your discount terms, the customer is giving you something of value so you can 'afford' to reduce the price by some percentage.

Careful analysis of your business costs allow you to calculate how much you can discount in given circumstances versus how much savings the customer commitment will give you. In this way, you can produce standard discount schedules for your selling staff, offering them flexibility when negotiating deals all the while staying within your business guidelines.

When to avoid special discounts

There are some times and some businesses where you must avoid discounting your basic product/service price. Why? Take, for example, the premium brand car or designer brand lipstick discussed earlier – the customer 'expects' to pay more for the accompanying status. If you lower the price, you reduce the 'exclusivity' of the purchase and thereby, your customer's status. You may experience a temporary increase in lower profit sales, but overall you will endanger your brand and market position.

Another circumstance when you should hold steady with your price is when you have a unique feature that the market needs and demand outstrips supply. A simple example of this situation is tickets to the final for Centre Court at Wimbledon. You could sell these tickets many times over, so why reduce your price? You may have select customers you wish to treat as 'special'. If so, either give them the tickets for free and hold the pricing for everyone else and/or give additional perks like free parking or a place in the hospitality tent. If you lower the price for an exclusive item for one buyer and your other customers hear about it, they will feel unvalued.

Both these examples focus on end consumers, but the advice holds true for business-to-business sales as well. In the consulting business, this situation is a regular challenge – particular as many large consulting businesses often have multiple contracts within the same customer. Typically, the large consulting companies quote a 'day rate' for different types of consultants. These days rates may be discounted against a standard formula of volume or time commitment by the customer. But what happens if a customer demands a bigger discount? There is the danger that if the company discounts for one piece of business, the customer will start to demand similar rates for all the ongoing contracts.

Worse still, word gets around in the market sector that someone got lower rates without having to give the standard concessions and then everyone demands reduced rates. In order to keep 'goodwill', prices have to drop everywhere and the profit margins take a nosedive.

So, what do consultancies do to fight this trend? The easiest response is to 'hold the base price' and offer 'free bodies' for a certain task. All consultancies have times when there is no work for some of their consultants and these consultants still receive a salary. Why not use them for a limited amount of time to do 'free work' in a customer if it secures a 'deal' – it costs the consulting company nothing and the customer gets extra value.

Other ways to discount

There are other ways to effectively offer a discount without altering your apparent basic price. A common example of this approach is at fast food restaurants when you pay a small amount more and get an extra-large or 'supersized' portion. The additional food or drink involved does not add much to the fast food company's cost, so the extra payment equals extra profit.

Bundling of product/service is another common strategy. Continuing with our 'fast food restaurant' as an example – you can order all your items – hamburger, fries and drink – and pay for each item separately or you can buy a 'meal' and get these items for a lower price. Why price this way? Often, especially in today's health-conscious environment, customers might 'skip the fries' if ordering separately. However, if the fries are offered for only a few pence more it's often enough to tip the balance and the customer thinks: "Oh well, why not?" Even at a few pence more, the fast food restaurant is making a profit on the fries. And it's not just the food industry that uses this technique.

You can 'bundle' other products together – for example, extended warranty on electronics, or software 'bundles' sold when purchasing a PC. This feature has little cost to the vendor – a new PC, if properly built, will have little that can go wrong in the first year. If something was wrong with the original manufacturing, the retailer should always take back the hardware and return it to the manufacturer. However, giving a free warranty appears to many customers to be an 'added bonus'. And it is – to the vendor! This supplier now has your name on a list and will try to sell you an extended warranty, collecting payments from you for years to come. In the retail world, bundling helps maximise the value of a sale during any customer purchase.

And 'bundling' can include services, contract terms – there are many options. "Buy now, pay in 12 months", "Interest-free credit" can be used in the consumer and business markets alike. Payment terms and timing are often critical for customers who are large businesses and might have budgeting issues with the timing of payments. Perhaps they have spent this year's budget but know they will have more money when the next financial year begins; It can even work the other way around.

In some businesses and many government departments, individuals try to use up all the budget in a given financial year. An example comes from a woman who ran a consulting business and did most of her work for government departments. She was recently paid a year in advance for work they could NOT even specify, merely to use up departmental funds. Be warned, in these instances there must already be an existing relationship and trust between the vendor and supplier as, technically, your customer is 'bending' his/her organisation's rules.

The key factor with 'bundling' is that you try to add things that your customer will value or buy that have little value to you. If you can't afford to 'advance the money', don't offer long-range payment terms. If you can, there may be times when it wins you the business.

Value-based pricing

So what's it worth to you? What's it worth to your customer? That's the question. We have already discussed one way of 'value-based pricing'. For some people having a right 'brand' of car was worth £10,000 to £15,000 extra and for some women wearing the right brand of lipstick was worth an extra £20. For this extra money consumers bought 'intangible benefits' – they felt 'good' being associated with this product. This brand-based 'value-based pricing' is difficult to use until you have established yourself as a premium brand; however, there are other valuable features you can exploit and use to price your offering. How much more will you pay for the convenience of an item bought from your corner shop rather than a cheaper supermarket? The extra price reflects the value to you of being able to purchase the item late at night or, perhaps, without having to get into your car. Emergency plumbers who will respond to a 'call out' will charge a premium because of the 'value' to you in having them respond at any hour of the night or day. The challenge in pricing is to determine 'how much more' an individual or business will pay for this convenience? What's it worth?

At the beginning of chapter 7 we talked about using information about costs, customers and competition to help you determine the best price. However, if you take a value-based approach, you can think of determining your price in a slightly different way:

- Creating value
- Calibrating value
- Communicating value
- Capturing value

So how do you go about it?

There are a number of ways to determine the value. A crude method is to keep raising your price until sales fall. With this 'fall' you can guess that you have reached the maximum price above which customers will not be pushed. At this point, you have more choices – reduce the price to a level where you achieve the business you desire OR keep raising the price until those few customers who pay the higher price make up for your lost sales in terms of revenue and profits. It's a risky strategy.

To more clearly understand value-based pricing you must examine how customers make buying decisions. The way that the decision is made will depend on where the decision maker stands in solving his issue or exploiting an opportunity – in other words, how well he or she understands his need and whether he/she has a clear idea of how to satisfy it.

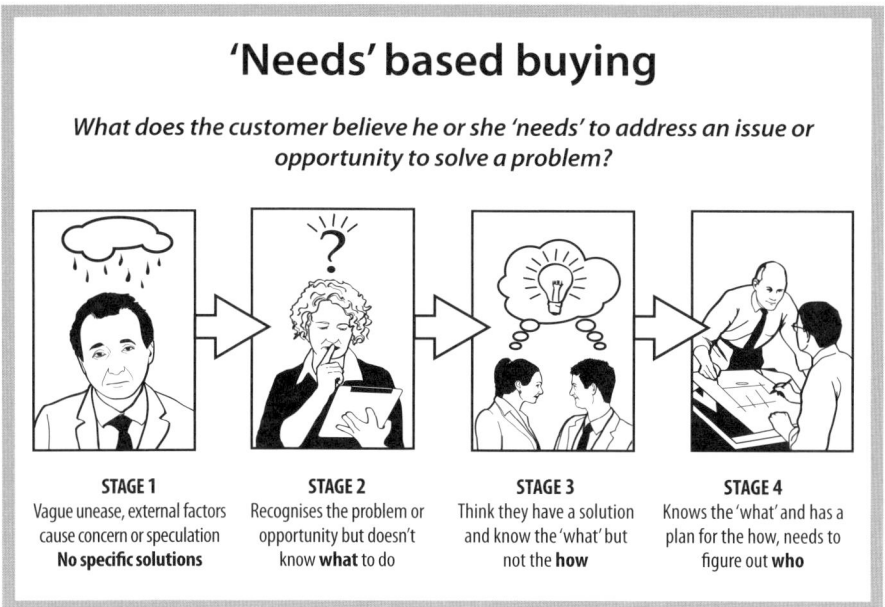

'Needs' based buying

What does the customer believe he or she 'needs' to address an issue or opportunity to solve a problem?

STAGE 1
Vague unease, external factors cause concern or speculation
No specific solutions

STAGE 2
Recognises the problem or opportunity but doesn't know **what** to do

STAGE 3
Think they have a solution and know the 'what' but not the **how**

STAGE 4
Knows the 'what' and has a plan for the how, needs to figure out **who**

You have had a brief introduction to the buying process or 'buying cycle' in chapter 6 when you looked at customer opportunities and issues and how these might be turned into customer needs. In essence, the 'buying cycle' describes how a person/company moves from a vague feeling to a clear idea about an opportunity or issue, and the journey of trying to define what's needed to deal with an issue or to take advantage of an opportunity. As a final step, late in the buying process, the buyer decides how to deal with the situation and who can help.

During the first stage of the cycle, either 'unease' or a vague 'inspiration' about an opportunity disturbs the decision maker, but a solution is not fully formed. At this stage the individual is unlikely to buy something to satisfy an undefined feeling, BUT he or she is vulnerable to suggestions and ideas. Advertising is sometimes designed to appeal to these vague worries by identifying the 'feeling' and then, during the advertisement, leading the observer through the opportunity or issue resolution to the solution and, finally, a specific supplier.

If your sales person becomes involved at stage 1 or stage 2, not only can he/she play a role in helping to shape the eventual solution (or 'sale') but the customer also discloses lots of information about 'value' during the process. If the sales person is able to quantify this information, it can help you to 'add' this value to your final price. Sales involvement that starts at stage 3 can also provide your sales staff with useful information and some ability to 'shape' a deal. However, by the time the customer has reached stage 4, if your company has not yet been involved it will be very difficult to develop a value-based price for your solution.

Developing a value-based price

Another way of developing a value-based price is open to businesses who sell 'solutions' – solutions often involve a mixture of both products and services. Examples include:

- selling and implementing a new software application in a business
- designing and building an oil rig or specialist building or room, like an operating theatre or research laboratory
- personal coaching that includes both diet advice and exercise

These 'solutions' focus on 'outcomes' rather than the specific pieces of the offering. So, as an example, let's look at the software implementation in more detail. To achieve a successful implementation the customer might need:

- Software
- A variety of IT specialists' help to install on hardware and integrate with existing software systems
- Business consultants to advise on how current company systems will be impacted and help with re-designing and optimising some of the business activities
- Implementation specialists and project management
- ...and possibly many, other specialists depending on the specific software

This sort of solution is complex and difficult to buy 'in pieces' – it's much easier to go to a single supplier who has done it many times before and understands what's needed. So, how could this experienced supplier price this solution?

First, of course, he or she needs to understand the actual costs. Then, because all these projects encounter unforeseen challenges, an element of 'contingency' costs should be added. If forced to quote 'fixed price' for the work, the business should always include an amount of money to cover 'contingency', but this value does not contain profit. To make a profit, the business must quote a number that includes a profit margin.

The reason to then consider value-based pricing is if you believe it will give you a higher final price as well as leverage to win the sale. First, let's look at how you might determine the value of a solution to the customer. Let us assume we wish to sell a computerised inventory management solution. With this information and appropriate discussions with your customer, you can begin to quantify the key, tangible benefits and confirm these individual values with your customer.

Let us say that you discover that the new, computerised inventory control system would allow the business to:

- Reduce staff at each depot by 50%
- Reduce wastage by 10% (total inventory costs)
- Enable better procurement terms due to better management information systems

Each of these 'benefits' can be converted into a cash saving for the customer when the benefits are achieved.

The next step is to uncover and agree with the customer that there would be:

- Loss of three staff at five sites ➡ total 15 staff at an average cost of employment of £30k/year
- Current wastage runs at £1m/year
- Procurement manager believes he could get better deals if he had more information at his fingertips. He estimates he could save 10-15% more during negotiations. He tells you he currently spends about £12m with suppliers each year

From these three examples alone you can see that when the company successfully implements the software solution, it can potentially save:

- £450k/year in staff savings
- £100k/year in reduced wastage
- £1.2-1.5m/year in reduced spend with suppliers

If this were a real case, there would undoubtedly be more savings, but you get the idea. These examples alone represent approximately £2m/year annual savings. Therefore, you could easily justify a £2m price tag for your work. £4m would also be easy to justify. Many companies don't look for payback until three, four or five years after the implementation of a project. Regardless of your costs, even £6m would be justifiable. After all, these three benefits come from 'cost reduction' – you will also hope to uncover and agree quantifiable 'opportunity costs' to add to the pricing equation.

What do I mean by a 'quantifiable opportunity'? Well, suppose you are speaking to the sales director of your customer and he tells you that he could double his sales success rate if he could rely on having necessary stock available in the warehouse – something their current systems don't support. He also discloses that his sales staff currently win three out of ten of the bids that come to them. He then goes on to reveal that a typical 'deal' is valued at £2m with a profit of 5% (yes, customers really will give you this sort of information!). So, three additional deals per year at £2m each is £6m more revenue with 300k more profit. At a minimum you can add £300k to the value of installing the software.

All these examples, 'cost savings' and 'opportunities costs', illustrate a minimum value that the customer could realise if he installed your solution. You can see that by collecting these numbers from various people in the customer organisation, you can begin to build a total value that you can use in determining how you price. In the end, your price can be 2%, 20% or 200% higher than your costs; it doesn't matter, just as long as you enable your customer to achieve these valuable benefits and you are competitively priced!

Calculating the 'value'

Typical areas of cost savings

- ▸ Decreased spoilage/loss
- ▸ Reduced headcount
- ▸ Decreased production time
- ▸ Decrease in time-to-market
- ▸ Increased efficiency
- ▸ Lower money costs (e.g. smaller/no business loans)

Typical areas of opportunity

- ▸ Increased win rate
- ▸ Increased sales
- ▸ Increased profit
- ▸ Increased customer satisfaction
- ▸ Improved management information
- ▸ Improved targeted marketing

If you do use value-based pricing, NEVER accept a contract where your payment depends on achieving these benefits. Why? Because as an outside company, all you can do is 'enable'. You have no control over how your customer runs his business. It's still up to your customer to implement the changes – for example, the sales director will still have to win three more deals and the head of operations still has to fire three people at each warehouse. Just because you have enabled them, it doesn't mean they will carry through with the activities. You have no control over these activities and therefore should not take payment based on them.

Sales approach

Your pricing strategy will shape your sales approach. As you can see from the following table, which shows key steps in quantifying customer benefits, it is virtually impossible to attempt complex, value-based pricing without deploying at least one sales person who can form relationships and ask questions throughout the customer organisation in order to build the value proposition. Furthermore, this sales person should be able to deal at all levels, from director to receptionist, with ease and credibility. Therefore, not only will you need a dedicated sales person, you will require a highly skilled individual who is numerate, understands business processes and engenders enough trust so that the customer will provide this business information.

Steps to quantify & confirm customer benefits

1. Identify potential problem areas and problem owners

2. Document the existing problems with the various managers/directors (e.g. inventory level, lost sales, customer returns)

3. Get customer to disclose values for current situations (e.g. value of inventory, % sales lost, number of customer returns)

4. Obtain benchmark industry figures – either from your customer or industry studies, or both

5. Ask your customer contact to give his/her best estimate of improvement with the use of your product

6. Summarise and play back what you have been told and gain agreement. For example: "If we were able to give you a system which did credit an instantaneous credit check, you believe you could decrease your 'bad debt' by 20%. From what you say before, your bad debt amounts to £1m/year, so this would be a savings of £200,000/year. Is this correct?"

7. Repeat this process with each issue and each problem-owning manager/director

8. Total the value of all benefits

At the other end of the scale, if your market position is that of 'lowest cost provider' and you provide a well-defined commodity item, such as toilet paper or light bulbs, it's not always necessary to have any sales staff. Advertising, your company brand and an easy, low-cost way to purchase – such as a website – is often sufficient. And you need to be lowest cost to exploit the web marketplace. Alternatively, if you have a large or very specialist product range and good availability, the internet can also be a good sales vehicle for your business and can enable you to grow to a dominant market position.

Look at Amazon. If you want a book, any book – new or used – often the easiest option is to check Amazon. The Amazon price is often the same as a high street shop – more in some cases – but in terms of convenience and breadth of selection, for books, Amazon sits in a dominant position. And Amazon is an example of where it's the 'whole offering' and not just the price that attracts and keeps customers.

As a business, SMEs typically sit somewhere in between the Amazon marketing strategy and the value-added offering approach described above. Any use of one-to-one selling always gives you the chance to sell 'added value', whether you reflect it in your pricing or not. The more distant your business from its actual customer, the more you will rely on brand to convey your offering's strength. If you invest in a 'prestige image' (and are successful with this approach) then your pricing can be higher.

There is no single, right answer that fits all companies.

However, it is well worth taking the time to work out your pricing policy because there is a good chance you could be making more money. As outlined earlier, start by reviewing and defining your marketing strategy, develop the appropriate pricing policy and then, make certain that your sales approach is right. Then, take the time and effort to communicate these strategies and policies so that your entire company understands them. And, when you have established guidelines and policies – review and enforce them.

The competition

You should always be aware of your competitors – their offerings' features, advantages and the companies' ways of doing business – especially new entrants to your market-place can be potential threats. By making the effort to observe what your competition does, not only can you counter threats but you might also learn something about your market, your customers and even a few clever business practices. One of my first 'learnings' as a rookie sales person was taught to me – indirectly – by a competitor.

• •

What the competitors can teach us…

Back to the early, start-up biotechnology company mentioned in chapter 2. I moved to Europe to help establish European sales. In the beginning, I sold research products across many European countries, driving from site to site, meeting researchers in universities, hospitals and research centres. The sales territory was large and diverse. This meant it was often weeks and weeks between visits – even more if the researcher happened to be away when I did the circuit of that institution. There was one Belgian institute where I had been trying and trying to convince an important market influencer to stop making the product himself and buy it from the US company. Then, one day, I returned to discover that the customer had stopped making the product himself, but he had now purchased it from a competitor!

"Why!?!" I asked. "Why did you buy it from them?!" The customer responded sheep-ishly: "Because the salesman was around more often than you." Well, I learned a lesson and, from then on, focused more time on key institutes rather than trying to see everyone. Not only did I learn a relevant business practice from a competitor, but I also learned a little bit more about what influenced the customer – "presence". If someone was around at the time the customer needed something, then that's the company that got the order.

Taking this approach one step further, I arranged to pay for and install storage freezers in the top labs and set up the biotech company's stock of products in these freezers. The arrangement with the customer was that he would only have to pay for what he took, but it would all be there, on site and convenient. Once a month I checked the stock to note the usage and sent an invoice. By installing a fully stocked freezer I had, in effect, created a 'constant presence' and the sales in this account skyrocketed!

• •

In the case study above, I, the sales person, learned from the situation and took action. But I didn't mindlessly copy my competitor – I took his tactics and went one step further. And I didn't need to go to the institute more and more often, just often enough.

What I needed was to have his 'presence' always there when the customer needed products. The point here is: observe your competition, learn from them, but do not mindlessly copy them. Try to match or better those things your competitors do that appeal to your customer but you can do in a different, even a better way.

What you can learn by being aware of your competitors…

Customer preference

Business practices

Your offerings' strengths

Your offerings' weaknesses

Competitive strategies

Finally, take care about how much you discuss your competitors with customers. If you show too much concern about a competitor's price, the customer will wonder why. Understand your own price and be able to justify it, and if your customer asks why you cost so much more than Company X you can simply say: "I don't like to say negative things about anyone. I will only speak about what I know and I know our margins and our product quality and frankly, I don't know how Company X can produce a similar quality item for that price." And leave it at that.

If, on the other hand, your customer wants to know why you are so much less expensive, a way of answering the question (as long as it's true) is: "Over the years our firm has invested in state of the art manufacturing systems (or distribution systems or whatever is appropriate) and, year after year, have ruthlessly driven down are costs while maintaining our quality." There are many good reasons why you might offer a comparable or better product for a low price IF being a low-price provider is your market strategy. Whatever your reasons, know them so that you can respond honestly and definitively to your customer's question. Otherwise, a good competitor will try to use your lower price to suggest that your product is of inferior quality.

Finally, don't give your competitors free advertising unless you can capitalise from their market image. Be very careful about mentioning your competitors in any of your advertising or sales literature – it's usually NOT necessary and only provides your customers with the names of other companies they might ask for competitive quotes. In fact, often your customers are unaware of your competitors. So, why provide them with the company names?

One instance where you might directly or indirectly refer to competition is when you can benefit from their brand or market image. Many years ago, the top two rental car agencies in the USA were Hertz and Avis respectively. For years Avis (without explicitly mentioning Hertz) ran an advertising campaign with the phrase "We Try Harder" suggesting that it was a good thing for customers to buy from the number 2 company. This situation is a good example of how Avis capitalised on Hertz's presence and strength in the marketplace to advance its own business.

Selecting a pricing policy

Where are you in your market now? Market leader? Sole supplier? New entrant to the market? Your pricing policy goes hand-in-hand with your marketing strategy and should support the image you wish create in your chosen market. You have already seen how a luxury car manufacturer decided that, in the UK, it wanted to be an exclusive brand and sacrificed market share for this brand image (but didn't sacrifice profit!). Whatever you choose, you cannot do so in a 'vacuum' – you must consider your market, your current market image and how your competition is perceived.

Whatever you choose, you must be consistent and everything: your business culture, sales approach, pricing, offering and market strategy must support your choice.

Common pitfalls

DO NOT:

1. Give away something that has greater value to you than to your customer
2. Fail to cost ALL your business costs when you calculate your baseline costs
3. Price your offering at 'baseline cost' or below
4. Fail to provide discount guidelines for all sales staff
5. Ignore the competition
6. Mention the competition in your sales literature –
   UNLESS it's part of your marketing strategy
7. Immediately drop your price in response to a competitive threat
8. Confuse pricing/discounting with 'negotiating' –
   winning is not always just about price

END OF CHAPTER 7 – SELF-ASSESSMENT

EVALUATE YOUR PRICING & DISCOUNT POLICIES - Tick 1 box for each question

QUESTION	Yes	No	Partly
1. Do you know all your costs, including 'cost of sale'?			
2. Do you regularly recalculate your baseline product or service cost?			
3. Do you have a pricing policy?			
4. Is your pricing policy communicated throughout your business, well understood and enforced?			
5. Does your pricing policy support your market strategy?			
6. Do you have a well-documented and enforced discount policy (even if your policy is 'no discounts')?			
7. Do you know about how your competition (products, business practices, pricing, behaviours, image in the marketplace)?			
8. Does your sales approach support your pricing policy?			
9. Do you know the value of your offering to your customers?			
10. Does your staff understand the difference between 'selling' and 'negotiating'?			

YOUR SCORE: Give yourself 5 points for every 'yes', 2 points for every 'partly' and '0' for every 'no'.

36-50 Points	⇒	Excellent – note areas where you didn't score 5 and plan to rectify if relevant to your business
26-35 Points	⇒	Good – you have some room for improvement. Check those areas in which you ticked 'no' or 'partly' and evaluate how you can improve your score
11-25 Points	⇒	You could do better – there is definitely room for improvement…
0-10 Points	⇒	Get help! You have lots and lots of opportunity to improve your income stream.

Part III

Your Engine Room – Keeping Your Selling Machine Tuned and Running

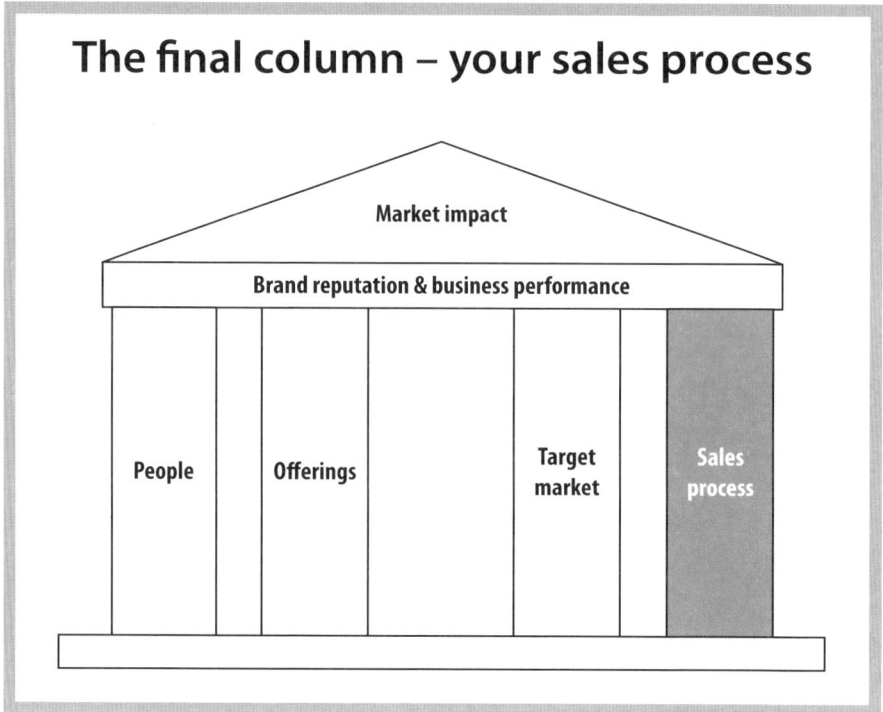

Introduction – How to get the most from your people, your offering and the market opportunity

By now, you already understand that successful selling is much, much more than merely hiring sales staff to knock on doors and arrange sales meetings. It is a complex process that can involve almost your entire company – and so it should. No matter how spectacular or unique your product or service, if no one buys it you won't have a business. There are a number of factors involved in getting it 'right':

- Your people as discussed in Part I
- Your target market and your offering as discussed in Part II

And the final supporting column – your sales process. The sales process is the 'back office' organisation and setup that helps you provide support for and management of sales activity.

Let's use a different analogy to illustrate what's meant by sales process. Let's say your business is 'a symphony orchestra' and your 'offering' is a musical performance. Your customers are the audience and your staff, the musicians – each with different skills and instruments.

So, what's missing in order for you to produce a fabulous performance? Three things: the 'musical score', the 'conductor' and off-stage technical support. The 'musical score' is the process the musicians follow in order to produce harmonious music. In other words, to the musicians, the score contains the rules that all the musicians understand and follow with respect to which note to play and when to play it. The conductor is the overall 'manager' who leads the musicians, controls the tempo and keeps on eye on all the professionals to make certain that they play together to maximum effect. Out of sight, 'off-stage technical support' – the stage hands, sound and light specialist – all work to support and enhance the orchestra's performance.

All these elements are necessary in order to stage a good performance. This section focuses on 'the score', 'the conductor' and the off-stage stage support – or, in business terms, 'the selling process', 'sales management' and sales support operations.

Like the musical score, a company sales process provides a common language and way of viewing sales situations that enables individuals to work together more effectively. A strong, defined sales process ensures that progress is defined, action plans for different stages are agreed and review points are built in. This structure ensures that everyone can quickly understand current sales situations and take any necessary actions. Such a process also pulls together the diverse skills in an organisation and helps them to work together effectively and efficiently.

Many businesses assume that having a 'sales process' means installing a customer relationship management (CRM) system. Certainly computerised systems can help, but they do not replace clear thinking about the sales process and how it needs to be tailored to suit the organisation. Many, many business installations fail to make this effort which is critical to ensure that the CRM system can be set up and used properly. So, in additional to your marketing strategy and pricing policy, use of your CRM systems and/or sales processes should be monitored and evaluated on a regular basis so that you can respond to opportunities and challenges.

Typically, any situation in which a customer might buy something from you is recorded as an 'opportunity'. Thus, a good sales process, whether computerised or not, can provide valuable management information about future sales, including:

- Volume – how much or how many
- Value – ££££
- Composition – which products/services
- Timing – when will offering need to be ready

Ideally, the more an opportunity has been 'worked on' and moves along the process, the closer it is to being won.

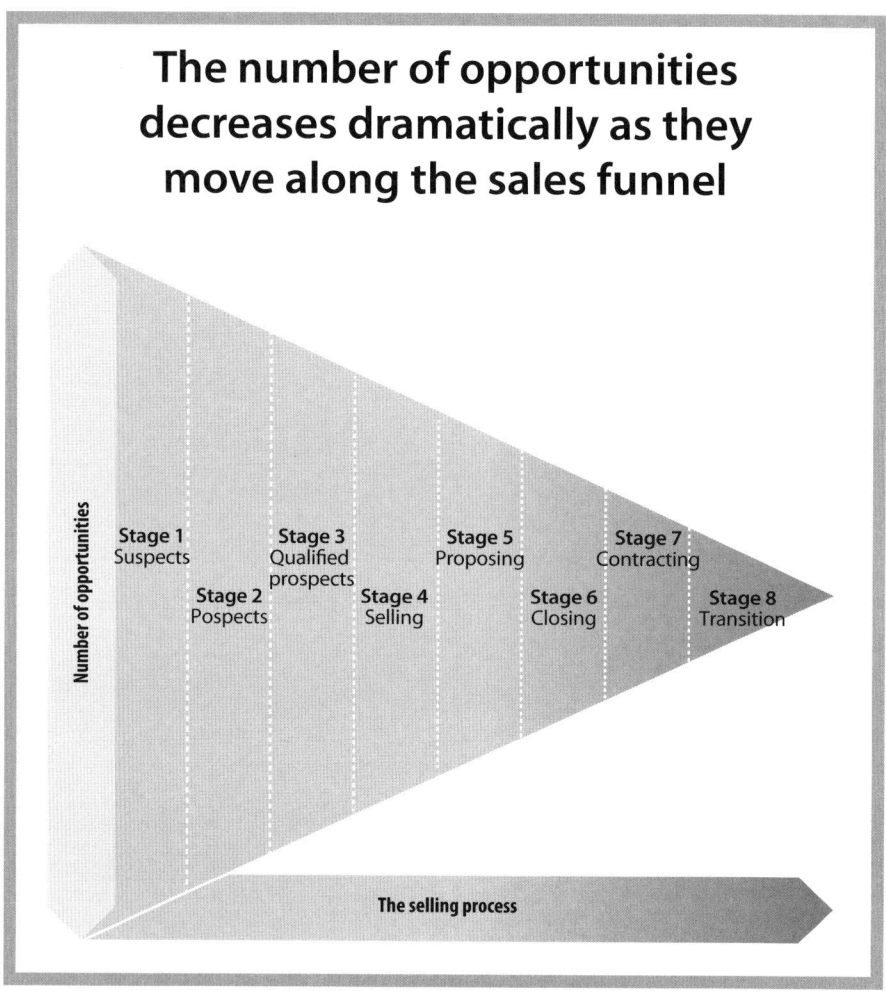

The number of opportunities decreases dramatically as they move along the sales funnel

Number of opportunities

Stage 1
Suspects

Stage 2
Pospects

Stage 3
Qualified
prospects

Stage 4
Selling

Stage 5
Proposing

Stage 6
Closing

Stage 7
Contracting

Stage 8
Transition

The selling process

A good sales process can also give you insights into market behaviours, shifting preferences and price sensitivity. Finally, a well-constructed sales process provides a good sales management tool.

The importance and use of a sales process depends on your market segment and offering and how your target customer makes buying decisions. Purchase of low-cost product by consumers has a relatively short buying cycle, while procurement of a complex business solution involving multiple products and services typically follows a more lengthy and complex buying process. In general, the more complex your offering, the longer the buying process and the more specialised the activities and skills needed at each step. Back to the orchestra analogy – you wouldn't expect a tuba player to be able to play the violin or a drummer to play the flute with professional skill – it's possible, but rare. So why would you think someone who specialised in high-level marketing and advertising could also negotiated complex contracts? Again, it's possible, but very, very rare.

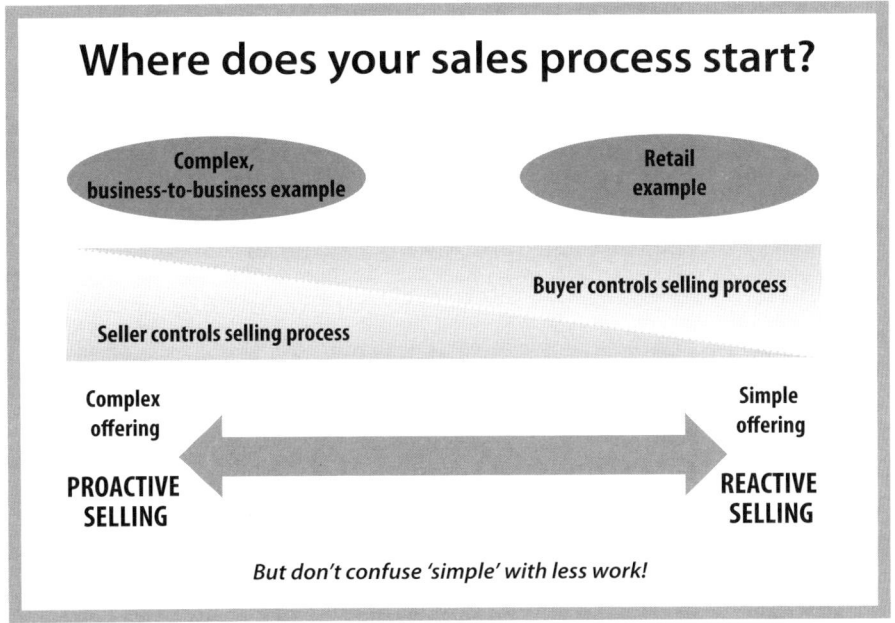

Where does your sales process start?

Complex, business-to-business example

Retail example

Buyer controls selling process

Seller controls selling process

Complex offering

Simple offering

PROACTIVE SELLING

REACTIVE SELLING

But don't confuse 'simple' with less work!

A long and complex sales process is like an orchestra playing a complex symphony – the sales process (or the 'score') enables the conductor to bring in the appropriately skilled musician at the appropriate moment. Sales management provides the same skilled leadership in your business environment. If your buying process is lengthy, then your sales process provides a valuable management tool to drive sales activities toward a successful conclusion. And the sales process should be managed.

'Sales management' means more than just giving someone the title and making this individual responsible for achieving revenue targets. Would you take this same individual, give him/her a title of surgeon, equip him or her with a scalpel and ask him to perform open-heart surgery? Of course not! That sounds ridiculous – someone's life depends on the outcome. Well, the life of your company depends on the outcome of your selling efforts, so make certain you have an experienced, well trained and equipped individual in charge of the process.

Finally, back-office sales support enables customer-facing sales staff to spend more time selling to the customer rather than back in the office doing paperwork. The more complex your selling process, the more time a sales person can spend inside your company rather than the customer's, getting information and gaining commitments from your production or specialist staff. There are more efficient and effective ways to manage these internal procedures and processes.

In reading this section you may think: "But this book goes on about lots and lots of staff – I'm only a small business!" The lessons in the next chapter – in fact, in all the chapters – apply to businesses of all sizes. If your company is larger, you may well have many people doing some of these jobs. If you have a small business, don't think of these descriptions as separate jobs, rather think of them as 'roles' and one person can play many roles. You must make certain that somebody in your organisation has each role covered.

Before you read the next section, ask yourself if you are getting everything you can from your selling machine. If not, the answer might be found in how you manage and drive your sales process. Very few businesses do everything optimally. Even the most sales-aware businesses have to make regular adjustments to tune their selling engine in response to changes in the market, competition or business needs.

In summary, a well-functioning sales process provides businesses with the ability to:

- Win more sales with less effort
- Understand opportunities and allocate the right resources
- Have a consistent view of the probable value and likelihood of future business
- Measure the success of individual sales people/teams

Test your company's process against what you read in Part III. What you learn here could directly impact your business performance.

Chapter 8

Your Sales Process

Top tips – Chapter 8

1. Understand how your prospects buy

2. Define a sales process appropriate to your business

3. Communicate, ensure 'buy in' and then, enforce this sales process throughout your company

4. Be clear what benefits your sales process brings to the business and all the individuals involved

5. List all 'opportunities' on the sales process to produce a 'sales pipeline' or 'sales funnel'

6. Use your sales process to provide management information – a sales funnel

7. Make sure only 'good data' goes into your sales funnel

8. Police your sales funnel for timely updates and data manipulation

What's the big deal? A sales person sells, somebody in the company takes the order, the offering is delivered and the customer pays. Why go to all the trouble to define a 'sales process'? Do all types of businesses need one? Is it really worth the effort? Of course it is and this chapter will explain all the reasons why it is worth the effort – whatever your business type.

In brief, a sales process maps on to your customer's buying process – which informs you of the likelihood that the customer will actually spend money with you. Therefore, it provides an important tool that allows everyone in your company to share a common understanding of how and when a prospective customer will buy and how much money this customer might spend. This shared view enables your employees to work together efficiently and effectively to close the sale and helps you to prioritise your resources and sales investment. For a high-volume, low-value type of business, the sales process can measure 'interest' in your product and how successfully you transform that interest into a sale.

In addition, any business that uses a CRM system will benefit from understanding the sales process in order to gain maximum value from these systems and engage all the users. Most leading CRM systems were designed to support a 'typical' sales process, so an understanding of this process will help you to extract maximum value from your CRM system.

Finally, no matter your market segment, all customer types have a buying cycle that should map on to the sales process, although the length of time spent in each stage does vary with market sector and sales approach. It's worth understanding how your customers buy and, therefore, your options in designing both a sales approach and sales process. This process is NOT just for sales staff – management information, resource allocation, production and distribution schedules, marketing activities can all benefit from the information supplied by a well-implemented sales process. No matter where your market focus, it's worth reading this chapter to get an overview so that you can understand how use of a sales process can maximise your sales effectiveness and business planning.

Let's start by understanding what you do now.

The sales process – a language of buying and selling

Do you currently have a documented sales process? When asked this question, many companies say "yes!" and then explain: "We installed 'System X', a leading CRM and sales system." While CRM systems can be helpful, they are not, in themselves, a sales process. These systems merely provide a place where you can record individuals' sales activities; they are NOT valuable unless everyone uses the system the same way and it is kept up to date.

A well-defined and implemented sales process is critical to providing you with insights about your marketplace, your customers and your sales team's performance and provides you with the information and tools to manage your sales staff and forecast product/service requirements. Deployed properly, this process can lead to a higher win rate, lower cost of sales and better use of resources. And, while a CRM system is certainly useful, you can also have a sales process without a computerised tool. So, what's the process? The typical computerised sales process has seven stages:

1. Identifying suspects
2. Selecting prospects
3. Qualifying prospects
4. Actively selling to the qualified prospects
5. Proposing a solution (your product/service)
6. Closing
7. Negotiating/contracting

In chapters 8 and 9 you will also find an important '8th stage' that is often neglected – 'Transition'.

The remainder of chapter 8 will provide an overview of the stages, and then chapter 9 discusses each stage in more detail. Not every business benefits from focusing equally on all the stages. If your business is retail and sells to the consumer or sells low-value items to a business market, focus on the very early stages (1, 2 & 3) and the final stages (6, 7 & 8). Should you run a 'solutions' business or sell one-to-one in a business-to-business environment, it's worth reading in detail about all the stages.

Before we launch into a more detailed discussion of the sales process, let's take a moment to a look at bit more closely at how customers buy and hope the buying cycle maps on to the sales process.

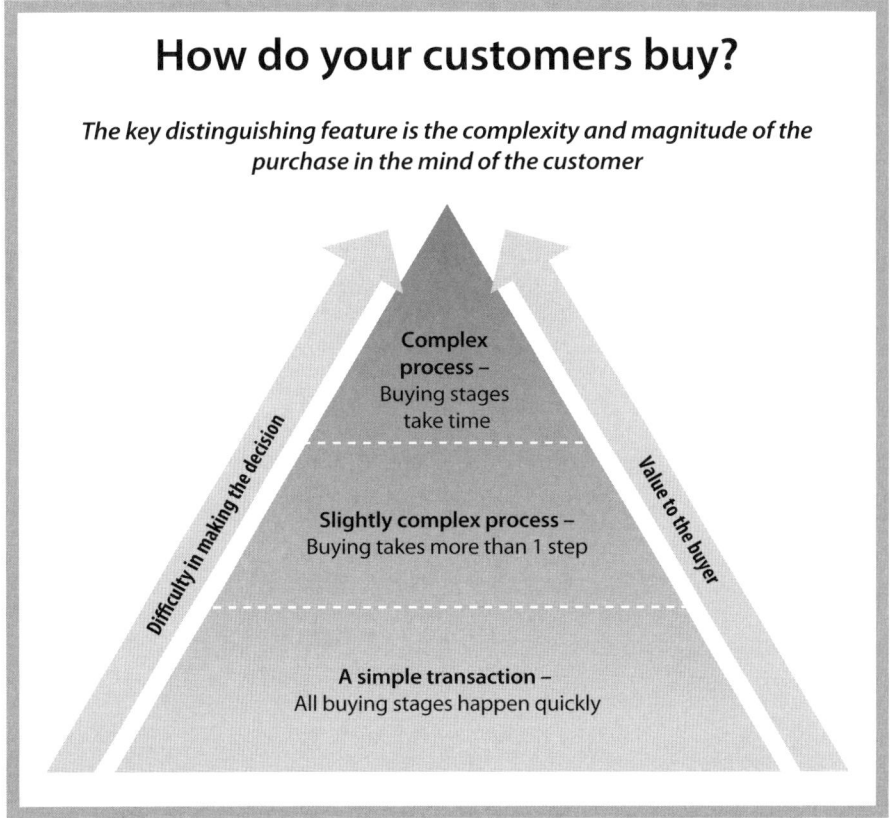

How do your customers buy?

The key distinguishing feature is the complexity and magnitude of the purchase in the mind of the customer

Difficulty in making the decision

Value to the buyer

Complex process – Buying stages take time

Slightly complex process – Buying takes more than 1 step

A simple transaction – All buying stages happen quickly

At its most fundamental, there are two variables that dictate how a customer will buy: how complex the decision process and how valuable the purchase is to the buyer. In general, 'valuable' equals 'money', but brand or status can also play a role. Complexity may be due to a purchase that requires customisation – such as purchasing a new extension to the house or buying a custom-made suit – and/or requires consultation or approval of others.

However, this diagram describes how customers buy once they have decided they need to buy something. The buying cycle actually starts a bit earlier.

The buying cycle

At its most basic, the customer buying cycle is made up of three steps:

1. Formulate need
2. Investigate options
3. Buy

Sometimes these stages last a long time and sometimes they happen all at once – in a single sales meeting, a trip to the shops or reading/listening to an advertisement.

The buying cycle

At its simplest, customers go through 3 Stages when taking a buying decision

Formulate need

Investigate options

Buy

The buying process starts again as a new 'need' is identified

When customers believe they understand their needs, they often begin the process at the second stage, or even the third. That's why being an existing supplier can be so useful – many customers simply 'buy' a requirement from the same supplier unless or until there is pressure to do something different. It's common behaviour – for example, unless you have a very specific need, you probably go to the same supermarket each week, even though you might have a choice of up to three or four other supermarkets nearby. You might not even check 'the special offers' and go to two or three different supermarkets in order to optimise your purchases, because your time is worth something. It's easiest to simply buy from the same supermarket that you patronised the week before.

So, when you are an incumbent supplier, this behaviour is good news, but what do you do if you are not?

Fortunately, there is something you can do. If you look again at the diagram of 'The Buying Cycle' you will note that, in this process, the buyer does all the work. The buyer formulates his or her own need, the buyer investigates options and the buyer makes the final purchase. In the example of the supermarket, all the supplier has to do is 'be there', have easy parking and provide a sufficient selection of quality goods to satisfy your needs. However, if and when the store is out of something, you will get back in the car and go to one of the other supermarkets. In this instance, the business is being 'bought from' rather than taking an active role in the selling process.

But imagine what would happen if the supermarket took a more active role. This approach is, in fact, what is happening when the leading quality supermarket posts a 'price match' comparison showing that its prices match a well-known low-cost provider. Also, the store can go some way to help if parking or crowds are a regular problem – for example, by offering online shopping and home delivery OR by offering 'self check' if you prefer to shop in person but don't want to waste time standing in queues. And, using the supermarket example again, when M&S and Waitrose first offered "Meals for 2 for £10" they both helped identify and articulate a need that their customers may not even have known existed.

In all these examples, you can see how supermarket retailers are taking a more proactive role in 'selling' to their customers and trying to influence and shape customer needs earlier in the buying cycle.

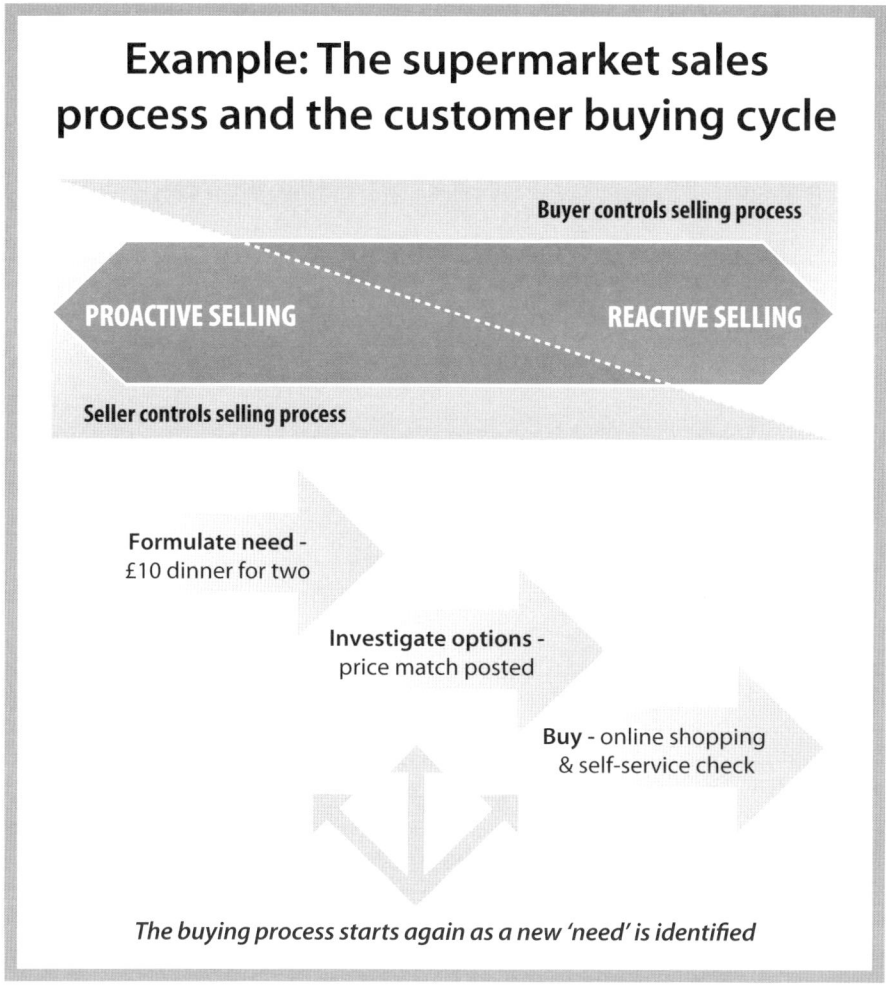

Example: The supermarket sales process and the customer buying cycle

Buyer controls selling process

PROACTIVE SELLING   **REACTIVE SELLING**

Seller controls selling process

Formulate need -
£10 dinner for two

Investigate options -
price match posted

Buy - online shopping
& self-service check

The buying process starts again as a new 'need' is identified

Let's look at a slightly more complex example. Remember the 'Customer issues' and 'Opportunities' that were discussed in Part II? Well, many customers first become susceptible to a 'solution' (or sales approach) very early in the buying cycle, just as they are aware they have a problem and are trying to formulate their need. Businesses can influence potential buyers at this stage. The challenge is: how to gain access to these individuals at this early stage in the buying cycle. Typically, when a 'buyer' at this early stage wants help, he or she usually seeks it by personal referral or speaking to a very trusted supplier or consultant.

At the opposite end of the cycle, the buyer/selling interaction is many steps removed from the individual who has the issue or opportunity. Often, rigid and very proscribed invitations to tender (ITTs) or requests for proposal (RFPs) are sent out by a procurement department. For the intermediate stages, larger companies often seek help from consultancies in order to formulate the need and understand options.

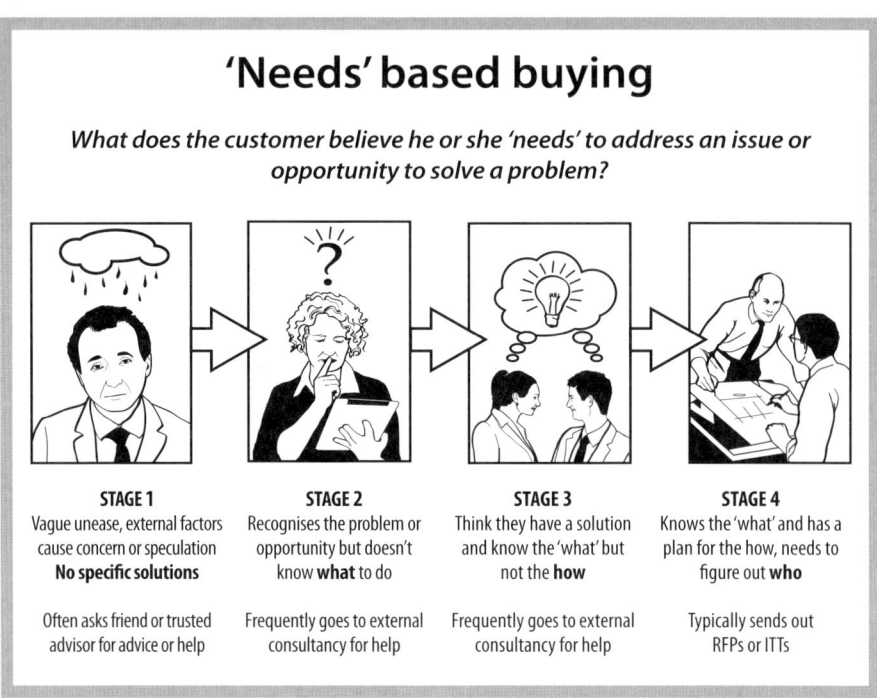

'Needs' based buying

What does the customer believe he or she 'needs' to address an issue or opportunity to solve a problem?

STAGE 1	STAGE 2	STAGE 3	STAGE 4
Vague unease, external factors cause concern or speculation **No specific solutions**	Recognises the problem or opportunity but doesn't know **what** to do	Think they have a solution and know the 'what' but not the **how**	Knows the 'what' and has a plan for the how, needs to figure out **who**
Often asks friend or trusted advisor for advice or help	Frequently goes to external consultancy for help	Frequently goes to external consultancy for help	Typically sends out RFPs or ITTs

Buyers can be influenced early in the buying cycle – an example

Advertising is sometimes designed to appeal to these 'vague worries' by identifying the 'feeling' and then, during the advertisement, leading the observer through the issue or opportunity to a 'solution' and then to the specific supplier who has commissioned the advert. A good example of this approach is TV advertisements for life insurance.

Most people – especially as they age – are vaguely worried about dying and most are also concerned about money and providing for the daily needs of a family or dependants. Many of these individuals will not have put the two concerns together to worry about what will happen to their family if they die. Life insurance commercials take them through this logic and then name a supplier and a cost for insurance – the price of which has been worked out to appeal to the target audience. At the end of the advertisement, contact details are provided to make it easy to buy.

This example represents a straightforward attempt at targeting people early in the buying process, taking them through the process using 'fear, uncertainty and doubt plus great expectations' and then asking for the business. In fact, some of the viewers might not even have had a vague sense of unease before seeing the advert. By capitalising on the buying cycle, the advert hopes to tempt many of the individuals watching straight into a purchase, so that potential buyers do not shop around and look at competitors.

Whether you are interested or not in life insurance, the selling lesson is clear – the earlier you become involved in the buying process, the more influence you have over how your customer defines the situation and structures a solution. However, not every-one sells to the consumer world, so not everyone can use advertisements to reach their customers. If nothing else, it's a very, very expensive approach. In general, it is only those with a direct sales force and higher value offerings that make the investment and get involved at the problem definition stage. For example, remember Paul Brennan, chairman and acting CEO of Zeus Technologies, the IT business that redefined itself as a Cloud computer supplier?

Zeus Technologies satisfies new and growing need in the 'Cloud' space

2004 was the beginning of 'Cloud' technology and not many vendors owned the 'Cloud space'. Zeus Technology's key product was software that acted as a web server and load balancer. So Zeus Technology began to focus on Cloud applications and repositioned itself as providing a 'traffic manager for the Cloud' – introducing the concept of PVC (physical virtual cloud) and shifting the goalposts in the marketplace. In this way, Zeus Technology began to sell 'futures' based on scalable entry into the Cloud world, where customers paid only for what they used. Thus, rather than taking on the global network hardware manufacturers in a head-to-head competition, Zeus Technology jumped ahead and began to sell the 'next generation' solution.

In this way, Paul turned his business around by helping his customers understand that what they **really** needed was a 'scalable' entry point for Cloud and not what was being offered by the traditional (very, very large) multinational suppliers.

A lengthy buying cycle

As an example, let's say your company sells high-value offerings to other businesses. These businesses often have a rigid procurement process in which you must participate in order to get the deal. Typically, the procurement or purchasing department will issue a request for proposal (RFP) or invitation to tender (ITT) or a similar request by a different name. Basically, you will be required to go through a lengthy and expensive process in order to be considered as a supplier.

What can you expect as a success rate? Well, even the best usually only succeeds in one out of 10 proposals. Furthermore, you will be responding to something that has already gone through most of the stages of the buying cycle, so – right or wrong – the customer believes he knows exactly what he needs and is just looking for a specific company to supply these needs.

Every time you go through this cycle, your costs of sale are high and your chances of winning are relatively low. Is there an alternative? Many times, yes. But it involves becoming involved with the buyer at an earlier stage of the buying cycle – ideally, when he/she is trying to define the problem. Those competitors who do become involved at this stage help the customer defining the solution.

Whether you do it or your competitor, only one company can fill this key relationship with the buyer. In this position, the buyer's solution can be built to emphasise your offering's strengths and minimise any competitor's strengths. In addition, sometimes such early involvement enables you to bypass the standard procurement process all together. In this way you have reduced your odds of winning from 10/1 to almost even odds.

Such an approach is very common in the full-service consultancy arena, and the success of this approach explains why many software solutions businesses have added management and business consulting arms to their businesses. Solutions suppliers typically get involved with the tail end of the buying cycle, while consultants help their clients with the earlier phases. In addition, consultants often interact at the highest levels of a business, with the decision makers. When these senior decision makers want a particular solution, they get what they want, no matter the procurement policies or standard company processes.

Selling 'high' has many benefits, but it's not appropriate for all business types. Let's look a little closer at how different business styles map their customer buying cycles.

Defining the customer buying process for your business

Different businesses expend the bulk of their resources at different stages of the sales cycle. Take, for example, a consumer retail business. This style of business tends to be 'bought from' rather than 'sold to'. Therefore, it's important that considerable effort is make to spread awareness by focusing on the 'suspect' phase, a first step when you target consumers your think might be prospects. Consumers tend to 'qualify' themselves, showing their interest once they are made aware of the retailer, either by entering a store or logging on to a web page. Many consumer retail businesses offer relatively low-cost items, so it is important to spread the net wide and have lots of suspects on which to focus.

These businesses do their 'selling/proposing' in one simple step – by having product displayed, priced and available – and 'closing' becomes the payment transaction. The TV advertisement for life insurance is a good example of the consolidation of these stages. However, the advert can go only so far and the deal isn't 'done' until the payment transaction is completed. Even in retail there is a 'transition' phase. Customers can return goods and will do so for a myriad of reasons, including a bad feeling that lingers from an incident during buying process.

At the other end of the spectrum, companies who sell complex deals, business to business, often invest a lot of time and money in the selling process and proposing a solution. These businesses must do everything possible to minimise their cost of sales and maximise their chances of success. So, before making this investment in proposing a solution, it's vital that such businesses thoroughly qualify the prospect and seriously ask: "Will this company buy? Does it have the money? Has the decision already been taken to go with another supplier?" 'Qualification', 'selling' and 'proposing' can be the most time-consuming phases for this type of sale. If the value of the deal is very, very large, then perhaps your company needs only one, two or a half-dozen such deals a year. If true, it's not important to generate a huge suspect list – 'qualified prospects' are a far more important measure of future business potential.

When and if they can, these businesses will try to have a high-level 'relationship' with senior managers/directors in the business to help influence the shape of the proposal. As mentioned earlier, a clever and strategic option is to have an additional offering that engages with the business at an earlier stage in the selling cycle. One example of how this can be done comes from my years at Capgemini – at the time, a full-service IT systems and business solutions provider.

....

Turning Capgemini into a solutions seller

I joined Capgemini UK (Hoskyns at the time) in the mid-1990s to help them raise their game in solutions selling. At the time, the business sold in pieces of IT solutions – business consulting, IT consulting, outsourcing – but didn't have a process to easily pull together these components as a single 'solution'. Furthermore, the company was organised for each of the business types and the way the business measured success made cooperation between these departments very challenging. As a result, most business came to Capgemini in the form of ITTs or RFPs, which had a win rate of 8/1, with a high cost of sale.

Working with a team of specialists, we mapped Capgemini's skills on to the target customer buying cycle and created a new sales approach. In order to test this approach, we identified a target market in which we knew businesses were experiencing 'pain' due to new government regulations. We then put together a 'solution' – one that used all Capgemini's major skill sets – that would resolve the prospective customer's problems. We designed a sales approach and briefed one person to go out into the market, 'cold call' and test the process.

Our approach? Obtain a sales meeting with the individual in the target business who should feel the most 'pain' as a result of the new legislation. In this case it was usually the operations director or sales director of financial services businesses. During the meeting, the Capgemini salesman was told to:

1. Confirm that our hypothesised business issues were genuine problems and causing this individual prospect's business pain
2. Explain that Capgemini believed it had solved similar problems for others, but didn't know enough about this particular business to guarantee it could solve the problem in this instance
3. Describe a consulting process that Capgemini used to find out the details and provide enough detail to confirm a solution – the process was called 'Scope' and delivered a 'scoping study'
4. Explain that the output of Scope would provide the prospect with enough information to go out in the market and obtain a solution OR, if he preferred, Capgemini could provide the solution

This process gained traction with the prospective customer very, very early in his buying process and put Capgemini in pole position to define the solution in terms that suited Capgemini. This approach isn't to say that Capgemini wasn't the best organisation to provide the solution; I firmly believed it was. Capgemini was merely engaging early in the process and making it easier for prospective customers to solve their business problems more quickly and effectively.

The approach, of course, also provided many benefits to Capgemini. In this example and future applications of the Scope sales approach, Capgemini was able to engage the business decision maker so early in the process that they often missed out on the tendering process completely and the resultant 'deals' were typically 5-10 times larger than using the standard approach. Finally, customers paid for the Scope process because it provided them something of value – but it also provided Capgemini with a paid for selling process and significantly reduced its cost of sale.

••

The Capgemini example, although from a large business, is equally applicable to smaller businesses – in fact, in many ways, it's easier because there will be far less politics and interdepartmental manoeuvring in your business than in a large corporation. What this example does show is that there are indeed benefits to defining your marketing and sales efforts against a staged sales process that has been mapped on to your customer's buying cycle.

The sales process – an overview

Defining your sales process is necessary in order to apply leadership and judgment and coordinate a huge number of activities, decisions and investment within your business. Look at the list of business activities necessary to close a single sale in the table below. Imagine these activities multiplied by 2, 10 or 30, depending on the number of sales staff you employ. Look and see where other staff – finance, operations, admin, marketing – also play a role. The sales process provides a useful tool and a common structure to manage all these individuals and activities. It's more than a selling tool – it's a business tool!

Summary – how business activities map on to the sales process

Stage 1	Stage 2	Stage 3	Stage 4	Stage 5	Stage 6	Stage 7	Stage 8
Invest in:	**Carry out:**	**Identify & qualify:**	**Produce:**	**Steps to produce proposal:**	**Close:**	**Negotiate:**	**Set up:**
Advertising	'Cold calling' (prospecting)	Who is the decision maker?	Sales plan, Buyer map,	Determine baseline costs and baseline price	Ask for the business!	Agreement & amendments on both sides if necessary	Post-sales activities
Suspect lists	Targeted mailshots	Is there money to buy? How much?	Resource plan &, if team selling, a arci	Do risk assessment	Can take the form of: presentation, proposal or both	Re-submit final proposal if necessary	
Website 'enquiry capture'	Prospect events	When will the decision be taken?	Sell to customer as per plan and buyer map	If value based pricing, put together 'customer business case' to justify value		Final contracts	
	Sales campaigns	Who else is competing?		Obtain internal approvals & sign-off			
		What happens if prospect does nothing?		Write proposal			
		How will decision be made?		Submit proposal			

So what should your staff be doing at each stage of this process?

The 8 Steps of the Sales Process

Look at the diagram (above) and you will find 'suspect' written at stage 1. What is a suspect? It is someone – a business or individual – who might buy your product or service. For an opportunity to be labelled 'suspect' there is unlikely to have been any contact between your business and the person or business listed. If you sell to very, very large organisations, while some departments might be labelled as 'prospects' because they are already customers, other departments or divisions could be considered 'suspects' if these departments had the potential to buy from you but you have never contacted them. Often, suspects may not even be aware of your company or its offerings.

When does a suspect become a prospect? Usually after more careful analysis or general qualification of the suspect list. For example, if you send an invitation to a 'marketing event' to everyone on your suspect list, anyone who responds with interest could be a potential buyer. Because you received a response, you know the individual has some interest in your offering or solution and is aware of your business. He or she is no longer a 'faceless' name on a list. So, at this stage the suspect becomes a prospect. He/she is interested in what your company provides, but you still have no idea whether he/she needs it or will buy it from you. However, beware! Some people are 'tyre kickers'. They like to go to seminars to learn things, to network and/or to get out of the office. Just because someone attended a seminar or asked for more information from you, it doesn't mean that person will buy anything.

Active work to further qualify the prospect moves the prospect name and sales opportunities from stage 2 to stage 3 – a qualified prospect. Properly carried out, this activity should remove any 'tyre kickers' from your list. In any case, you have to decide: will the person ever buy? If no, take the name off your staged sales list. Will they buy later? Then leave them as a prospect but NOT a qualified prospect – leave them at stage 2.

It is not until you have thoroughly qualified the prospect, and made certain that he/she has both the money and the desire to buy something, that the active selling – stage 4 – begins. For some businesses with more straightforward products or services, stage 4 and stage 5 melt together into a single step. However, for others with a more complex offering, hard qualification continues at stage 4 because lots of resources and money will be spent at the proposal production stage. For some businesses such as major IT solutions suppliers, specialist construction firms involved in major building projects and any bid to governmental bodies, the proposal stage can involve many specialists and take up to a year.

Stage 6, the 'close', occurs when you 'ask for the sale' and the customer says 'yes'. Be careful: many sales are lost between the 'close' and the signing of the contracts, which is the next stage. You have really only 'won the business' when you have a signed contract in hand! Finally, when the customer signs, he/she no longer has the 'power' of a buyer and it can leave him/her feeling uncomfortable. This stage – stage 8 – is the transition. Remember to continue to treat the customer with the same respect and attention you used during the selling process so you don't fall foul of 'buyer's remorse'.

Now, you may ask yourself: "What about my existing customers? Where do they fit into this sales process if I want to sell them something else?" You should use the sales process to map all your sales activities, even those to existing customers. List activities on your process map by 'sales opportunities'. So, for a new sales opportunity, even though you may call the prospect a 'customer' because he/she bought from you in the past, enter this opportunity on the list as a stage 2, prospect. In fact, everything on the list will be listed as opportunities so in some circumstances the same customer or prospect may be listed multiple times if there are many opportunities.

Doesn't everyone sell this way? In theory, yes! – but not in practice. Many SMEs behave as though they expect to be 'brought from' and if this is your business strategy, you are better off investing the bulk of your resources in effective targeting and awareness campaigns so that potential customers will know you exist and how to buy from you. The latter stages of the sales process are most useful for companies who want to proactively sell. Which type is your business? Do you 'proactively sell' or do you prefer to be 'bought from'?

For a clearer understanding of what I mean by 'proactive' and 'reactive' selling, go back to the early part of this chapter and re-read the section on the buying process.

Why is defining a sales process good practice?

There are a number of reasons.

A good understanding of the customer's buying cycle can help you to plan your marketing and selling strategy to best effect. Employing a sales process that maps directly on to your customer's buying cycle illustrates clearly how and where you can deploy resources to best effect to move activities toward contracting the deal. It will also help you refine your best sales approach.

Mapping your sales approach on to how your customers buy

Face-to-face selling

Channel sales or direct sales

Retail, internet, telesales

Size or complexity of the sale

Value of the sale

But, in addition to these insights, there are other, good reasons for defining, employing and embedding an appropriate sales process in your business.

First, the defined, staged sales process gives everyone in your business a common language to describe sales efforts and a common understanding of how close you are to winning (or losing) the business. It helps you or your sales manager to deploy the most effective person to carry out particular tasks in case a task requires specialist skills (e.g. contract negotiator). Also, in defining rules by which opportunities progress through the various stages, you can gain valuable management insight into the probability and potential value of your future sales.

When you use your sales cycle to describe your sales opportunities it is termed your 'sales pipeline'. Typically, as opportunities progress along the cycle, they tend to be fewer and fewer in number. For example, you might have 1,000 suspects, from which you derive 100 prospects. After qualification, you might have 30 opportunities remaining and so on along the pipeline until there are only three or four opportunities at the closing stage at any particular moment, and one under negotiation. This skewed distribution is funnel-shaped, so sometimes the sales pipeline is also called the sales funnel.

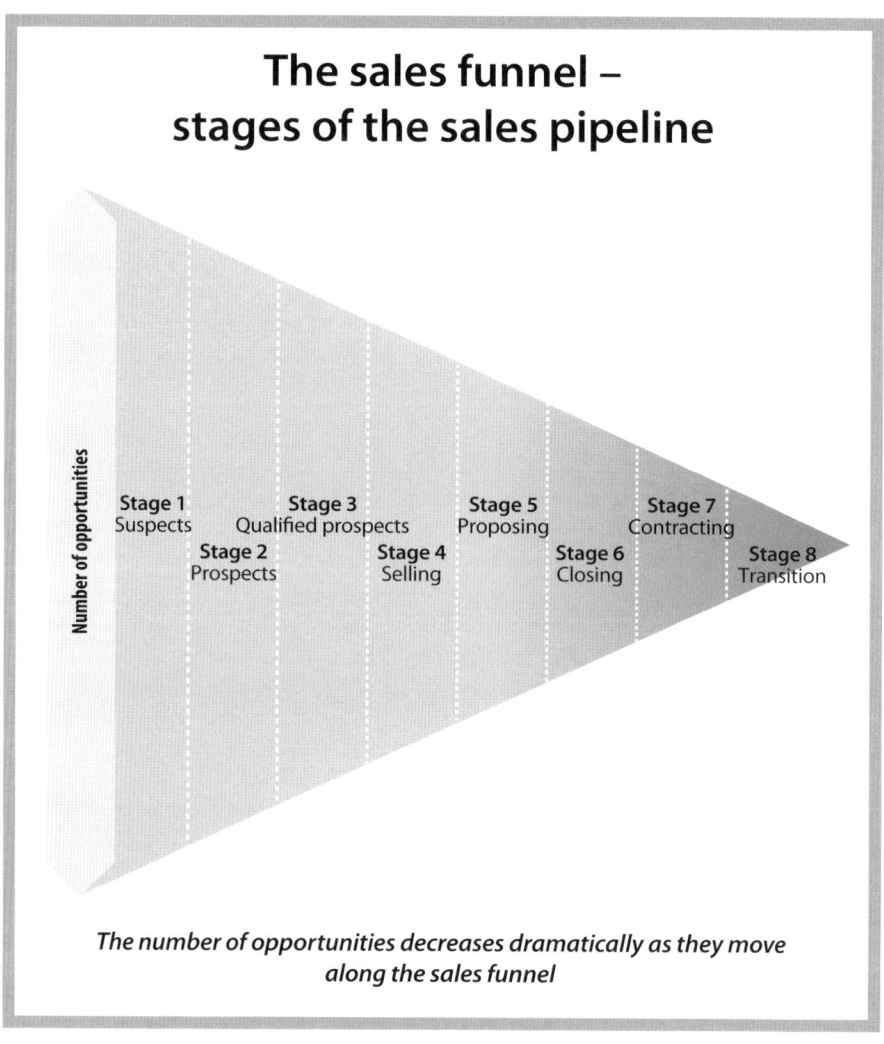

The sales funnel – stages of the sales pipeline

Number of opportunities

Stage 1
Suspects

Stage 2
Prospects

Stage 3
Qualified prospects

Stage 4
Selling

Stage 5
Proposing

Stage 6
Closing

Stage 7
Contracting

Stage 8
Transition

The number of opportunities decreases dramatically as they move along the sales funnel

Stages of the sales pipeline and information

When planning a strategy to cope with the current market climate, it's an excellent chance to adjust and finely hone business processes at all stages of the selling cycle. All information inputted into this process should use identical definitions and standards that are clearly communicated to all staff. It is critical that staff understand and believe in the importance of the sales process and understand the language and how to keep the systems up to date. Investing in such training more than pays for itself in terms of employee satisfaction, sales win rates and more efficient sales efforts. Therefore, a good first step is to establish standard definitions of what each stage of the sales pipeline means in your business, as well as the rules for progressing the sales opportunity from one stage to the next. You must also decide what information you want to capture.

Typically, businesses record data such as:

- The 'opportunity' being pursued
- Target company name or consumer name and address
- If a company, the name of the target individual within the company with contact details
- Date that information was put on to the sales pipeline and who inputted the information
- Date and nature of last interaction with the company (e.g. marketing or sales contact, letter or meeting – most online CRM systems allow you to link letters and, proposals and emails generated within your own business to the target company so that you have a record of all written interactions)
- The forecast value of this opportunity
- Forecast 'close' date and probability of winning
- Name of individual responsible for the sale
- Date of last contact

You can see from this list that, potentially, many individuals with varying roles in your company might update this sales pipeline. If you don't have a process in place to ensure both accurate and timely updates – as will happen if you have sales staff who spent a lot of time outside the office – this discipline can be a challenge. It is imperative that you invest in getting 'buy in' to this process. Regardless of how difficult it may be to capture, this information is still important. Checking whether a sales person made all updates should be a standard question at every weekly/monthly sales meeting.

Scan the list of the data collected for the sales pipeline. You will note that, in addition to descriptive information, it contains quantifiable input such as 'value of sale', 'probability of winning', 'close date'. When you populate the sales pipeline with data you trust, you can produce reports that give an excellent forecast of future business. You can also identify potential problems, with both individual performance and business management. However, to obtain any benefit from this information, it is vital that all users of the system have guidelines to help them – particularly for the quantifiable information. In particular, there are three critical areas where uniform standards should apply:

1. When to progress an opportunity to the next stage of the sales cycle
2. Definitions of how to apply % probability for success
3. How to forecast opportunity value

At brief discussion of typical sales funnel reporting provides an explanation and example.

The sales funnel report

Example of sales funnel report

Sales Funnel Report 30/06/2014	Opp 1	Opp 2	Opp 3	Opp 4	Opp 5	Opp 6
Opportunity	'Big bank'	'Small bank'	Retail shop	Builder	County council	Insurance
Salesman	Joe	Jane	Mark	Hannah	Raj	No sales assigned
Date of last sales action	25/02/2014	30/05/2014	15/06/2014	23/06/2014	02/06/2014	Mail shot – 1/2/2014
Estimated deal value	£6m	£2m	£500k	£800k	£200k	0
Probability of winning	20%	60%	80%	40%	40%	0
Stage in sales funnel	3	4	5	4	5	1
Length of time at this stage of cycle	12 months	1 month	1 month	3 months	4 months	24 months
Estimated close date	31/05/2014	30/11/2014	01/09/2014	15/11/2014	31/10/2014	N/A

The sales funnel report shown above lists data extracted from six fictional opportunities for a business. Six examples are used to illustrate key points, but in reality most sales funnel reports have tens, hundreds or even thousands of opportunities listed. This example lists the opportunity and the salesman associated with the opportunity. All the rest of the information is quantifiable and consists of:

- date of last sales activity
- estimated deal value
- probability of winning
- stage in sales funnel
- length of time at this stage of the sales funnel
- estimated close date

There are, of course, many other things that can be reported, but these provide critical information and are most susceptible to manipulation by employees or misleading management reports if they not monitored carefully. Let's discuss each in turn.

Date of last sales action

This information is intended to help you assess at least three different things:

1. At the end of the sales cycle, how much effort it has taken to 'close' a particular opportunity
2. If an opportunity sits at the at early stages of the sales funnel, how long it has been since you last contacted the potential customer
3. Assess individual sales staff activities and performance

If you have a computerised CRM system – and in today's marketplace there are cost-effective ways of buying CRM systems for even the smallest business – it should link documents, emails and comments to this field of activity. That means that anyone in your organisation – finance, customer service, sales, your factory foreman – can input a note about the nature of the contact associated with a given sales opportunity. Sales people can input a brief report after meetings or phone calls and all written communication can be automatically linked to the opportunity. In sum, you can create a complete picture of all interactions by everyone in your company and observe these activities over time.

Estimated deal value, probability of winning and estimated close date

These first two columns should always be examined together. Typically, the sales manager/director generates a first cut sales forecast by multiplying:

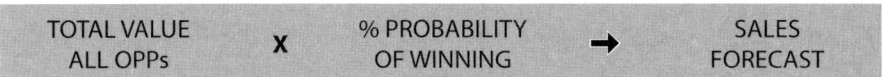

| TOTAL VALUE ALL OPPs | X | % PROBABILITY OF WINNING | ➡ | SALES FORECAST |

This value provides the total sales forecast and is also known as the weighted revenue forecast because of the percentage win probability is factored into the total amount. The report can be further refined month by month or quarter by quarter – whatever makes sense in your business – including factoring in the estimated close date. If you wish to use this information for business decisions, it is critical that you:

- **Decide how to attribute a £ value to any opportunity using a consistent approach.**
  Specific rules will depend on the type of business you run, but there should be consistency between your sales staff in how opportunities are valued. Under no circumstances should a value be provided for stages 1 or 2 (suspects and unqualified prospects) of your sales funnel because such numbers are meaningless.

- **Define different % probabilities**
  Most businesses that use the sales funnel in earnest only use five or six percentage values because, in fact, greater precision is not possible. How you define each point will depend on your business. However, typical, standard definitions are:

  0%   – Not qualified (stages 1 & 2)
  20% – Qualified, but the selling process is still in early stages OR qualified, proposed, but your proposal is one of more than five being bid.
  40% – Selling (stage 4)
  60% – Proposing (stage 5) – unless you are one of more than five competitors, in which case the probability should be lower
  80% – Opportunity 'won' but contracts NOT yet signed
  100% – Opportunity 'won' and 'contracts signed'

  These percentages are only indicative of 'how' the system might be defined. It is well worth doing a planning exercise to set up or confirm that your business is using % probability in a way that best supports your business.

- **Define 'close date' means and make strict rules about how often this date can be changed.**
  'Close date' is one of the key bits of information used to produce the sales forecast. While businesses that respond to tightly defined tendering dates can input relatively accurate data, other types of organisations might have long, complex sales cycles with close dates that can only be estimated and then 'refined' as the initial date approaches. In sales organisations, this is the date that moves most often and as the 'close date' gets closer, it's often moved out a few months further.

Stage in sales funnel and length of time at this stage

These two columns should be evaluated together to be used as a sales management tool. For example, something sitting at stage 1 (suspects) for 12 months is not unusual. Eventually, you might want to consider removing the opportunity, but chances are you aren't expending much effort or resources and this opportunity doesn't contribute to your sales forecast, so it's not a problem to leave an opportunity listed at stage 1. If, however, something has been sitting at stage 5 or 6 for say, 12 months or more, the situation should raise alarm bells. It is not usual for opportunities to sit at the proposing or 'sold but not contracted' stage for more than a year. Now, you may ask why alarm bells weren't already ringing. In a well-run sales department, these warning bells would have been noted well before 12 months and there would be a good explanation if such a situation found its way on to the sales funnel.

However, in organisations that do not use the sales funnel for management information or who have no rules for the input and movement of information, it's possible to lose this level of discrimination. Problems that should be easily spotted will be missed, business will be lost and sales efforts wasted. If you have a sales funnel, take the trouble to make it accurate and then use it as the management tool it is!

Interpreting the sales funnel example

So, with just six opportunities and a little bit of background, what kind information can you obtain about business and sales performance (see previous table again) Try it yourself! Assuming that these deals are all that's going on in this company, what can you tell me about expected business revenue in the next quarter? Year? Beyond a year? Are there any details that give you cause for concern? What are they and what would you do next? Which opportunity is your 'top priority'?

Now for the answers.

There are two answers to the first question about expected business revenue. You can obtain the first by simply adding up the total revenue forecast (£6m + £2m + £500k + £800k + £200k + 0) and give £9.5m as a response. However, this is not a number on which to base all your business planning. This number assumes that you win all the deals at the forecast revenue value. A more realistic assessment would be to provide a weighted forecast by taking into account the percentage probability of winning. This answer is:

20% of £6m + 60% of £2m + 80% of £500k + 40% of £800k + 40% of £200k + 0

Or, doing the sums:

£1.2m + £1.2m + £400k + £320k + £80k + 0

Which is equal to £3.2m – that's compared to the £9.5m value for the unweighted sales funnel. While it 'feels good' to use the higher number, it's not realistic and weighting appropriate to your business should always be factored into the equation.

If you break down this forecast over time, all the opportunities are forecast for the next 12-month period. Unweighted and weighted forecasts over the next four quarters look something like:

	Q1 2014 (July-Sept)	Q2	Q3	Q4
Unweighted revenue	£500k	£3m	0	£6m
Weighted revenue	£400k	£1.48m	0	£1.2m

Displayed as revenue forecast over time, this information clearly shows problems ahead. There is no revenue forecast at all for Q3 (Jan-Mar 2015) and all the revenue for Q4 relies on winning a single, big deal.

Next, areas for concern? A big concern is the length of time – 12 months – that opportunity 1 has sat at stage 3 (qualified prospect) of the sales funnel. While there are possible explanations for a qualified opportunity sitting at this stage without any sales activity, it would be very, very unusual – particularly an opportunity that is the largest by far of anything on the funnel. Such a situation should prompt further investigation. Check the 'close date'. It's given as 11 months away.

Hmmm! This is long enough away to avoid too much management interest, but still within a 12-month period so that the weighted value would appear on sales reports. Again, this date alone should flag concerns but, combined with the length of time spent without active selling activity makes it highly suspect. Finally, you notice that the last time there was any sales activity for this account was 25 February 2014 – more than three months beforehand. For an opportunity of this relative value (the highest on the sales funnel), one month is too long without customer contact. This whole situation screams for investigation.

Where to focus immediate efforts? 'A bird in the hand' is good advice here – secure the business that is about to close. Make certain that this deal has the appropriate help and resources to ensure a successful conclusion.

What next? Yes, put some resources on the Q2 deals, but also take a look at what can be done to generate some more prospects and then qualified prospects. A look at the sales funnel report shows that there was a mailshot last February – almost five months ago. What was the outcome of that mailshot? Have there been any follow-up activities? Did it generate leads? A next step is to investigate these outcomes and either follow up earlier leads that were neglected or initiate activities that generate additional prospects.

Capturing information – the challenge

From this simple exercise you can see just how important a tool a good sales funnel can be. The example does not mirror every business type, but some variation will support management in any business. When done well, it looks simple and obvious, but there is skill and experience required in designing both the sales funnel and the sales process so that whatever your business, they provide the means to capture both market and management information.

There are many, many details you can attempt to capture as opportunities move along the sales process. However, the more data you capture, the more time someone must spend recording the information and keeping it up to date. Therefore, there is a trade-off between what you capture and the time and effort expended to do so. There is also a trade-off between how detailed the report and how difficult it is to assimilate the all-important 'big picture'.

A final word of warning – keep it clean!

No matter how disciplined the organisation and how well defined the rules for data, all sales pipelines/funnels need a periodic review. When a named individual on the prospect list changes companies, dies or gets promoted, your information becomes outdated. Similarly, businesses reorganise, titles change, departments merge or close down – all these changes too should be updated on your pipeline so that the information stored is still useful. The more information you store, the more cumbersome such 'sales funnel cleansing' will be. However, it's still worth doing.

Why? First, it's not professional to regularly mis-address communications to your customers or prospective customers. It happens sometimes, of course, but it shouldn't be an acceptable way of doing business because it shows a lack of respect for the individuals you hope to contact. In addition, if your employees know your sales funnel is filled with errors it can influence their motivation to keep their own data up to date and accurate. Finally, if management reports are filled with errors – even names and addresses – then the rest of the data is looked upon with suspicion.

Some questions you should ask...

Sales funnel health – check list

Question	Yes	No
Has your sales funnel been updated to reflect changes to your target market?		
Has your sales funnel been updated to reflect changes to your offerings?		
Are all sales staff listed current employees?		
Do you know how long – on average – different opportunities stay at different stages of your sales funnel?		
Are there any opportunities of stage 3 and beyond that have been on the sales funnel for more than 12 months? Do you know why?		
Do you know which opportunities have moved to a new stage since your last report?		
Do all your opportunities contain complete data (names, addresses, values, etc.)?		
Do you know what opportunities are expected to close in the next 3 months, and their value?		

Any 'no's should prompt investigation and action

Common pitfalls

DO NOT:

1. Leave 'tyre kickers' on your sales funnel. There will always be individuals who will ask for information, attend your seminars, take up your sales person's offer of a free lunch – do all these things without any intention of buying. Remove them from all sales lists (except a 'tyre kickers' list!). Otherwise, you will forget and, over time, someone else will waste time and money trying to sell them something.

2. Load databases on to your sales pipeline/sales funnel without going through and cleaning up all the entries. Unfortunately, such care is seldom taken. It is all too common for someone in a sales or marketing department to load lots and lots of unchecked data into the 'suspect' stage (stage 1) and then, never deal with it again. Loading the suspect and unqualified prospect stages (1 & 2) is also a favourite trick used by less than scrupulous sales staff and sales management to make it seem like there is lots going on in terms of sales activity when in fact

there isn't. The theory is that if there are lots and lots of names there must be lots and lots of opportunity. It's not necessarily true — well-qualified names, yes, but suspects and unqualified prospects mean nothing in terms of forecasting sales. The volume of data also makes it more challenging to use the sales pipeline information to manage the sales activity as effectively.

3. Put a 'value' (other than 0) in the forecast line for a 'suspect' or unqualified prospect. Any other value is just wishful thinking and not a value around which you can build a business.

4. Let opportunities sit at stage 3 or beyond for long periods of time without a management review.
   Another difficultly arises when individuals manipulate sales figures using 'movement along the sales cycle'. Loading online sales systems with lots and lots of prospects which high-value sales and low probabilities can keep a sales manager off a sales person's back. Check length of time in a given stage and/or continued extension of forecast 'close date' to determine the legitimacy of any given opportunity.

5. Fail to define and closely monitor the 'close date' field. It is vital to keep an eye on this date to get a realistic picture of when the business will genuinely be 'won' — after all, your company gets no revenue until the deal is done. It is common practice in some organisations for sales staff (and their management) to 'manage appearances' by keeping opportunities at a late stage of the sales funnel with a high probability of close and then, keep pushing the close date into the future. This gives impression of lots of revenue coming in (sales stage x % probably) which never actually 'closes'. Such 'manipulation' of the sales funnel cannot happen if changes are strictly monitored.

END OF CHAPTER 8 – SELF-ASSESSMENT

**EVALUATE YOUR SALES PROCESS & YOUR CUSTOMER'S
BUYING PROCESS** - Tick 1 box for each question

QUESTION	Yes	No	Partly
1. Do you understand how your customers buy?			
2. Do you have a 'fit for purpose' sales process?			
3. Is your sales process well defined and understood by everyone in the business?			
4. Is your sales process actually used and are your staff clear about the benefits and 'bought in' to using it?			
5. Is your sales process mapped on to the way your customers buy?			
6. Do you have definitions for all data put on to the sales funnel and have you trained your staff in these definitions?			
7. Do you monitor the accuracy and timeliness of all information added to the sales funnel?			
8. Do you monitor how long something remains at various stages of the sales funnel?			
9. Do you monitor changes in the 'close date'?			
10. Do you use your sales funnel reports for management information?			

YOUR SCORE: Give yourself 5 points for every 'yes', 2 points for every 'partly' and '0' for every 'no'.

36-50 Points	⇒	Excellent – note areas where you didn't score 5 and plan to rectify if relevant to your business
26-35 Points	⇒	Good – you have some room for improvement. Check those areas in which you ticked 'no' or 'partly' and evaluate how you can improve your score
11-25 Points	⇒	You could do better – there is definitely room for improvement…
0-10 Points	⇒	Get help! You have lots and lots of opportunity to improve your income stream.

Chapter 9

Your Sales Funnel

Top tips – Chapter 9

1. Don't waste sales time on 'suspects'

2. Qualify 'hard' to focus your best efforts on opportunities you can win

3. Use 'trial closing' to qualify and to uncover objections

4. Ask for the business

5. 'Selling' and 'Negotiating' are two very different skills

6. Use your own contracts wherever possible

7. Remember, the deal isn't 'won' until the contracts are signed!

8. Don't suddenly change your attitude to customers after the deal is signed

Do you use a CRM system? Do you sell a complex product or service that requires technical input? Does it take a long time and many steps in order to sell your product or solution? If you answered 'yes' to any of these questions, read on. Other indications that this chapter will prove useful include:

- Use of team selling techniques
- Employing sales staff to sell business-to-business
- Employing a direct sales force to sell high-value or complex retail products
- Customer has a long, proscribed and complicated buying process
- Buyer map is big
- Customer decision makers are distributed over multiple locations, especially foreign
- Customer decision makers are a combination of business and technical people
- A sales strategy that focuses early in the customer buying cycle

Read this chapter for interest only if your business:

- Focuses on consumer retail
- Uses the internet as its main selling tool
- Sells high-volume, low-value products via volume channels (e.g. internet or catalogue)
- Provides administrative support only for franchisees and VARs

If you are one of the latter group of companies, there will be some items of interest and possible use, but using all the techniques described in chapter 9 will be cumbersome and probably not worth the investment of time and effort. It would be better to read through and select what you think might help, focusing particularly on phases 1 & 2 (suspects and prospects) and phases 6 & 7 (closing the sale and contracting).

On the other hand, if your business falls into the first category then you should use the entire sales process in earnest. Do it right and it provides you with a sales funnel – a powerful tool for your business. But you can (and many people do) do it wrong. When the process is followed diligently, it provides considerable management information about the effectiveness of marketing, future sales forecasts, sales performance (both by individual and the overall business) and can profile sales by service/product type and market if the system is set up accordingly.

The remainder of chapter 9 will focus on the sales process to:

- Outline what should happen at each stage of the process
- Identify the information that should be collected as the sale proceeds
- Discuss how to use the information to build a sales funnel
  which can be used for forecasting and sales management
- Introduce a few advanced selling techniques and
  terms that illustrate good ways to:
  o Collect relevant information from the prospective customer
  o Progress the sales process on to the next stage

Let's begin at the first stage: suspects.

Building your sales funnel – suspects – stage 1

Typically, stage 1 – 'identifying suspects' – consists of developing a list of anyone who could potentially buy your product or service. Even within your existing customers, you may have departments you treat as 'suspects' for future business. For the data to be meaningful to your business, you should provide tight guidelines for what constitutes a 'suspect' and who within your organisation may enter this information on the system. It is rarely cost-effective for sales teams to focus on suspects. Often it is marketing departments or specialists who focus their efforts on the suspects in order to convert some to the next stage of the process, which produces 'prospects'.

Tips for producing good suspects:

- Review your targeting process
- 'Clean up' existing list (remove duplicates, update company
  details, remove old or defunct information)
- Get referrals/names from your existing customers
- Check out appropriate 'handbooks', organisation membership
  lists – anything that provides a comprehensive list and address of
  companies/individuals who are likely to want your offering
- Investigate your own employees' employment history and
  personal connections as a source of potential contacts
- Deploy appropriate marketing campaigns/events
- Include marketing as part of the sales planning process

Creating a list of suspects is the 'first cut' in narrowing down who might actually buy from you. It should NOT be everybody or all companies in the market, but it could still be a large list of potential candidates. In this way you can narrow down your suspect list to a more manageable number around which you can more effectively deploy sales resources and marketing effectively.

Suspects are consumers or businesses that may not even know you exist and, in all probability, have never purchased anything from you or had contact with your business. Remember Revive, the company that offers 'Smart Repairs' to car bodywork? Potentially, the company could have focused on anyone in the UK who owned cars. But Mark Llewellyn, the CEO, approached the market a step at a time and focused on used car dealerships first. In this way he could focus on fewer suspects, with each suspect potentially netting him multiple cars and repeat business.

There are other things to watch out for if you want to have a meaningful list of suspects and use this data for management information. Even at the stage of 'suspects' these data must be 'good data'. You should never assign a 'close date' or 'sale value' to any opportunities listed in the suspect phase. Any reports you produce will give artificially exaggerated and misleading sales forecasts.

Issues at stage 1:

- Pipeline cleansing (redundant, inaccurate, obsolete data)
- 'Loading' the pipeline
- Lack of single ownership of an opportunity

The first two issues have already been discussed at length, but it's worth discussing 'ownership' in a bit more detail. The 'owner' of an opportunity should be accountable for the accuracy and timeliness of all information. If new opportunities are added ONLY by the sales person responsible for closing the sale, ownership is clear. However, in some organisations there are no hard and fast rules about who adds information and new entries, so it's not obvious who added the data or who is responsible for data integrity or progressing the sale along the stages.

Furthermore, marketing activities can complicate matters still further. Sometimes a marketing person takes all responsibilities for 'stage 1' opportunities. This situation can result in two potential problems. How and when does 'sales' take over the responsibility? If this ownership is not made clear, a potential (and frequent) complication is that the sales person enters the name and opportunity on the system for a second time. Won't reports spot such duplication? Often not.

Consider the following example:

My name could be entered as: T.H. Howard, Tamara Holm Howard, Dr. T. Howard, Ms T. H. Howard and on and on with other permutations – and that's if it's spelled correctly! Howard is a common surname, so it's possible that all these variants could be four different people. Establishing clear 'ownership' and rules about data entry can help to keep the data 'clean' and maintain the accuracy of your reports.

If you have marketing staff, yes, they should be involved at stage 1 – that's not the issue. The issue – if you have more than one person involved – is to ensure a smooth transition between stage 1 and stage 2, when your sales staff should take over.

Prospects – stage 2

It is at the prospect stage that, if you have more than one person handling sales and marketing, the sales professionals should first become involved. A prospect is someone – a company or individual within a company – who has clearly indicated a possible need for your product or services.

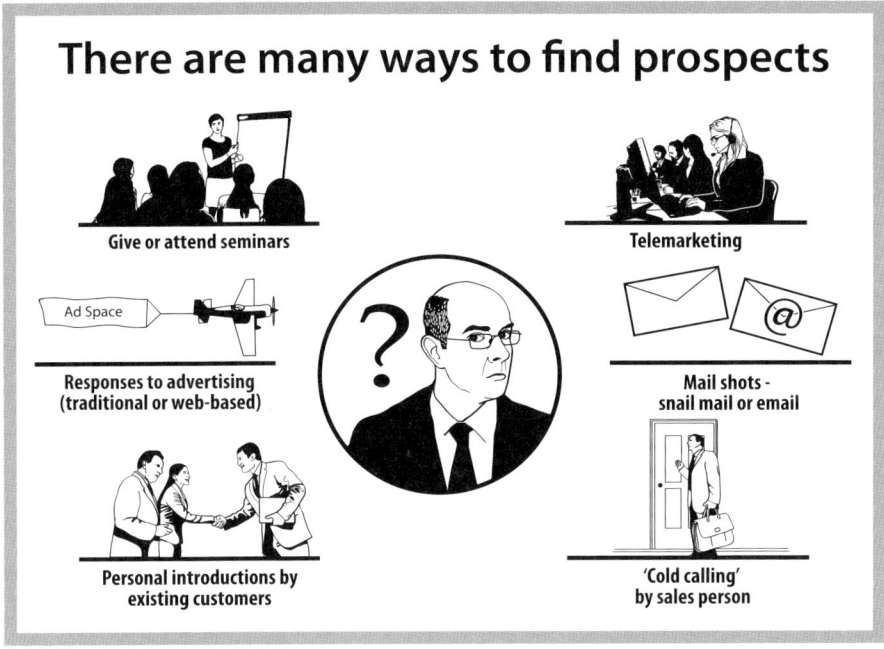

There are many ways to find prospects

Give or attend seminars

Telemarketing

Responses to advertising (traditional or web-based)

Mail shots - snail mail or email

Personal introductions by existing customers

'Cold calling' by sales person

An individual may have 'ticked a box' on a form, attended a seminar or requested information from your company. You may have obtained the name via a database of your key competitor's customers. At stage 1 you now know the name of someone who has interest in your offering and who knows about your company. What you don't know is whether or not this person will or can actually buy anything. It's now up to someone – usually a sales person – to qualify the opportunity.

Ready Steady Store (RSS) – the start-up self-storage business we discussed in earlier chapters, used its warehouse staff to convert 'suspects' into 'prospects'. For RSS, the suspects consisted of everyone in the local area – businesses and consumers alike. So local RSS employees went out into the community. They posted flyers, set up stands at supermarkets and local events – doing everything possible to make the local residents aware of RSS. This activity proved to be a very effective process for turning suspects into prospect.

By stage 2, ideally your sales person is certain that the prospect knows:

- That your company exists
- Something about your product and/or service

Next step? Qualify.

Qualifying prospects – stage 3

This section is the longest in the chapter because qualification is so important. It is after the qualification stage that a business may invest significant time and money in pursuing the sale. In fact, many businesses introduce a 'management review' at this stage to assess opportunities before they pass this hurdle. Qualification itself may take only one or two meetings or phone calls – but doing it properly saves substantial effort later in the sales process and increases your chances of winning the deal.

Prospect qualification

KEY QUESTIONS:

▶ Who? ⟶ Who makes the final decision?

▶ What? ⟶ What criteria will be used to make the decision?

▶ How? ⟶ What is the decision making process?

▶ When? ⟶ Is there a time by which the decision must be taken?

▶ How much? ⟶ Is there a budget? If yes, how much?

After speaking to a qualified prospect, the sales person should always be able to tell you:

1. **Who** will make the final decision? Ideally, it will be the person who has made the inquiry or who has spoken to your sales person, but this is not always the case. An experienced sales person will also find out who else might be involved in taking the decision – 'recommenders' as well as people who might be against purchasing anything.
2. **What** decision-making criteria will be used to evaluate your proposal? This question can also inform your sales person about others at the customer who might be involved in the evaluation.
3. **How** will the decision be taken? Will it be by committee? A short list? And who is involved at each stage?
4. **When** does the prospect expect to make a decision? How firm and how critical is this timing?
5. **How much** has the prospect budgeted to make this purchase? Some prospects are coy about discussing budgets, but it is essential that you agree on an approximate figure in order to understand whether the company has set aside enough money.

In addition, the sales person should be able to describe what customer issue or opportunity is being addressed and what your offering can do to address it. The discussion should also highlight competitive threats and focus on your business's added value and USPs(unique selling points).

Prospects may 'fall' at this hurdle. Some remain prospects until some future date when contact is re-established to see if circumstances have changed. Others should be removed from the sales funnel. That's OK – there is no shame in removing a name from the sales list if a prospect does NOT qualify as a potential purchaser. It is better to focus attention on those prospects who might actually buy something rather than waste time on those who won't. However, both sales staff and management alike panic when the prospect list shrinks, so both are tempted to keep unqualified and 'disqualified' prospects listed on the sales funnel. If your company has no – or very few – qualified prospects, you should know as quickly as possible so you can take remedial action to increase the number of genuine prospects.

Once a sales person has developed a 'qualified prospect', the selling can begin in earnest. At this point the sales person should be able to forecast an approximate value for the deal and a timeframe and probability for successfully closing the business. If sales cannot do so, then it is likely the prospect is not well qualified or the sales person is inexperienced. An experienced sales person can take this qualification meeting much, much further and might even move the process a long way toward closing!

The qualification sales meeting

So, what else can happen in the qualifying sales meeting? In fact, if your sales person is well prepared, the sales process can begin at this stage. Therefore, when the prospect becomes a 'qualified prospect', the sales person should continue asking questions in order to gain as much information as possible to prepare a sales strategy and plan – sometimes even 'close' the business!

Additional questions useful in structuring the selling process

ADDITIONAL QUESTIONS:

▶ What will happen if the customer does nothing?

▶ What are they doing to meet their 'needs' now?

▶ Who else is the customer considering? (Your competition)

▶ How will the customer decide between suppliers?

▶ What experience does the customer have in making this sort of purchase?

▶ Is there anyone in the customer's business who doesn't think they should be making this purchase?

▶ What will this purchase enable them to accomplish and what's it worth to them?

Additional questions can focus on understanding how important timing is to the customer. Will it cost them money or lose them business if they don't 'buy your offering' by a particular date? If so, how much will it cost them? Obtaining these dates and numbers directly from the prospect provides you with the basis for business a cost justification for your proposal – or a 'benefits case'.

Quantifying benefits

This early sales meeting is also an excellent chance to collect 'numbers' so you can produce a 'benefits case' to accompany your proposal. In the last chapter (see *'Value-based pricing'*) you will find a detailed example of how to use this kind of information. Quantifying benefits and producing a benefits case is a very, very strong tool. An experienced sales person can use this initial conversation to obtain lots and lots of information that will help structure and price the subsequent proposal.

Furthermore, the sales person should always ask what will happen if the customer does nothing, using this question to understand, among other things, if there is anyone in the customer's business who is 'against' making any buying decision. In fact, as a way of summing up the discussion, a good sales person can even try to 'close' the sale there and then; it rarely succeeds at this point but 'trial closing' as it's called, is a useful technique to uncover still more information.

'Trial closing'

So, what is 'trial closing'? Let's start by defining 'closing': closing the sale means 'asking for the business' and getting the customer to say 'yes', you have won the deal. You may not have a contract yet, but you have the customer's agreement that you won the business.

'Trial closing' is when you ask for the business in order to understand what outstanding issues must be dealt with before the customer will buy. When a sales person employs a 'trial close' he or she doesn't expect the customer to say 'yes' – trial closing is an excellent way to uncover outstanding 'objections' to buying from you – objections that customers might otherwise be loath to voice.

The most common way to use 'trial closing' – when appropriate – in a qualifying discussion is for the sales person to sum up the discussion and then ask for the business. If we use the installation of a new, Cloud-based stock control system as an example, then a trial close might be:

"So, if I could show you a way to prove we install a new stock control system that can be managed from any location at any time, at an acceptable cost, would you buy from us?"

The possible answers can range from:

"Yes, if you could show me that now, I would buy now!" to "No, we still need to get funding for the programme." Or: "That's a ridiculous question – how can you prove that to me?" This last question is a great one, because the sales person can turn it around and ask: "What would I need to do to convince you?" and then, once he or she has an answered the question, trial close again.

If and when you are genuinely speaking to a decision maker, this approach is rarely a problem. Those customers who get annoyed are often the ones who do not have the authority (no matter what they claim) to take the decision on their own. This information, too, is extremely useful to the sales process and it's worth uncovering early.

Preparing for the sales qualification meeting or phone call

It should be clear from the discussion so far that, for a 'sales meeting' to go well, whether by phone or in person, the sales person should spend at least as much time in preparation as spent with the prospect. Ideally the sales person should think through how the discussion might go and plan for various outcomes. If the deal is worth a lot of money, in addition to a Plan A, there should always be a 'fallback' or Plan B. Scenario planning should be part of the skill set of any experienced sales person.

The following table offers a check list of the minimum preparation that should be completed before any serious qualification meeting. It is always useful to know how many people from the prospect's business will be attending the meeting, as well as their names and positions with the company. Any time there is more than one person in the meeting it will radically alter the nature of the sales encounter. For example, the 'trial close' is rarely effective when there is more than one person in the meeting. The bottom line? Find out as much information as possible BEFORE the meeting and then plan accordingly.

Preparation for the qualifying sales meeting

Sales Activity	Done
1. Investigate all past interactions between your business and the prospect's company	✓
2. Get background on the prospect's company	✓
3. Get any background available on the prospect	✓
4. Investigate competitor's position in the prospect's business	✓
5. Understand current 'issues' in prospect's marketplace	✓
6. Obtain list of 'references' where your company has been successful	✓
7. Prepare 'next steps' for 'best case' scenario outcome	✓
8. Prepare 'next steps' for plan b scenario outcome	✓
9. Re-confirm date, time and attendees in the meeting 24 hours prior	✓

It's always worth preparing for success. In the earlier story about Capgemini and the Scope selling process, everyone involved was keen to test where the hypothesis about market segment issues and sales approach would work in the insurance sector.

•••

Always prepare for success when trial closing

The sales person who made this first, qualifying sales call on the financial director did everything right. He confirmed the prospect's issues and pain, and he got the FD to give him financial information about how much it would cost the business if the problems weren't solved. The sales person did all the right reference selling by suggesting similar solutions Capgemini had delivered for others and mentioned various companies' names. He then said: "Of course, I don't know if we can do it for you – no reason why we can't – but we don't know enough about your business processes and computer systems to propose a firm solution. However, we have a process that takes 6-8 weeks and will tell us what needs to be done to fix your problem and how much it will cost you. At the end, you will have a possible solution and know the costs and risks. You can then go to any leading supplier to get a proposal – but of course, we would be happy to bid too!" The FD was quiet for a moment and then asked: "How much will it cost [the Scope process] and when can you start?"

•••

In this instance, the 'Scope sale' was won on the first, qualifying sales call. Why? Because the salesman understood the customer problem – and it was a big problem that would stop the business dead in its tracks – and could offer a low-risk, creditable next step. He effectively asked: "If I could show you a way to understand and solve your problem, would you buy?" Though unlikely, the salesman had prepared for this outcome and so he won the sale – and much, much more business followed.

Selling – stage 4

You have already heard about the qualifying questions: "If I could show you a way to... [solve the identified problem], would you buy?" and "What would I have to do to convince you?" In addition, the sales person should have asked: "Would I have to convince anyone else?" and if the answer is yes, ask the next question: "What would it take to convince them?" Fundamentally, the rest of the 'selling stage' focuses on providing the 'proofs' and 'facts' the prospect requested when he/she answered this question.

Typically this activity consists of:

- Creating a sales plan
- Identifying all the decision makers/recommenders and blockers
- Building a 'buyer map'
- Populating a plan with activities that address the concerns/actions of all these individuals
- Mobilising internal (your own) resources – as needed – to assist with the sales process
- Collecting information from within the prospect to support your proposition

It is also worth mentioning that, no matter how rational the business, people make the final buying decision and people are not always rational. Any good sales plan includes activities that deal with the prospect's company politics and non-rational issues as well as building a traditional, business-based sales proposition. These political and emotional elements dictate 'who' is consulted in the prospect's business and how the sales process is carried out. The whole selling process is NOT simply a matter of collecting data – it's a series of individual engagements or 'battles' that must be fought in order to win the deal.

The end result should be a general agreement within the customer about their 'issue' and a common view of the solution (your proposal) – a solution that should have been, to a large extent, moulded and crafted by your sales person or selling team. At the same time, the sales person or selling team should have built trust and confidence while engaging with the prospect's key staff.

When carried out properly, this work puts you in a good position to respond to the next phase in the sales process, stage 5: 'proposing'.

Proposing – stage 5

By this stage in the process, both prospect and sales people plus sales support staff are actively engaged trying to win the business. Not all companies need a substantial proposal process – some require little more than a well-thought-out contract and tariffs, whereas others can require entire teams of specialists to address specifications and answer requirements. But even web-based and 'bricks and mortar' retail businesses 'propose'.

Think about what it feels like when you are a customer. What do you want to know? What's available? Size and colour? Delivery? Price? Availability and 'return' options? Incentives to buy now? Businesses that state these features clearly and in a way that grabs the customer are, in effect, proposing. If your business sells this way, read through the list of items that should be included in a proposal and check that your material covers these details. Without a direct sales force, the quality of this 'proposal' material will directly affect your success and how quickly you close a sale.

Proposals to the public sector probably represent the most extreme example – often requiring teams of specialists to produce volumes of paper in order to secure business. Quite a few small businesses do not pursue public sector work because the cost of pursuing a sale is too high. Those businesses that do respond usually have a well-thought-out, efficient process for responding to prospect requirements.

If your business does require significant proposal work and risk assessment, how slick is this process? Do you have 'standard paragraphs' that may be reused to save time and effort and minimise risks? Do you use the same team to produce proposals each time so that you can capitalise on their experience? A sales person will and should always promote his own opportunities and shout loudly for these resources, but it is really a business judgment to decide how sales support resources should be deployed. Does your management review the opportunities to decide whether it is worth the business effort to bid? Lengthy proposal production can suck company resources into the process, drawing individuals away from other, perhaps more lucrative opportunities.

Approach to producing a proposal:

- At the beginning, state clearly and simply which is the overall objective of your proposal (the 'problem definition')
- Keep everything to a minimum and keep it simple

- Set deadlines and timing
- Ensure that your proposal protects you as well the potential customer
- Remember to incorporate the necessary legal requirements – usually by reference
- Try to keep the legal jurisdiction to your own country
- Write contracts in your native language
- Use the most appropriate format to win the business – a proposal can take the form of a letter, a presentation, a lengthy document or even, a multimedia deliverable

Having said that the form of the proposal may vary, the content should include:

- Executive summary
- Brief outline of the reason for the proposal (summary of requirements)
- Description of product/service provided
- Delineation and definition of timeframes (e.g. deliveries, period that service is provided, times of day and days of week)
- Defined service levels if appropriate
- Details of when product/service is deemed 'accepted'
- Description of pricing and discount criteria – if appropriate
- Reference to your standard terms & conditions documents

It is also a good idea to include a separate terms & conditions document that contains the more heavy 'legalese' and rarely changes. It is in your general terms & conditions that you define your standard terms of business – such as definition of a working day, limits of liability, IPR ownership, warranty of product or services (if relevant). Standard contract and Ts & Cs will be discussed in more detail later, but they should not vary from customer to customer. What will vary are the unique terms (price, timing, committed individuals) you propose for a specific opportunity.

Closing the sale

'Closing' is the term used to describe agreeing the business or winning the sale. If you run a retail or web-based business, identifying the initial 'close' is straightforward – it's when the customer hands over the payment details and the transaction is completed. However, some retail businesses – both web and bricks and mortar – have high rates of returns, so these businesses should not really consider the deal 'closed' until the return period is over.

In a sales force-based business – whether you use agents or your own staff – the 'close' can be slightly more complex and the 'winning moment' can be a series of up to three steps – even more if you sell to a recommender who then must 'sell on' to the decision maker. To ensure that you always win the business, it is important to recognise these steps.

Stages in closing the sale

The first 'win' occurs when your key decision maker says 'yes'. A big mistake is heaving a sigh of relief and then focusing your efforts on other business. You don't have a contract yet! Sometimes your customer contact will qualify his or her 'yes' with a "Of course, my board will need to ratify a contract of this size." That means you still have more selling to do. You should stick close to your contact and help him or her if you can.

A common 'assist' is offering to help write the board paper or proposal. Not only does this effort help your contact, it also ensures that you have some control over what's being presented to the other decision makers and potential blockers. In fact, you may discover that you have to start a mini-sales process all over again, but focused exclusively on the board (and with the assistance of your contact). Whether you invest a lot more time or the decision gets a 'rubber stamp', the message is clear. Don't stop selling, and keep your focus on the customer.

Finally, there is the contract. If you use your own contracts (and you should if at all possible) immediately after your contact says yes, you should confirm whether or not signing will be a straightforward process or whether someone else (i.e. the customer's legal department or solicitor) will need to be involved. If yes, send blank forms of the contract to the legal expert to start that process moving. If there are going to be legal issues, its best to get them sorted before the board meeting so that the contract can be signed as soon as possible after a positive board response. The longer this final step is dragged out, the more likely it is that something else will delay the final step.

With each step you heave a sigh of relief and break out the champagne, but remember, the deal is never finally 'won' until the contract is signed

When to 'close'

When should a sales person try to 'close'? The honest answer is 'as soon as possible', as long as he or she doesn't expect an immediate 'yes'. It is worth delving into a few advanced sales techniques to help illustrate some issues around 'closing'. Because the act of buying is emotional as well as rational, closing techniques can uncover both a customer's emotional commitment and emotional 'blocks'.

The example presented earlier under 'Qualification' is an example of 'closing' early in the sales process. You understood that when the sales person effectively asked during the very first meeting "If I could show you a way...would you buy?" it was, in fact, a form of closing. And throughout the sales process, a sales person can use the 'trial close' or another type of 'close' — the 'assumed close'. An example? Let's assume someone is considering buying a car or a new patio set – simple products provide the easiest illustrations. When speaking to a potential buyer before a commitment has been made, a sales person might ask: "So, will you be using the patio set for lunch or for dinner?"

Like the 'trial close', the 'assumed close' helps uncover unexpressed concerns about the purchase, and it goes a step further. In a business-to-business sales process a common 'assumed close' is to ask: "What time of the week [or day] is best for delivery?" It asks the buyer to picture himself in the situation after the decision has been made. Saying 'yes' to buying is very difficult for many people and moving them past this key emotional milestone makes it easier to finally contract the business. Why? Because after successfully 'picturing' their family sitting around the patio furniture eating dinner and the sun shining, somewhere in their 'emotional mind' they have already made the purchase – they can picture the family enjoying a barbecue and it 'feels' right.

The patio set sale was just a simple example, but this approach works just as well with big, complex, business-to-business sales – get the prospect to imagine how it will be after the new product or service is in place. By the time you are ready for the final 'close', signing the contracts become a matter of form – the emotional element to procurement has already been appeased.

As discussed earlier, whether selling to an individual or a group within a large company, it is dangerous to think about selling as merely a rational process – both buyer and seller go through a series of both rational and emotional stages and these phases must be acknowledged and accommodated in order to be a successful selling company.

Contracting and negotiating – the final hurdle

At this point, you have one last hurdle to jump and then you have won!

Yes, there are the occasional instances when less scrupulous prospects may string you along and enter negotiations in order to gain better terms from someone else; in this instance, you are merely being used to batter down someone else's price and your time and sales efforts have been wasted. An experienced sales person or negotiator will see this situation for what it is and only waste his or her company's time and money if some benefit can be extracted from the situation. How can you tell?

- Well, the first step is to ask again: "If we meet these terms and price, do we have a deal? Can we shake on it?" Most people – but sadly, not all – baulk at lying directly to your face. A nervous response or failure to respond should ring warning bells.

- Ask direct questions about who else is in the running for the business and how a final decision will be taken. Don't be afraid to probe.

- If the remaining competitor is an incumbent supplier and your company is NOT, be suspicious. Why wouldn't the customer choose an existing supplier? If there were a big problem, this competitor wouldn't have been asked to bid.

- Finally, after a lengthy sales process, you will have some advocate in the company – ask them for a realistic assessment of the situation.

You can't always get it right. Luckily, most of the time, this situation will have already been identified during qualification or selling stage. However, this situation does happen, occasionally because the sales person has no other opportunities and fears for his or her job so, from a personal point of view, it is better to appear to be selling than to confess that the business should have been qualified out. Good sales management should be able to spot such a situation and avoid wasted efforts.

So, assuming you have succeeded and are near the finish line with only one final hurdle, what can you do to ensure that this last step is not a mis-step?

First, recognise that there is a big difference between 'negotiating' and 'selling'. Many businesses make a serious mistake in not acknowledging this distinction. Negotiation is about agreeing the terms of a sale so, in effect, the sale is almost 'won' pending mutually agreeable terms. Negotiating usually occurs at the very end of the sales process after much hard work by selling staff or sales teams who have driven the process this far. The final step is about understanding how flexible both businesses will be in agreeing the terms of the sale and remember, it's usually not just about money.

In some businesses, notably consumer retail, there is very little room for negotiation – the product is the product, with little room for changes. Perhaps discount guidelines provided to the sales staff can offer some financial incentives to buy. In this instance, there is little flexibility, so there can be only small concession and little negotiation. Most complex negotiations occur between two businesses or organisations or when a business offers a bespoke service or product.

In fact, in some situations, contracting is a long, drawn-out process and critical to the success and profit of a deal. For this type of business, 'negotiating skills' and 'selling skills' are not the same thing and sales staff do not always have both. The skills that got you this far are not necessarily the same skills that will take you through the negotiation. Negotiators must understand the legal implications of contractual terms, while sales staff need not have these skills to be successful. Negotiators should also have the clear authority to give concessions on behalf of their company and you may not wish to concede this authority to your sales people.

Negotiating can be so important that some companies use a different specialist to negotiate contracts. In smaller businesses, the commercial or managing director will often (and should) step in to play this role. Other companies understand this distinction and do not involve their sales staff in the final negotiations, but then make the mistake of believing that because 'contracts are legal' a solicitor should be employed at this stage. Solicitors are trained in legal issues, not commercial negotiations. While it is true that some solicitors have gained significant experience in commercial areas, most have not, and it is 'the law', not commerce, that is their formal area of expertise. By all means obtain legal advice from a solicitor if necessary, but don't expect one to carry out your commercial negotiations.

Some small businesses send the financial director on the basis that negotiation is about money and the FD is the money expert. Once again, many (but not all) financial directors grow from an accountancy background and accountancy in itself is not ideal training for contract negotiation. Besides, negotiation of contracts is not just about money!

So, if it's not only about money, what else might be involved?

The list depends on the particular business. Deal-breakers include: additional, specific features, delivery times, cost of after-sales support, access to specific, named specialists, payment terms – to name but a few. Some of these 'demands' might have great value to a potential customer and little value to you. These are the areas in which you can horse trade with least cost to the business.

Negotiation tips

- ▶ Use a qualified and empowered business person to do the negotiation

- ▶ It is not just about price – uncover and quantify other features that are important to the buyer

- ▶ Always trade

- ▶ Use your own contracts where possible

- ▶ If you must use buyer's contracts, check them carefully and seek to modify them if the terms are onerous

- ▶ Try to ensure that any negotiation feels like a 'win/win'

Contracts

Ideally, a contract is a good thing. It clearly spells out terms and obligations for both the buyer and seller in order to avoid misunderstanding. A good contract is good for both sides. Sadly, not all businesses work this way so you must take care. In a perfect world, you already have a set of standard terms and conditions (Ts & Cs) that have been reviewed by a reputable commercial solicitor. If you do not have a standard contract or haven't had your contract reviewed by a solicitor, you should.

All areas important to the business process should be clarified in these standard Ts & Cs – including, but not limited to, things like:

- what constitutes the product/service
- definition of 'working day'
- confidentiality
- intellectual property
- limits of liability

...to name but a few. Specific details of 'the deal' may form a variable section in the contract or be appended as a separate schedule. It is most important that you specify which country's legal jurisdiction rules your contract.

Areas to define in your standard contractual terms and conditions

▸ Working days/times

▸ Confidentiality

▸ Time limits of the contract

▸ The product or service being purchased/sold

▸ Ownership of the product, service, process, output

▸ Liability

▸ Standard obligations of buyer

▸ Standard obligations of seller

▸ Cancellation and/or postponement terms

▸ 'Rectification' clauses & penalties

▸ Payment terms and currency

▸ Reimbursement of expenses

▸ Country under whose jurisdiction the contract falls

Plus any items which are standard and unique to your industry

Where possible, use your own contracts rather than those provided by your customers – customers' contracts are invariably constructed to favour them, not you. If you are forced to use a customer contract – and sometimes it's unavoidable – make certain that you negotiate appropriate clauses to protect your own interests. And just because it's not your contract, it doesn't mean it can't be amended, either within the body of the contract or with an accompanying side letter. It is far better to use your own contractual terms and have strict guidelines about who can negotiate terms and how these terms may be amended.

Transition

Excellent! Your customer said 'yes' and signed on the dotted line. What could go wrong now? Well, with only a bit of effort on your part, nothing. However, many customers feel a bit nervous once they've taken a decision. How can you ensure that the decision 'sticks' and that the buyer remains happy that he or she purchased from your company?

First, whether you sell business-to-consumer or business-to-business, continue to make the customer feel special. No matter how small the spend, both the internet and email make continued communications a very cost-effective way to maintain good feelings.

Whether you've sold a big deal with a sales team of dozens or sold a rubber duck over the web, you can always:

1. Thank them for their business and let them know that it is valued
2. Explain what happens next
3. Inform them about delivery or start date
4. Ask for feedback about how it felt to do business with your company

If possible, do these things in four separate communications – in any case, more than one. Each communication reminds them that you are doing things on their behalf and validates that they took the right decision in purchasing from you. Again, when you mention things about delivery or project start-up, mention things that happen after the delivery. You can talk about "bathing with your rubber duck" or ask: "Which room will we assign for joint planning meetings?" Both these sentences invoke a time when the product is delivered and working or the project has begun and, as with the 'assumed close', moved the customer emotionally to a time when the product or project has already begun. By taking the customer well past the moment of decision and making him or her feel valued, it decreases your chances of bad feeling with loss of future business and/or cancellation of the original contract.

Common pitfalls

DO NOT:

- Suspects ⇒
  o Load the sales funnel with arbitrary lists of names and addresses
  o Let anyone load names on the sales funnel without
    insisting on an owner for each opportunity listed

- Prospects ⇒
  o Let prospects whose opportunities have failed the qualification
    process remain on the prospect list. If there is another, different
    opportunity, fine – add it to the list as a new opportunity. But
    if you have qualified it 'OUT', take it off the list. Far better to
    honestly discard names where no business is likely and focus sales
    efforts on those opportunities most likely to yield revenue.
  o Fail to properly qualify at an early stage and do so systemically and ruthlessly.
    You will only create unnecessary work for yourself and staff if you continue
    to pursue opportunities that you won't win or can't sell profitably.

- Proposing ⇒
  o 'Just mail' or drop off your proposal. Always try, if possible, to present
    it – with summary – to the decision maker so that you can gauge his
    or her reaction. Better still, discuss drafts of the proposal with your
    key customer contacts and incorporate their input if relevant.

- Closing ⇒
  o Forget to 'ask for the business'! Believe it or not, may sales people fumble
    this last step – they find it very, very difficult to ask: "So, will you buy?"
    Make certain that whoever you employ to do your selling is able to 'close'.

- Negotiating →
  o Let untrained sales staff conduct complex negotiations without help.
  o Let your procurement specialist conduct complex negotiations without help.
  o Ask a solicitor (unless appropriately skilled) to carry out your closing negotiations.
  o Give away something that you value more than the customer values.

- Contracts →
  o Use customer contracts unless absolutely necessary.
  o Let sales staff write 'side letters' qualifying your contract Ts & Cs.
  o Let sales staff make 'amendments' without going through a management process.
  o Make amendments without a full understanding of the legal implications.
  o Forget to include an 'anti-poaching clause' in your contract if your staff work on your customer's site. (You should include something similar in your employment contracts as well.)
  o Forget to ensure that your contracts protect your own intellectual property (IPR) unless you sold it as part of the deal.
  o Forget to make it clear who owns the IPR of any joint work that's undertaken with a customer.
  o Accept a foreign country as the legal arbiter of the contracts unless absolutely necessary or you have good legal representation in that country. A very pragmatic reason to avoid this situation is the cost – if you have to defend yourself or enforce your contract in a foreign country it will usually cost you far more than doing so in the UK.

END OF CHAPTER 9 – SELF-ASSESSMENT

EVALUATE YOUR SALES FUNNEL - Tick 1 box for each question

QUESTION	Yes	No	Partly
1. Do you categorise your sales opportunities into a sales pipeline?			
2. Do you have a target list of suspects and/or prospects?			
3. Do you have a process for qualifying and/or categorising your most important prospects?			
4. Do you take as proactive a sales approach as possible for your market segment and business type?			
5. Is the whole of your organisation aware of what's happening in your sales funnel and 'bought in' to ensuring that it is up to date and accurate?			
6. Do you have a slick proposing process?			
7. Have you ensured that 'buying' from you is as easy as possible?			
8. Do you use your own contracts for sales transactions?			
9. Does your business recognise the difference between 'selling' and 'negotiating'?			
10. Do you have a process and policies to make certain that your customer stays satisfied after completing the purchase?			

YOUR SCORE: Give yourself 5 points for every 'yes', 2 points for every 'partly' and '0' for every 'no'.

36-50 Points ⇒ Excellent – note areas where you didn't score 5 and plan to rectify if relevant to your business

26-35 Points ⇒ Good – you have some room for improvement. Check those areas in which you ticked 'no' or 'partly' and evaluate how you can improve your score

11-25 Points ⇒ You could do better – there is definitely room for improvement…

0-10 Points ⇒ Get help! You have lots and lots of opportunity to improve your income stream.

Chapter 10
Managing the Selling Processes & Sales Operations

Top tips – Chapter 10

1. Give someone the overall responsibility for achieving sales

2. Make certain at least one person on the executive team is accountable for sales targets

3. Selling can cost money – make certain that you have allocated sufficient funds to pursue your revenue targets

4. Establish an opportunity review process when sales support staff, funds and/or equipment are in short supply

5. Offload office-based tasks to different employees so that sales staff can focus on selling

6. Monitor sales effectiveness

In the previous two chapters you read about the selling process and how selling activities change as opportunities move along the sales funnel. Who manages this process in your business? Who is responsible for the sales bottom line? Is it the same person? Whoever is accountable should be given the authority to lead and manage the sales and sales support processes.

Do you remember reading in the earlier chapters how you can empower your sales staff by providing slick, back-office support to field-based sales? If your business uses field-based sales people, how do you manage this back-office support or 'sales operations'? Managing these activities need not require extra staff, but it does require an understanding of what must be managed and a well-defined list of the responsibilities attached to the role. In some organisations, a sales or marketing director takes this job, but in others it falls to the managing director. No matter who, someone must do the job and do it well or you will lose money and waste effort.

Let's start by looking at sales management in a bit more detail.

Sales management

Sales management consists of more than just demanding regular reports from the sales staff and ensuring that sales numbers add up to targets. Effective sales management contains a subset of all the components required to run a successful business, including:

- Leadership and tactics
- People
- Planning and forecasting
- Managing the sales process
- Sales territories
- Judging where best to deploy resources
- Coaching and supporting sales (the team) about sales strategy and tactics
- Goal setting (sales targets)
- Obtaining appropriate support for the selling process
- Ensuring product/service supply to satisfy potential orders

In larger organisations there is often a separate individual, or even teams, responsible for each area. However, in smaller businesses there is rarely the luxury of so many staff, so one individual may play multiple roles. Typically, in SMEs, many of these activities are shared between different directors and, while such a setup can work, it is also fraught with pitfalls unless the separate roles are clearly defined, executed and well understood by all. Sales management is about managing processes and making judgments, but it's also about the more challenging and ambiguous aspects of motivating people. Does this emphasis feel like overkill for your organisation? It's not. While you probably do not need to hire separate individuals for each task, you should make certain you cover all the activities with appropriate, existing employees.

Paul Brennan provides a clear example of someone who understood and applied his learnings from a large corporation to many successful SMEs, including Zeus Technologies.

••

Zeus Technologies – managing a new sales approach

You may remember, Paul Brennan joined Zeus Technologies as CEO in 2004. When asked about the key to his successes, he starts his story by crediting IBM with many of his key business practices: "My training and time at IBM taught me that life becomes easier if one applies a few standard processes and procedures to a business. IBM also gave me insights into man management as well as business management." As discussed in an earlier chapter on marketing and service offerings, Paul's first step was to assess his market and offering.

In addition, Paul regularly gave 'state of the nation' presentations – both scheduled and impromptu – to the whole company, making sure that every employee felt involved in and a part of Zeus Technologies' challenges and successes. He went on to emphasise: "An inclusive approach makes people feel like they are part of the business and its success. This is key to successfully managing people and effective teams."

••

You can see that Paul understood that managing both people and processes were critical. He defined new roles for back-office staff to play a part in the sales process, modelling it after IBM's traditional approach of pairing up a sales person with a technical specialist – the systems engineer – who had also been trained in IBM selling techniques. Paul managed the process and gained outstanding results.

So what exactly gets managed?

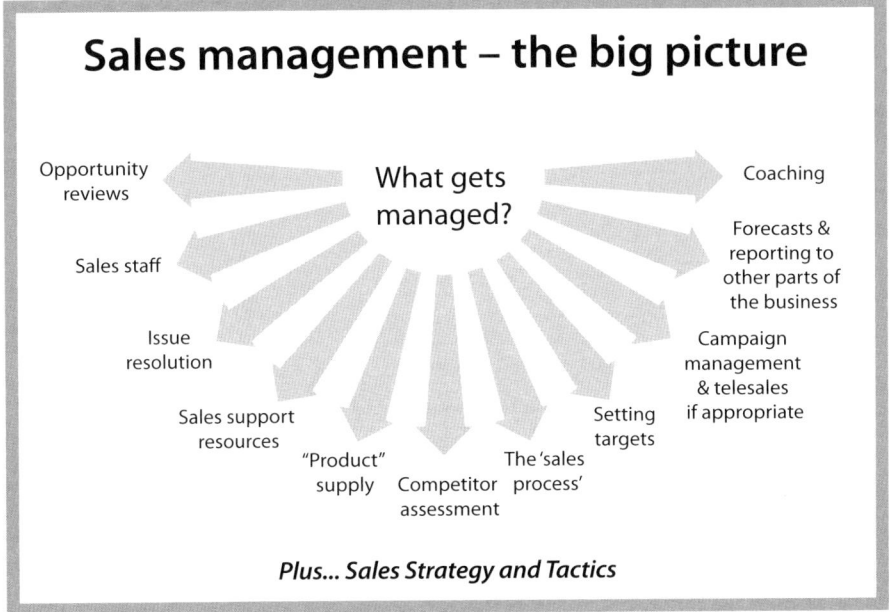

Sales management – the big picture

Opportunity reviews

Sales staff

Issue resolution

Sales support resources

"Product" supply

Competitor assessment

What gets managed?

The 'sales process'

Setting targets

Coaching

Forecasts & reporting to other parts of the business

Campaign management & telesales if appropriate

Plus... Sales Strategy and Tactics

In some organisations, portions of financial and contract management also fall under the sales management remit.

Let's look at these areas in a bit more detail to understand the typical tasks, objectives and what 'good' looks like'.

People management

This function includes the management of sales staff and any sales/technical support staff involved in the sales process. Sometimes this management is complicated because someone else has the direct line management of part of the team. People management is as much about the 'irrational' as the 'rational', and involves personal coaching as well as business direction, so face-to-face, one-to-one and group meetings are critical.

As a team – sales, sales support and sales admin – you should try to bring together all the staff in regular group sessions at least once a quarter. Such gatherings can be used to report successes, thereby increasing morale and thus productivity, and they can also be used to impact information about new offerings or business processes. Most importantly, such meetings help cement a common culture and help the back-office staff feel a part of the selling process. All good stuff. So is it worth all this effort?

Well, Vertex thought so. Remember from earlier chapters how Vertex refocused its marketing and service offering efforts on a tightly defined, public sector opportunity? In doing so, Vertex transformed itself into a 'selling organisation'. In addition, Vertex made some changes to its selling process and management and, once again, provides an excellent example.

Vertex redesigned its selling organisation and management

To more effectively address its target market, Vertex redesigned the sales organisation – dividing sales into two distinct activities: account management, which has overall responsibility for existing business – both renewal and growth of this business as well as overall customer satisfaction; and business development, a role that carries the responsibility for new business selling. The roles are different and the rewards and measurements differ accordingly.

A small, sector-specific team composed of account managers (for existing accounts), sales staff (for new business) sales support staff, marketing and technical and delivery managers, as appropriate, drives and manages the selling process. There are regular, bi-weekly 'sales' conference calls that include all these people and all contribute to the discussion, offering expertise that ranges from 'customer insights' to 'operational impacts'. All new opportunities now go through an 'opportunity review' process to ensure that:

- business resources are appropriately deployed
- sales staff pursue only appropriate opportunities
- the best possible sales tactics are being used

There is also now a monthly account meeting for this group that enables them to produce a shared plan and review all activities against this plan. 'Best practice' is also shared in these regular meetings. This meeting is also a good venue for sharing market intelligence gathered from both the 'delivery' and 'selling' perspective. This approach builds 'one team/one common understanding'.

Today, even with a much smaller sales force/account team, far more time is spent on preparation for sales meetings and bids. In addition to 'opportunity reviews', bi-weekly meetings and monthly account meetings, Vertex also holds quarterly strategy meetings. It is in these meetings that the business is able to share information to better target its services to up-to-date customer needs and changing market conditions. Campaign planning is also covered during these sessions.

Finally, before any 'bid' is submitted, there is relentless review. Presentations are rehearsed and reviewed twice before the real event. This approach has had an enormous impact on the quality of the final product – and a significant benefit is that the 'final' presentation must now be prepared before the first rehearsal, rather than 'just in time'.

. . . .

All the activities at Vertex didn't just 'happen' – they were all managed by someone in a function accountable for sales revenues. The sales manager kept an eye on the sales process, ensured effective communication between everyone involved and did so in a way that made individuals feel committed and responsible for the success of the sale.

Vertex – though a SME in its sector – is a large business, but you don't have to be large to have to 'manage' many sales resources; nor do you have to employ directly everyone who sells for you. Remember Nexsan from earlier chapters? It offered next generation in storage racks/cabinets to systems integrators in the information services market. Martin Boddy started this business with nothing – no money and product on the drawing board. So, what need did he have for a sales process and sales management?

Martin's approach at Nexsan offers a good example of how sales management can be deployed to obtain maximum performance in a business with very few employees and minimal sales staff. To supplement employee efforts, Nexsan used VARs – and similar techniques could easily be applied to franchisees.

• •

Nexsan manages its VARs for successful growth

Martin used his old connections from early business days to find a salesman from a complementary US company. This salesman understood the Nexsan offering and had a business relationship with many of the prospective Nexsan customers. This US salesman had also developed a comprehensive sales lead system to support VARs (value-added resellers). Using this system to 'register VARs' so they could sell the Nexsan product, he was able to get VARs to cooperate, rather than compete for various opportunities. With this cooperation, all parties were able to maintain a healthy profit margin rather than engage in a price-cutting war with each other.

After a short time, VARs became such an important selling tool that Nexsan set up systems and events (e.g. training, communication, new product launch) to better support this VAR network! By this stage, Nexsan finally added 'storage disks' to the configured 'racks' they provided. There were now two key target resellers – VARs and systems integrators – and by 2007 the business had grown to £50m turnover.

• •

Martin, through his US sales manager, managed and supported his VARs. In this way, rather than competing with each other – a common situation in the third-party sales arena – the VARs each focused on winning business at a profitable margin. 'Win/win' for everyone involved.

Management of sales people

What's unique about managing sales people? Aren't they just like any other employee? In many respects, of course they are, but there are some factors that you should bear in mind about the role: Sales staff:

- are the 'face of your company – often the only representative that your customer may meet
- hear feedback about your business, offerings and competition
- spend a lot of time outside the office
- are usually target-focused and motivated to achieve these targets

The sales management role ('sales manager') should motivate and inspire as well as assist sales staff. A sales person's good attitude and feelings about his or her employer get reflected in his/her dealings with customers. Any bad attitudes quickly show through and reflect on your business. Inspired and happy sales staff have a direct impact on your market image and your bottom line.

A 'sales manager' should also 'listen' and collect information to feed back to the rest of the business. Perhaps your product is being superseded by one from the competition. If so, you can be sure that your sales staff will be the first to know. Maybe the new person in customer service needs additional training around telephone skills – any negative feedback and a sales person with a good customer relationship will hear about it. Listen and your organisation can take action and nip any problems in the bud.

Finally, in addition to obtaining customer feedback and motivating the sales person, there are operational details to go over during meetings. Topics covered should include:

- Deals to be 'closed' soon
- Sales deals in the sales pipeline
- Feedback about competitor offers or tactics
- Discussion of how to expedite internal issues (e.g. delivery times or product complaints) where needed
- Administrative discussions as appropriate re:
  o Expenses
  o Written reports/updates
  o Behaviour problems/disciplinary actions

In addition to regular weekly or monthly meetings, sales managers should schedule different special meetings that cover:

- Updated training around new product/service and/or business changes
- Account and/or territory planning so that information can be included in a forecast

If you follow these practices, there should be no surprises around your sales results or the market/customer situation. Sales managers should also manage any sales campaigns, deploying appropriate resources and ensuring that the rest of the business can cope with increased sales volumes and any temporary changes in business terms and conditions.

Sales 'territories' – dividing up the opportunity

Another key function of sales management is to divide up the sales opportunities in order to best service all the potential business. Every sales person should have an assigned 'territory', whether geographical, business type or simply a list of accounts. If a business has only one person who sells, a defined territory is less important. But as a business grows and adds new selling roles, a sales manager should make certain that the 'territory' assigned to each person offers the business the best chance to win sales.

How does this work?

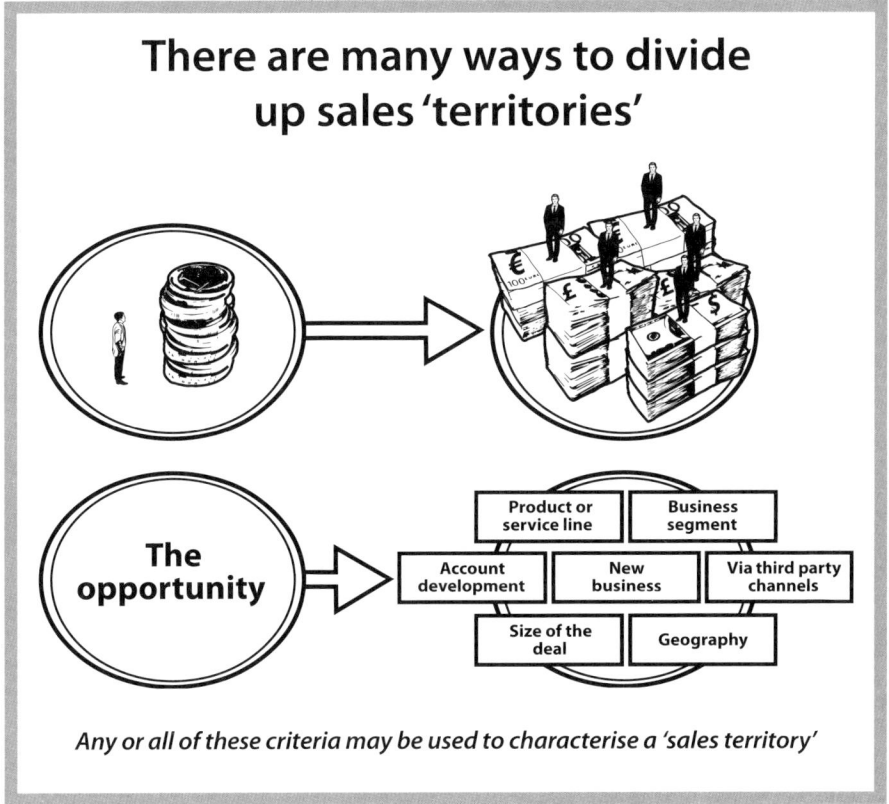

There are many ways to divide up sales 'territories'

	Product or service line	Business segment
Account development	New business	Via third party channels
Size of the deal	Geography	

The opportunity

Any or all of these criteria may be used to characterise a 'sales territory'

There are many ways of 'dividing up' the opportunity. In chapter 1 you read about the difference between 'new business' and 'account development' sales, and dividing sales opportunity in this way is often the first step in creating 'sales territories'. Some businesses with multiple product/service lines may elect to have a separate sales person for each offering. For example, purveyors of business software may have one specialist for accounting software and another for inventory/stock control software sales. Care must be taken with this approach, of course, because two or three sales people from the same company might call on a customer in a short space of time. Some businesses divide sales territories into business groupings – for example, all finance companies go to one sales person and all manufacturing companies go to another. There is no single, 'right' approach.

The best approach depends on your business – its maturity, offering and your growth aspirations. The idea behind sales territories is to:

- Optimise the deployment of your sales resources
- Balance the opportunity between appropriately skilled individuals
- Drive growth by acquiring new customers
- Drive growth by increasing sales in existing customers
- Ensure that two or more of your staff are NOT competing for the same opportunity

Whatever approach, someone with a sales management role must understand the potential opportunities allocated to each sales person.

Sales campaigns

A sales campaign is a focused selling effort, usually around a specific theme ('better service', 'lower price', 'end of line special offer', 'new release'). Typically, a business temporarily puts increased efforts into selling in this particular area.

A successful sales campaign needs:

- A well-defined proposition
- Target market
- Communication about the 'offer' both internally
  and to the potential customer base
- Resources to implement and manage the campaign overall
- Resources to follow up and manage the interest generated by the campaign

The Vertex case study from chapter 5 is repeated in full here because it illustrates a good example of a well-run sales campaign.

•••

Vertex focuses on 'Citizen Services' for a successful sales campaign

The challenge was: how to discover opportunities at an earlier stage? With only around 50 appropriate 'deals' per year in this sector, Vertex decided to do some research and take a more targeted approach.

First, Vertex more clearly defined and delineated its customer proposition. The business decided to focus on delivering "Citizen Services through Government" when it became clear that Vertex possessed neither the strength nor the capacity to be good at everything. So, with this in mind, if opportunities arose that did not encompass Citizen Services, Vertex would not bid. An added benefit was that by tightening up the definition of its service it could better describe it to its potential customers, making it 'easier to buy'.

Next Vertex decided to proactively investigate its market for potential opportunities. To do so, it focused on two areas:

1. Organisations
2. Specific individuals within organisations

For example, in the UK, there are around 500 local councils, but with a little bit of research it became clear that only those councils with a £200m budget or greater were in a position to buy Vertex services. A further cull was made because some of these councils did not offer 'Citizen Services' as defined by the Vertex service offering.

Finally, in the remaining list of potential customers or 'prospects' Vertex checked each council's 'propensity to be a buyer' against two different criteria: first, if larger competitors already held a strong position within the council it was unlikely that they would change supplier, and second, there were some councils that held a philosophical objection to procuring services from the private sector. This prospecting approach winnowed out still more of the potential 500 prospects, leaving a final list of around 80 councils who might buy Vertex's 'Citizen Services through Government'.

With the refined list of 80, Vertex then built a marketing campaign in order to create awareness within this target list where it was virtually unknown. Again Kieron Brennan reminds me: "Getting noticed is different from what you want to sell," and at this stage what Vertex wanted to was to get noticed and to begin a relationship and discussions with the appropriate individuals within these 80 councils. After three months, Vertex had engagement with 25% of this target list. A typical success rate for a good campaign is less than 5%. Clearly, Vertex was doing something right.

So, for Vertex:

- The proposition was: Citizen Services.
- The target market was: specific local councils who passed Vertex's qualification criteria and then specific named individuals within these councils.
- Communication included a pre-sales marketing campaign to raise awareness and communication and reorganisation within its own organisation
- Resources – Vertex did a lot of planning and preparation before embarking on the campaign. In his management role, Kieron made many judgments about refining the market, selecting targets, and then decided which sales staff should be deployed to qualify and pursue any opportunities. Kieron emphasised: "Don't be afraid to take the time to research your marketplace. It will save you time, effort and money in the long run."

Vertex ran this campaign with only one salesman, plus help from marketing and management. Because of the detailed planning and careful qualification discussed earlier (see chapter 5) Vertex was able to focus its efforts on those councils who could and would buy the offering. It worked for Vertex – it can work for you!

Empowering your sales staff

How much time should a sales person spend in your office and how much out with customers or trying to get new business? The answer? Ideally, the salesman should spend as much productive time as possible trying to close more business. When he or she is not in the office, you have to trust that the sales person is working – if you don't, hire someone you trust. What matters is that the sales person closes good business.

What many companies do in order to maximise sales efficiency is deploy other staff to handle some of these tasks. As mentioned earlier, less expensive telesales personnel can be used to reduce the 'cold calling' time of sales staff.

When a large proposal is required, some businesses deploy specialists to write the bulk of a lengthy proposal while the sales person 'tops and tails' with specific detail to tailor the bid to the prospect or customer's needs. Such businesses also deploy staff to write and manage 'standard' inserts/letters/proposals that can be quickly tailored to meet a specific sales opportunity. Using this approach has the advantage that the standard material can be pre-checked by a legal specialist and thereby minimise legal exposure for the business.

Sales support and support staff

You will hear it again – it's an important message: every administrative task a sales person performs takes up time that could be used finding more business, selling or closing a deal! A good first step for any business is to look carefully at how its sales people spend their time and to determine whether any of the time can be freed up to do more sales work. There is no hard and fast rule. Precisely how any business will benefit and what type of sales support makes commercial sense depends on the type of business and the complexity of the selling process.

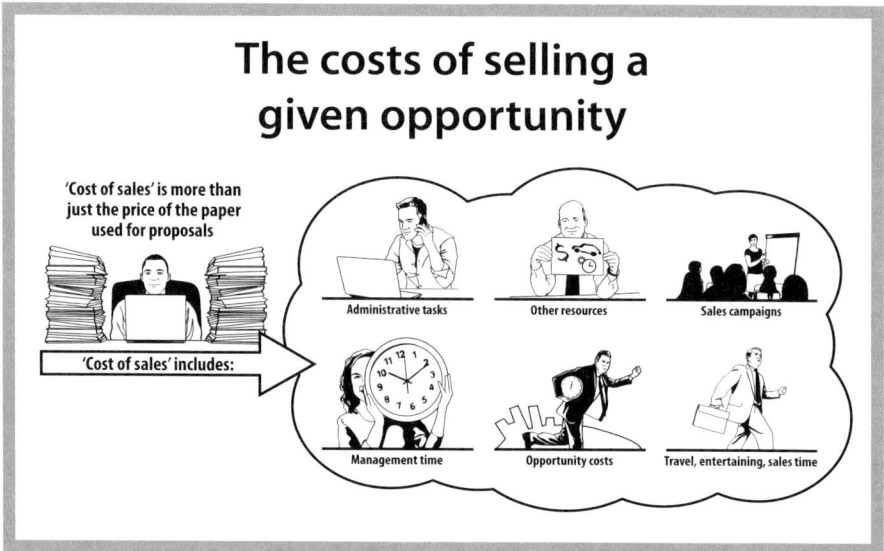

Regardless of your business type, bear in mind that the philosophy behind providing sales support is to free up the specially trained, prospect/customer-facing individuals so they can spend as much time as possible in front of potential customers. To this end, sales support is usually office-based and better able to handle office-based, company issues. Such help, properly implemented, not only reduces your costs but also increases your probability of a successful sale.

So, more specifically how can office-based staff help?

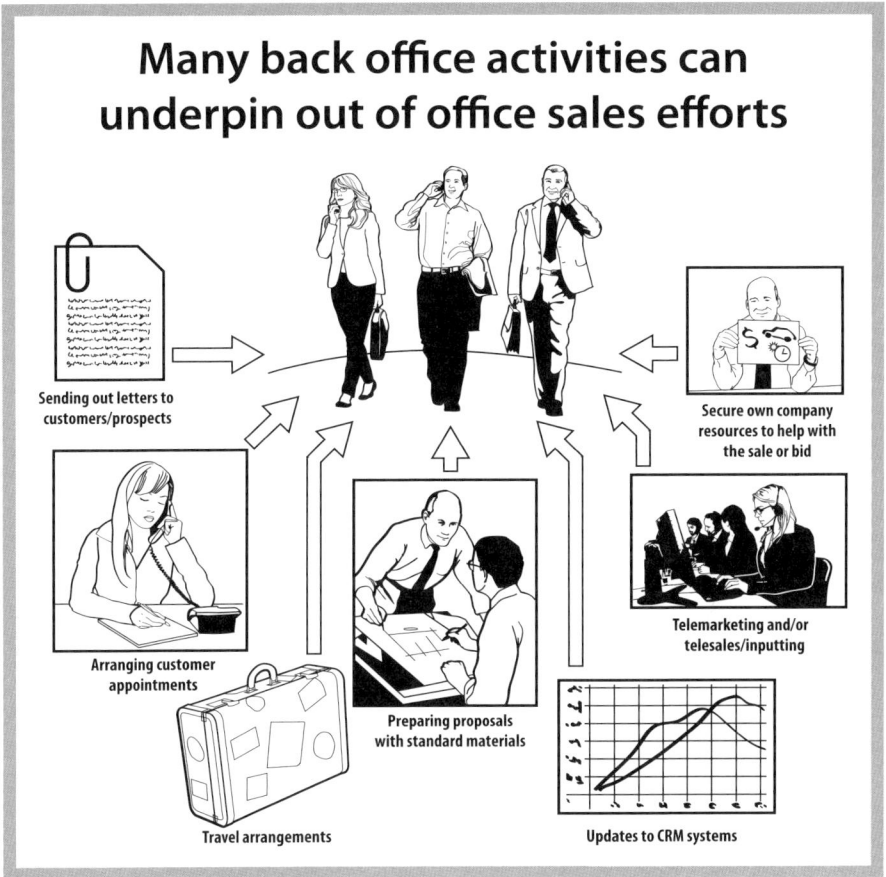

Many back office activities can underpin out of office sales efforts

Sending out letters to customers/prospects

Secure own company resources to help with the sale or bid

Arranging customer appointments

Telemarketing and/or telesales/inputting

Travel arrangements

Preparing proposals with standard materials

Updates to CRM systems

Activities can range from:

- Appointment making for the sales staff
- Sending out standard follow-up letters, documentation
- Inputting data into company CRM system
- Proposal preparation
- Bid management
- Technical resource allocation
- Delivery expediting
- Travel arrangements, hotels and room bookings
- Contract preparation
- Any back-office aspects of customer problem resolution

You can see from the list that while some of these activities are administrative, others can require specialist skills and knowledge about the rest of your organisation. Many businesses let their sales staff do all these tasks, as appropriate, but if you do you should ask yourself these questions:

- Who costs me more – my sales person or an administrator?
- How would I prefer my sales person to spend his/her time
  – arguing with my warehouse manager or resources director
  OR out of the office dealing with potential customers?

- Do I have time to read through every proposal, letter or quote in detail to ensure that my sales person hasn't inadvertently left the business open to unnecessary risk?

A last point: Most business executives respond that, of course they want to do their best to free up the sales person's time to sell. But often this raises a niggling question in the backs of their minds – is that what's really happening? How do I know the sales person isn't just going home early? You don't, and that's why a good sales manager and management process are so important. When a salesman is not spending enough time face-to-face with customers or prospects, a good sales manager will soon find out.

So, who manages all these diverse activities? If you have a small office, then the sales manager/director will oversee the whole process. The various tasks may not belong to any one person but are, perhaps, divided among different office-based staff. In some instances, one individual is hired to do everything and often given a general 'marketing' role. In a larger organisation or one with a complex sales process, there may even be a separate manager who directs sales operations.

There is no hard and fast rule about how you should organise to support the process. The details will depend on your sales approach, your offering and your target market. However, there are some guidelines that can help:

- Produce a 'Commercial ARCI' for your business. Remember, someone should have the accountability for each task (see example ARCI).
- No one person should directly manage more than 6–8 sales staff. Five direct sales reports would be optimum. Too many direct reports and the job does not get done properly – there just isn't enough time.
- Acknowledge the issues that arise in 'matrix management'. In other words, when a member of your staff must divide his or her efforts between the sales effort (managed by the sales manager) and 'the day job' (managed by someone else). There will always be a struggle, but clear lines of management, accountability and an ARCI can help.

ARCI offers a simple tool for clarifying roles and responsibilities

ARCI provides:

► Clarity about who does what

► Commitment / no hiding

► Resolution of conflicts

► A way to get stuff done!

Example: ARCI				
Activity	Anne	Brian	Claude	David
	(Technical lead)	(Sales lead)	(Sales support)	(Financial support)
Prepare risk assessment	R	A	I	I
Get technical sign-off	A/R	C	R	C
Complete costings	C	R	R	A
Write executive summary	I	A/R	R	R

Top Tips

► Only one A is possible

► A person with too many A's needs to delegate, otherwise he/she will become a bottleneck

► Multiple R's possible, so work can be delegate

► A person without A's might have a support or expert role; otherwise look carefully at the role and contribution. Ask yourself: Should this person be on the team?

Now, having reminded yourself about the ARCI tool, use the 'one size fits all' ARCI form below and re-label the roles to represent your business. Now try filling it in for your business.

Example: ARCI for management of key sales activities in a small business

Tasks	Commercial director	Managing director	Finance / operations director	Technical / production director	Customer service mgr	HR manager
Sales management, including reports and forecasting						
Sales support						
Technical support						
Campaign management						
Campaign follow-up						
Administrative support						
Sales funnel management						
Opportunity review						
Proposal production						
Contract management						
Customer service						
Marketing						

Work through the tasks:
- *Assign 1 'A' for each*
- *Assign R's where individuals will be directly involved*
- *Assign C's where activities will have direct impact on an individual's business area*
- *Anyone else get's an 'I'*

In a small business, there should be lots of R's and very few I's

Is there currently someone responsible for all these tasks? Is the 'right' person doing them? Could other managers or directors help? Again, be honest. No one will see your answers but you. Most small businesses do NOT have a single individual accountable for all these activities. For others, the accountability is all piled on to the managing director, who gets little assistance from the others. Remember, the days of the 'hero sales culture' are over (if they ever really existed). If you want to create a selling culture, you must get everyone involved. Dividing the tasks among your managers/directors and clearly distributing the accountability appropriately help to embed such a selling culture.

Sales operations

'Sales operations' encompasses the entire process of running, supporting and managing the sales process (as distinct from 'sales management'). As you know if you have a formal, documented sales processes, the activities are numerous and varied. Ideally, sales operations manages all the sales support activities, produces reports (against plan) and keeps an eye on the prospect pipeline. Sales operations is also an area that might manage the day-to-day activities of special sales campaigns.

Typical sales operations outputs

▶ High-level sales forecasts

▶ Management of sales plans

▶ Production/management of sales templates (e.g. presentations, offer letters, price lists)

▶ Proposal production

▶ Updated sales collateral

▶ Technical resource commitment for the sales process

▶ Telesales/telemarketing

In most organisations with a sales function, there are some sales materials produced centrally that sales staff can give or show to customers during a sales meeting. Typically, these items include:

- Product/service description sheets
- Price lists
- Discount/special offer criteria
- Company description (as written for a sales situation)
- Contracts/terms & conditions

In addition, for any organisation that produces lengthy proposals, there should be some 'standard', approved material that can be inserted into proposals.

What should be standard?

- Product/service description
- 'Boiler plate' (approve paragraphs that have been updated regularly to be slotted into proposals) to include topics such as:
  o Company overview
  o Product overview
  o Why us?
  o Customer reference material
  o Standard disclaimers
- Proposal letter template
- Proposal template
- Contract templates

Providing these standard and up-to-date 'inserts' and 'templates' not only saves time and money in proposal production, but can also significantly reduce your contract/business risks. If you 'sell' anything, somebody in your organisation is already producing documents that cover these topics. In fact, many different staff or sales people might be producing different versions of these documents, all covering the same topics. Apart from efficiency, why should you care?

All these documents potentially go out into your marketplace. Do they say the same thing? Are they are correct and up to date? If they are wrong or even just different, what do you think this does your company image? All material that comes from your company, no matter who produces them, represents your business in the customers' eyes. It's well worth taking the time and the care to manage this image. After all, what would you think of a company whose sales material was inconsistent, out of date or contradictory? What does that say about the company?

Whether you use one person, 'part' of one person or a cast of thousands, it's worth setting up and maintaining these standard sales documents and templates. In addition, remember to give someone in management the responsibility for both sales and sales support processes so that a senior employee is accountable for managing the processes and ensuring the quality of the materials. If nobody is 'accountable' it won't happen.

END OF CHAPTER 10 – SELF-ASSESSMENT

EVALUATE YOUR SALES MANAGEMENT & OPERATIONS
- Tick 1 box for each question

QUESTION	Yes	No	Partly
1. Does someone in your organisation have the accountability for managing and achieving sales?			
2. Does your nominated sales accountable person have the authority and skills to fully carry out the diverse sales management tasks?			
3. Does your business have an opportunity review process and, if so, do your other senior managers/ directors play a role?			
4. Is there a back-office sales support function in your company?			
5. Do all your senior management/directors play a role in supporting the sales process?			
6. Do you run and follow up on targeted sales campaigns?			
7. Does your sales manager hold regular, weekly sales meetings with his or her sales staff? Sales support staff?			
8. Do you use your sales funnel to forecast future business?			
9. Does your sales forecast feed into your annual business plan?			
10. Does your sales management accountable person possess good people and coaching skills?			

YOUR SCORE: Give yourself 5 points for every 'yes', 2 points for every 'partly' and '0' for every 'no'.

36-50 Points	⇒	Excellent – note areas where you didn't score 5 and plan to rectify if relevant to your business
26-35 Points	⇒	Good – you have some room for improvement. Check those areas in which you ticked 'no' or 'partly' and evaluate how you can improve your score
11-25 Points	⇒	You could do better – there is definitely room for improvement…
0-10 Points	⇒	Get help! You have lots and lots of opportunity to improve your income stream.

Chapter 11
Putting It All Together

Top tips for success

1. Select an appropriate sales approach(es) for your business

2. Ensure everyone in your business feels a part of the selling process and your business's success

3. Manage your selling process – be as proactive as business allows

4. Make a plan to tackle your areas of business weakness

5. Continue to use the chapter quizzes in this book on a regular basis to test your business

6. Don't rest on your laurels – regularly evaluate your market, offering, people and processes and implement improvements

7. If you can't do it by yourself, get help

Unless you are the sort of person who likes to skip to the end of a book to read the last chapter first, you have now gone through the whole book, done practical examples and completed all the End of Chapter Self-Assessments. Use this chapter to gather your thoughts and give your business an honest evaluation. Then... do something! Don't make the mistake that many of your customers doubtless make and believe that by doing 'nothing' you are not making a decision. By doing 'nothing' you are making a choice too and it is not necessarily a safe option. The world doesn't stand still. So, let's take a closer look at what you might do.

Start by reviewing your End of Chapter Self-Assessment scores – look at them as a whole. The End of Book Self-Assessment is designed to help you identify key problem areas, so have a look.

END OF BOOK –SELF-ASSESSMENT		
EVALUATE YOUR BUSINESS – Tick 1 box for each question		
Part I →	Your people and your sales approach	
Part II →	Your market and your offering	
Part III →	Your sales process, sales operations and sales management	
Section	**QUESTION**	**Points**
	1. Enter your score from Chapter 1	
	2. Enter your score from Chapter 2	
	3. Enter your score from Chapter 3	
	4. Enter your score from Chapter 4	
	5. Enter your score from Chapter 5	
	6. Enter your score from Chapter 6	
	7. Enter your score from Chapter 7	
	8. Enter your score from Chapter 8	
	9. Enter your score from Chapter 9	
	10. Enter your score from Chapter 10	
	ENTER YOUR TOTAL SCORE HERE:	

There is a possible total score of 500 points. How did you do? Be honest – no one else will see the results and it's your business we are discussing.

Results descriptions

1. 451–500 points
450 points or higher is excellent. Next steps depend on where you lost any points. If they were evenly spread throughout all the sections, then go back to the questions and identify areas for refinement. Don't rest on your laurels, but you are doing very, very well. Keep up the good work!

2. 401–450 points
This is a good score. You are definitely doing most things right. Most people who achieve this score did so by losing a few points here and there, so it's not always easy to know what to do. Use the individual tests at the end of each chapter to assess what areas you need to improve and then do something about it. If you lost most of your points in one particular area, the fix is more obvious. See the 200-300 points section below for hints at how to tackle improvement.

3. 301–400 points
You probably have the basics well covered, but there is lot of room to raise your game. See the 200-300 points section below for ideas on how to develop an improvement plan and then implement it.

4. 201–300 points

This score is 'the average' – it puts you in a similar situation to that of your typical competitor. Do you want to be 'average'? Wouldn't you like to get an edge on the competition and sell more?

Take a look at where you lost the points. Also, it's not merely a question of the total number of points – the balance is important.

Did you lose points predominantly in the ▨ section? Then you need help with your sales management and/or sales processes. These are all things under your own control and can be improved with a bit of effort by you and the rest of your organisation.

Was it the ▦ section? Take a close and honest look at your company culture. Does it support revenue growth? Do all your employees 'believe' in your offering and happily tell friends and acquaintances all about it? Are you using the best sales approach for your business?

Perhaps you lost the most points in the ⊠ section: service offering and target market? If so, take a careful look at both. It's well worth getting appropriate, external help with this review. Remember, you need to aim to hit a target, and to do so you need to know where your target stands. Otherwise, you depend on your potential customers finding you and/or figuring out for themselves why your offering is right for them. To do so involves a lot of effort and most potential customers just won't do it.

5. 101–200 points

If you aren't feeling pain in your business, then the good news is that you have lots of scope for improvement. In fact, you might have so much to tackle that it would be dis-ruptive to make too many changes all at once. Prioritise and create a plan to implement the changes suggested in each section of the book. Start by focusing on your market and your service offering, then make certain you are deploying the best sales approaches for your offering and marketplace. Finally, put in place appropriate management and business processes and internal communications (regular meetings, updates etc.).

Now, the challenging part while implementing these changes: try to involve the whole business. It's a great opportunity to create your own sales culture. Create a business case to justify any spend and get help. Be honest: do you currently employ individuals with any of the skills to make these changes without going outside your business? By making appropriate adjustments to just about any aspect of your business, you should see a rapid and measurable improvement.

6. Less than 100 points

Get help. By making appropriate changes to just about any aspect of your business you should see measurable improvement. See the previous paragraph for a good approach to fixing things.

What next?

No matter what your total score, from now on you should test yourself regularly, every 6-12 months if possible, depending on what's happening in your market and your industry. The market and competition don't stand still. Customers' tastes change. If you sell into a 'fashion market' then change is a constant and you must review your business even more regularly. Based on the score of your final test, you should now develop an improvement plan. Then, do something! Implement the plan. If you need temporary help, get it! If the external help isn't useful, try someone else but don't give up on making the changes.

And start measuring. Look for and record the benefits – both tangible and intangible – that you achieve by making these changes, and keep the rest of your business informed. After all, your employees will feel the impact of any changes, so let them know the upsides as well and make them feel part of any success.

A roadmap for success

Briefly, there are five steps to creating a powerful selling organisation. The first focuses on your product or service offer and your target the market segment(s). You may start with either, swapping the first and second positions depending on what's driving the business opportunity.

If you create or renovate your product or (re)design your service, you need to ensure that it still applies to your target market. If not, then you need to find the appropriate market or have another look at your offering. On the other hand, if you have you noticed a crying need in a particular market or markets, then you might try to create an offering to satisfy this need. All this 'redesign' may sound complex, but it doesn't need to be.

A simple example may be found in supermarkets. For years, breakfast cereal producers did just that: manufacture and package breakfast cereals. After a few years, these manufacturers recognised that smaller boxes sold in 'variety packs' capitalised on a need in the catering industry where hotels offered breakfast buffets. In recent years, in response to changing market demands, these same suppliers took their cereal and, with slight modification, repackaged it as 'breakfast bars' to appeal to a new market segment.

From this example you can see that businesses who continue to thrive never stop working on these first two activities – target market and service offer – adjusting and refining the offering to fit the target market and refining the target market after testing the response to the offering.

The next steps to building a powerful selling organisation

Product/service
offer

Market
segment(s)

Step 1
Clearly *define* target
market(s) & configure
product/service offer
to appeal to market

Sales approach & sales process

Step 2
Select appropriate
sales approach(es)

Step 3
Build your
sales process

Sales management & sales support

Step 4
Appoint & empower
build sales support

Step 5
Communicate
the changes

At the same time as re-examining your target market and adjusting your offering, remember to determine how you will approach this market. Does the new offering or target market need a new sales approach or will the old one do? Don't just do what you have always done because you have always done it. If you need to make changes, do it! And your work won't stop once you decide how you will sell your offering. As we have discussed earlier in the book, you must now set up support and management systems within your own business to underpin this sales approach. And all the while, you should lead your business through this change by communicating your new direction to all your employees and involving as many as makes sense in the change process.

Finally, don't forget to communicate these changes. Make certain that everyone in your business understands what you have changed and then let the market know.

Although it looks straightforward, changing the business can be challenging. What do you do if you want to change only some parts of your selling machine without putting the rest of your business at risk? And how do you manage the change if it involves altering your image in the marketplace?

How to manage change

Let's start by discussing 'change' within your own business.

Although critical to the ongoing success of most businesses, managing change is not straightforward. Why? Because it's not just about changing processes and rational measurements, it's about changing employees' behaviours and dealing with their emotional responses to change. It is a fact that most people view any change as a threat. Any successful change project recognises these emotional elements. Adding to this pressure, most employees will have to carry on with their day job while implementing change, so there is additional effort. If you remember to address a few key areas, you can successfully lead your company through change and toward your new or revised objectives.

Common obstacles to change...

People – 90% of the time have something to do with unhappy people. However, the obstacles may vary:

▶ Working days/times

▶ Poor communications

▶ Poorly defined roles

▶ Lack of initial 'buy in'

▶ Unclear or lack of 'common vision' about where change is going

▶ Doing it 'to them', not 'with them'

That's why it takes both leadership and management to implement successful business change

The key to successfully managing change combines strong leadership and management with clear and consistent messages, plus involvement of and communication to everyone affected by the changes.

Leadership vs. management

Volumes have been written on this subject, but the important point for this discussion is the leadership and management are different and that your business will need both to help you make necessary changes in your business. You might not find both skills in one person – in fact, you may need to seek external help for one or the other. The important point is to recognise that you will need both to be successful.

Leadership vs. management

Leadership is about:

▶ choices

▶ direction

▶ inspiration

Management is about:

▶ process

▶ execution

▶ discipline

Both *are about people and results and neither is very much good without the other*

How your business changes impact your customers and marketplace

Another factor to consider is how your internal changes impact on your customer and/or how changes in your market strategy might be viewed by potential and current customers. What do I mean?

Well, let's discuss the most straightforward situation first: your business contact with customers. Say, for example, you have reorganised all your customer-facing staff in order to create an effective 'machine' and the people who formerly worked in customer service now have a different job or additional responsibilities. What happens in your changed organisation when a customer rings your customer service department? Will the customer get the response he or she expects?

An example of how internal reorganisations for a business's benefit can impact the end customer in a negative way is computerised answering systems. You have probably experienced these systems yourself: the electronic voice that answers your phone call saying: "Press 1 if you want X and press 2 if you want Y." There are times when these are very useful – reporting stolen credit cards or a dangerous gas leak, for example. In any case, these systems are certainly very efficient for the companies who implement them. Of course they are! The customer now does all the work previously performed by one of their employees. Many customers, however, are not so happy and often become frustrated and annoyed at not being able to speak to a human being.

Confusing/mixed messages to the market

Automated answering services and large call centres are not the only way that internal changes can impact your marketplace. Implementation of new pricing policies and repackaging of your service offers to address different segments can cause anger and confusion too. Think of the times you have paid 'full price' for an item – a suit, a plane ticket, perhaps a holiday – only to discover that if you had waited a day or a week you might have paid substantially less. How does it make you feel? Are you happy with the supplier?

This sort of thing also happens in the business marketplace when a supplier introduces a new product that replaces the old or has a 'special offer' or sales campaign. In 'fashion-based' markets, which includes things like clothing but also automobiles and some electronics, many companies have overcome the potential dissatisfaction by 'institutionalising' special sales. Car dealerships offer 'deals' just as new models are announced, while retail business regularly announce sales at set times of year in order to shift last season's products. Customers know what to expect and rarely pay full price just before a known sale unless there is a compelling reason, such as Christmas, to make a purchase.

Finally, if you sell business-to-business, remember that your customers may talk to each other. Also, customers' employees change companies and could well end up working at different customers of yours. You must consider very carefully how you word your pricing offers so that one customer doesn't end up feeling he has been charged more for the same product or service.

Implementing business change: A check list of activities & issues

Have you figured out how to:

- ▶ Implement change without impacting 'the bottom line'
- ▶ Create a common 'vision' of what you are trying to achieve
- ▶ Involve and delegate to the appropriate people
- ▶ Clearly define and communicate all roles and activities appropriately
- ▶ Coordinate activities across organisational boundaries
- ▶ Encourage appropriate behaviours
- ▶ Manage diverse interests
- ▶ Generate and populate a benefits case or business case
- ▶ Drive change the change programme while everyone can continue doing their day jobs
- ▶ Communicate these changes to your customers
- ▶ Ensure your customers value the changes

And all of these activities must be addressed to ensure success!

A key point to understand is that such dissatisfaction is NOT just about money. For those who care that the price has changed or a newer product is now available, it's a question of feeling 'cheated'. The buyer thinks: "Surely the sales person or the company knew – why didn't they say something and let me make an informed choice?" This situation leaves a bad impression in the customer's mind and, more importantly, bad feelings. It will now be much harder to sell him anything in the future than had he never bought anything at all! And worse, he could spread bad reports about your business and affect the buying choices of other potential customers.

Many of these mishaps can be avoided by the use of a sound and comprehensive marketing plan that incorporates new product/service launches, pricing changes and sales campaigns and includes well-planned communications – both within your business and to potential customers. The very best rule of thumb is to put yourself in your customers' shoes and ask yourself : "How would I feel?"

Finally, understand why you are making these changes. Put together a business case or benefits case, then stop for a moment to consider: "Are these changes worth it?" If yes, carry on and your business will be in better shape. And don't forget to refer to the original business or benefits case to make certain you achieve what you set out to do!

Conclusion

Well, that's it. You have now covered everything you need to do to build a high-powered and successful selling machine for your business. You have covered a lot of material – entire books have been written on topics covered in each chapter. Remember, you haven't even touched on basic selling skills – however, books and courses abound on this topic already, so you can investigate your options if your business needs these skills. If you knew all this material already, congratulations! Pat yourself on the back – you are one of a very small, select group of managers/directors in SMEs today.

Most readers will have found something new in at least one of the sections. Please follow the advice at the beginning of the chapter and take steps to improve your selling effectiveness where appropriate. Measure your efforts and measure your results – prove to yourself it was worth the investment. Even when the economy is poor and the market is 'tight' it pays dividends to invest in appropriate marketing and sales.

Finally, use this book as an aide memoire, a check list for you to use to make certain that you are doing everything possible to sharpen your commercial position. You may well know all these techniques but lack the skills or resources to make the necessary changes. In such circumstances it is well worth the investment to source a commercial specialist who can help you to implement your ideas.

Good selling!

Index

Who's Paying for Lunch?